Y0-BVQ-578

Designing Performance
Assessment Systems
for
Urban Teacher Preparation

Designing Performance
Assessment Systems
for
Urban Teacher Preparation

Edited by

Francine P. Peterman
Cleveland State University

LAWRENCE ERLBAUM ASSOCIATES, PUBLISHERS

2005   Mahwah, New Jersey   London

Lawrence Erlbaum Associates, Inc., Publishers
10 Industrial Avenue
Mahwah, New Jersey 07430
www.erlbaum.com

Cover design by Kathryn Houghtaling Lacey

Library of Congress Cataloging-in-Publication Data

Designing performance assessment systems for urban teacher preparation / edited by Francine P. Peterman.
    p. cm.
    Includes bibliographical references and index.
    ISBN 0-8058-4929-7 (cloth : alk. paper)
    ISBN 0-8058-5384-7 (pbk. : alk. paper)
    1. Teachers—Training of—United States. 2. Teachers—Rating of—United States. 3. Competency-based education—United States. 4. Education, Urban—United States.   I. Peterman, Francine.
LB1715.D46   2005
370'.71'1—dc22   2004053200
                                                              CIP

Books published by Lawrence Erlbaum Associates are printed on acid-free paper, and their bindings are chosen for strength and durability.

Printed in the United States of America
10 9 8 7 6 5 4 3 2 1

Contents

Preface

Colleges of education throughout the United States today are engaged in the complex task of designing performance assessment systems to track student and institutional progress. Their endeavors are a response to two strong currents running through the field of education—one arising from particular perspectives on learning and understanding and the other from views on how standards are set and how progress toward standards and toward federal and state mandates for teacher education accountability are assessed.

This accountability movement is not new. As Zeichner notes in the first chapter of this book, the history of American education has been riddled with accountability measures that delineate what teachers should know and be able to do. The premise of this book differs from the underlying premises of traditional accountability measures. We propose (a) that educator learning is of the utmost importance in having a positive impact on student learning and (b) that context matters. The term *educator learning* as we use it here intentionally includes, but is not limited to, teachers, teacher educators, teacher candidates, inductees, parents, administrators, and others responsible for students' and teachers' learning and development. Thus, in this book, we authors situate urban teacher assessment in a historical context, detail distinguishing characteristics of urban settings, and suggest a sociocultural theory of teaching and learning and a set of design principles to frame performance assessment systems for urban teacher preparation. In addition, we document our efforts to prepare and assess urban teachers in case studies, analyzing our efforts in light of the historical, theoretical, and analytical frameworks provided.

Designing Performance Assessment Systems for Urban Teacher Preparation cul-
minates 6 years of vital dialogue and focused, local activity in which teachers
and teacher educators from institutions in the Urban Network to Improve
Teacher Education (UNITE) engaged. UNITE is a special interest group of
the Holmes Partnership.[1] In particular, representatives from 6 of the 19
UNITE institutions agreed to develop a volume that addresses our concerns about urban teacher preparation and the teacher assessment proto-
cols each of us was required to design and implement in our home
institutions. This book is the result.

Part I presents the historical context that was examined for this work
(Zeichner, chap. 1), a theoretical framework to undergird teacher preparation assessment (Conway & Artiles, chap. 2), and design principles to guide
the development of assessment systems (Peterman, chap. 3).

Part II details, in four case studies, our struggles and success in designing
and implementing these systems (Marquez-Zenkov, chap. 4; Genor, chap.
5; Kalnin & Pearson et al., chap. 6; Cokely & Murrell, chap. 7). In Part III,
the concluding chapter, Navarro (chap. 7) discusses the importance of context and current trends in assessment practices in urban teaching.

Each contributor to this book has played a key role in urban teacher
preparation and in the design and implementation of a performance assessment system that in some way addresses the complexity and demands of
urban teaching. We were not always in agreement about what beliefs and
theories should underpin the work, nor were we convinced that "urban"
means the same thing for each of us. This reflected, to some degree, the fact
that our respective institutions are situated differently, representing a variety of settings and serving different school populations. In addition, although each of our institutions was engaged in partnership to prepare
urban teachers, these partnerships differed in terms of the nature and focus
of collaboration:

> 1. Cleveland State University, a midsized state institution situated in a
> midsized urban city, prepares more than one third of the teachers hired
> by the Cleveland Municipal School District, the 6th largest urban district
> in the nation. The University's relatively new Masters of Urban Second-
> ary Teaching program (only 3 years old when the case was prepared) fo-
> cuses on a 14-month, 5th-year program that places interns who intend to

---

[1]The Holmes Partnership, a network of more than 90 universities, schools, community
agencies, and professional development organizations, was established in 1997 as the reor-
ganized Holmes Group. Focusing on partnering institutions creating high quality professional development that significantly supports school renewal and increased student
learning, the Holmes Partnership links schools of education with schools, districts, and their
communities to simultaneously strengthen teacher education and schooling.

be urban teachers in partnership schools where teacher and university mentors support interns' professional development.

2. University of Wisconsin–Madison, a large, research-oriented university, is situated outside a major metropolitan area but provides teachers to Milwaukee and Chicago and involves its teacher candidates in suburban contexts that mirror the socioeconomic and cultural diversity of larger urban settings. The university simulates working in an urban setting by identifying schools where the cultural, socioeconomic, and linguistic diversity matches those of the larger cities where graduates might be employed. It has introduced an electronic means of assessing teacher performance.

3. University of Minnesota–Minneapolis, a large, research-based state institution that prepares most of the teachers for its city, is in a large urban setting where the population is differentiated more significantly by culture than by race. The University has a long history of collaboration with the school district, which includes the development of a performance assessment system that was completely aligned with state and district standards for teachers' licensure and professional development.

4. Northeastern University, a midsized private institution in one of the largest most diverse cities, situates its internship in a charter school. Northeastern's program was in its infancy when the case was written. Its purpose was to detail the nature of the negotiations that take place when teachers, interns, university faculty, and other community members engage in dialogues to construct a notion of the "community teacher" that will guide preparation and assessment practices.

In each case, the partners engaged in urban teacher preparation and struggled with the expectation that we would arrive at shared understandings of teaching and learning and the urban contexts in which these occur. It is the nature of these struggles that we seek to illuminate in the case studies—with particular attention to the complexity and demands of teaching in urban school settings and to the task of developing responsive assessment systems geared to preparing the best teachers for such schools.

Over the course of three meetings a year for 6 years, we met as representatives of our leadership development teams in UNITE. To guide our initial discussions, we focused on two chapters from the most recent *Handbook of Research on Teaching* (Richardson, 2001): Gallego, Cole, and the Laboratory of Comparative Human Cognition provided a deep understanding of a sociocultural perspective on teaching and teacher education and its implications for working in urban settings and for designing assessments for teacher candidates who would work there; Moll proposed a theoretical stance on teacher learning and teacher preparation that requires teacher candidates, mentors, teacher educators, and others involved to engage in continuous dialogue, activity, and reflection about learning to teach. Moll's perspective established a critical foundation for thinking about learning to teach—one based on engaging all participants in questioning the inequities found in our settings and our own roles in establishing, continuing, and addressing these inequities. Promoting the development of this critical edge in educator learning is perhaps the most distinguishing contribution of our work.

The theories and practices provided in this book present an argument for, and invite, critical examination of teacher preparation and assessment practices—in light of both the complexities and demands of urban settings (the poverty, diversity, and bureaucracy that define them), and the theories of learning and learning to teach that guide teacher education practices. This dynamic approach to learning to teach distinguishes our stance on urban teacher assessment as one that can help address social justice issues related to gender, race, socioeconomic class, and other differences and at the same time promote the professional development of all educators engaged in the process of learning to teach. We believe the contextually bound, sociocultural stance presented in our book promises greater teacher and student achievement.

ACKNOWLEDGMENTS

This book would not have been possible without the ongoing cheerleading and support from UNITE, especially Ken Zeichner and members of our workgroup engaged in the important work of preparing urban teachers; our editor Naomi Silverman; our muses, Ken Howey and Sandra Hollingsworth; our families and friends; and Kristy Sweigard and other staff members who diligently kept us on task.

Partial funding to produce this manuscript was provided by the U.S. Department of Education, Agency #P336B990072, Office of Title II Teacher Quality Grant: The Milwaukee Partnership Academy to Improve the Quality of Teaching, Dr. Nancy Zimpher, Director. In addition the U.S. Department of Education, Agency #P336C020018, Office of Title II Teacher Quality Grant: The Cleveland State University Quality Urban Educators Program. However, the contents do not necessarily represent the policy of position of the U.S. Department of Education.

REFERENCES

Gallego, M., Cole, M., & The Laboratory of Comparative Human Cognition. (2001). Classroom cultures and cultures in the classroom. In V. Richardson (Ed.), *Handbook of Research on Teaching* (4th ed., pp. 951–997). Washington, DC: American Educational Research Association.

Moll, L. C. (2001). Through the mediation of others: Vygotskian research on teaching. In V. Richardson (Ed.), *Handbook of Research on Teaching* (4th ed., pp. 111–129). Washington, DC: American Educational Research Association.

Richardson, V. (Ed.). (2001). *Handbook of Research on Teaching* (4th ed.). Washington, DC: American Educational Research Association.

About the Contributors

Alfredo Artiles' scholarship focuses on the intersections of culture, learning, and disability. He has presented his scholarship or worked as an advisor/consultant to organizations/programs in the United States, Europe, Latin America, and Africa. Recent publications include: (2003), "Special education's changing identity: Paradoxes and dilemmas in views of culture and space" *Harvard Educational Review, 73*, 164–202 (2003); "Culturally diverse students in special education: Legacies and prospects." In J. A. Banks and C. M. Banks (Eds.), *Handbook of research on multicultural education* (2nd edition). San Francisco, CA: Jossey-Bass (with S. Trent & J. Palmer, 2004); *English Language Learners with special needs: Identification, placement, and instruction*. Washington DC: Center for Applied Linguistics (coedited with A. Ortiz, 2002). Dr Artiles received the 2001 Early Career Award from the American Educational Research Association's Committee on Scholars of Color in Education. He is a principal investigator for the National Center for Culturally Responsive Educational Systems (NCCRESt, with J. Klingner, E. Kozleski, & C. Utley).

Micky Cokely is the Director of Field Placements at Northeastern University's School of Education. She is responsible for coordinating field placement for prepractica, student teaching, and internships, training Northeastern faculty to supervise practicum, selecting and mentoring cooperating teachers, and teaching practicum seminars. Prior to joining Northeastern University, Ms. Cokely was an educational consultant at Children's Hospital, Boston, a teacher, special education administrator, and coordinator of student service learning in Montgomery County Public Schools, Maryland; an Instructor at Johns Hopkins University, Maryland; and a teacher and director of parent and professional development at Gallaudet University, Washington, DC. Ms. Cokely holds master's degrees in guidance counseling and speech language pathology and completed advanced coursework in special education administration.

Paul Conway is a College Lecturer in the Education Department at the National University of Ireland (NUI), Cork, and a Visiting Scholar in the College of Education, Michigan State University. Prior to returning to Ireland, he was Assistant Professor of Educational Psychology and Human Development at Cleveland State University. He is Coeditor of *Irish Educational Studies*. His research interests are in teacher education, sociocultural learning theories, and ICT policy in education. Recent publications include: "Learning in communities of practice: Rethinking teaching and learning in disadvantaged contexts" *Irish Educational Studies*, (2002); "The journey inward and outward: A re-examination of Fuller's concern-based model of teacher development," (with Chris Clark, 2003); *Teaching and Teacher Education*; and *Gender politics and 'Exploring Masculinities' in Irish Education: Teachers, materials and the media* (with Máirtín Mac an Ghaill & Joan Hanafin), Dublin: National Council for Curriculum and Assessment (2004).

Michèle Genor is an assistant professor of education at Teachers College, Columbia University in the elementary preservice program. Along with teaching in the program, Genor collaborates in coordinating work with supervisors and cooperating teachers, supervises student teachers, and acts as a liaison to New York City schools. A member of the Executive Board for the Professional Development School Partnership, she acted as interim director during 2002. She is also currently co-facilitating a Spencer doctoral seminar on teacher education and has recently traveled to Afghanistan to support their Ministry of Education's development of curriculum and teacher training programs.

Julie Kalnin, originally a high school English teacher, has been working in teacher education since 1996. She has co-authored a book that examines literacy instruction and assessment in urban schools. Other publications focus on writing pedagogy, the induction of urban teachers, and teacher professional development and evaluation. Since coming to the University of Minnesota, Dr. Kalnin has worked with the Minneapolis Federation of Teachers (MFT) and the Minneapolis Public Schools (MPS) developing teacher induction support. This partnership secured grant funds from the state of Minnesota to create the Minneapolis New Teacher Project. This project supports first and second year teachers in Minneapolis in learning about action research in their classrooms, an important part of teacher assessment in the district. Kalnin currently works as a staff development specialist at Nora Classical Academy, a charter school.

Peter C. Murrell, Jr. is Professor of Urban Education at Northeastern University in Boston, Massachusetts, where he also directs the Center for Innovation in Urban Education. He is a teacher and researcher in human learning, cognitive development, urban pedagogy, and the social–cultural contexts of human performance and school achievement. He is a member of several national initiatives on teacher assessment, including membership on the board of examiners for the National Council for Accreditation of Teacher Education (NCATE) and the International Recognition in Teacher Education (IRTE), and the National Commission on High Stakes Testing. Dr. Murrell is the author of *Like Stone Soup: The Role of The Professional Development School in the Renewal of Urban Schools* (AACTE Press); *Community Teachers: Teacher Preparation for the Renewal of Urban Schools and Communities* (Teachers College Press); and *African-Centered Pedagogy: Creating Schools of Achievement for African American Children* (SUNY Press). Dr. Murrell's research focuses on: (a) *learning environments*—qualitative studies of human learning in cultural and community contexts; (b) *achievement performance*—learning achievement in urban-focused professional development schools; (c) *practice-oriented education*; and (d) *cultural and racial identity development* and their relationships to school achievement.

Virginia Navarro, an assistant professor in the College of Education at the University of Missouri–St. Louis, has coauthored a series of articles on the social construction of identity. She also writes about school/university partnership work and recently co-edited a book of partnership case studies for the Urban Network to Improve Teacher Education. Dr. Navarro teaches child development, qualitative research methods, and sociocultural (Vygotskian) theory.

Donna Pearson is the Family Education Coordinator in the Department of Work, Community, and Family Education, and a research associate for the National Research Center for Career and Technical Education at the University of Minnesota. For the past 14 years, she has been involved in all phases of teacher education at the University of Minnesota, including serving as the Coordinator of Clinical Experiences for the initial teacher licensure programs in the College of Education and Human Development. In that role she coordinated the development of the College's formative assessment for preservice teachers. Dr. Pearson's research interests are focused in the area of teacher preparation and development. Most recently, she has been involved in a national research project focused on the enhancement of mathematics in Career and Technical Education classrooms.

Francine P. Peterman, PhD University of Arizona (1991) is an associate professor and urban teacher educator who serves as chair of the Department of Curriculum and Foundations at Cleveland State University. Peterman writes about urban teaching and teacher preparation, standards for urban teacher education, inquiry-based teaching and learning, and the invention of cultures and practices that support renewal that is socially just. Her roots, in teaching in Miami, Florida for 12 years, keep her grounded in her work in schools, where she prepares educators for the complexities and demands of urban teaching.

Ken Zeichner is Hoefs-Bascom Professor of Teacher Education and Associate Dean of the School of Education at the University of Wisconsin–Madison. He has published widely on issues of teacher education, teacher learning, and practitioner inquiry. Recent publications include "The Adequacies and Inadequacies of Three Current Strategies to Recruit, Prepare and Retain the Best Teachers for All Students" (Teachers College Record) and Teacher Research as Professional Development for P–12 Educators in the U.S. (Educational Action Research) and "Pedagogy, Knowledge and Teacher Preparation in Closing the Achievement Gap" (ASCD).

Kristien Marquez-Zenkov is an assistant professor in the literacy area of the Teacher Education department at Cleveland State University and assistant dean of field services. He is a veteran urban teacher and administrator, and now serves as the codirector of the Master of Urban Secondary Teaching (MUST) program, and coordinates professional development school partnerships with high schools in the five Cleveland-area urban school districts. He is currently piloting an urban induction project for entry year and early career teachers, directing the redesign of the College of Education field programs, and is co-director of a photography project through which city students are sharing what they believe are the purposes of high school. His recent publications have concentrated on the impact of the standards movement on city teachers, students, and communities, and he is co-authoring a book on urban professional development school partnerships.

Part I

THEORETICAL FRAMEWORK

Chapter 1

Learning From Experience With Performance-Based Teacher Education

Ken Zeichner
University of Wisconsin–Madison

One of the distinguishing characteristics of teacher education in the United States is its lack of attention to history. Over and over again during the last 50 years, we have seen the emergence of different waves of teacher education reform emphasizing different views of teaching, learning, knowledge, schooling, teacher learning, and the social order (Liston & Zeichner, 1991) with minimal attention to how the allegedly new reforms being proposed are connected to things that have gone on previously. The idea that we might learn something from our experience over time with different approaches to teacher education is rarely acknowledged, and is even more rarely developed into analyses of how we might benefit from our experience.

Currently, teacher education is once again at the center of a national debate in the United States on teacher quality and its relationship to the success of our system of public schooling. Two conflicting views of the desirable future for teacher education frame much of what is happening in the United States. On one hand, advocates of what is referred to as the "professionalization agenda," building on the recommendations of a series of reports on teacher education reform since the 1980s (e.g., NCTAF, 1996, 1997), are calling for an end to emergency teaching licenses, for higher standards for entry into and exit from teacher education programs, the adoption of content and performance standards, performance-based assessment systems, and external examinations of teachers' content knowledge for teacher licensing, mandatory national program accreditation, National Board Certification for teachers, Professional Standards Boards in each state, and a host of other things such as extended teacher education programs and professional development schools (e.g., Darling-Hammond, Wise, & Klein, 1999).

On the other hand, advocates of deregulating teacher education, such as those associated with the Fordham Foundation and the National Council on Teacher Quality (e.g., Ballou & Podgursky, 1998, 2000; Kanstoroom & Finn, 1999), have proposed greater ease of entry into teaching through alternative routes, a greater emphasis on content knowledge and school-based experiences, less emphasis on methods courses and educational foundations courses, and an end to what they see as a higher education monopoly on preservice teacher education. The American Board for Certification of Teacher Excellence and its "passport certification" is the organizational apparatus that the deregulation camp has developed to further its agenda for teacher education reform.

As a result of these debates, two kinds of reforms are occurring simultaneously in U.S. preservice teacher education. First, on the professionalization side, as a result of either state education department mandates or the new performance-based voluntary national accreditation mechanism (National Council for Accreditation of Teacher Education [NCATE], 2000), most teacher education programs in the United States are being transformed into a performance-based mode with explicit sets of teaching and content standards that graduates are required to meet prior to receiving an initial teaching license (e.g., Garvin, 2003). These standards are usually assessed by examining evidence accumulated in teaching portfolios that is often supplemented by external examinations of teachers' content knowledge administered by the states (Darling-Hammond & Snyder, 2000; Zeichner & Wray, 2001). The teaching standards for initial licensing in many states were designed to be compatible with the more advanced standards of the National Board for Professional Teaching Standards (NBPTS, 1994).

The federal government has gotten into the act as well with its recent and punitive Title 2 requirements that have resulted in teacher education report cards ranking college and university teacher education programs according to the test scores of its graduates.[1] This ranking of teacher education institutions by the pass rates of their graduates is not a new practice. Table 1.1 shows a ranking of teacher education institutions in Wisconsin in the 1860s according to test scores, which was published in the *Wisconsin Journal of Education* (WJE, 1863).

On the deregulation side, to meet severe shortages of teachers in certain fields such as special and math education and the sciences, and in certain

---

[1]See www.title2.org for the current teacher education report cards.

TABLE 1.1

Summary of Averages

	Whole No. Examined	Int. Arithmetic	Written Arithmetic	Algebra	El. Sounds	Spelling	Analysis	Grammar	Composition	Reading	Geography	Physical Geography	Physiology	History	Theory and Practice	Penmanship	Total
Racine High School	6	78.3	87.5	81.7	78.3	86.7	61.7	69.2	60	85	66.7	73.3	75.8	72.5	66.7	75	74.4
Lawrence University	7	75.5	86.4	73.5	68.5	86.4	75.5	77.1	71.4	78.5	56.4	62.9	73.5	65	72.1	77.1	73.5
Allen Grove Academy	13	77.7	76.2	75.5	78.8	80.4	66.5	67.7	52.3	83.1	73.5	68.1	66.2	62.3	62.3	79.6	71.4
Platteville Academy	11	76.8	78.2	64.5	76.3	86.3	60	70.9	62.7	83.2	55.9	63.2	55.4	48.2	65.9	79.5	68.5
Wisconsin Female College	6	72	78.3	67.5	48.3	69.2	73.3	65.8	65	78.3	63.3	67.5	65	63.3	75	62.5	67.7
Fond du Lac High School	4	72.5	72.5	83.7	71.2	81.2	51.2	68.7	63.7	76.2	57.5	50	65	41.2	68.7	80	66.8
Evansville Seminary	20	68.5	74	61	72.7	74	53.2	56.7	57	72.5	61	64.2	62	66.2	70.7	75.5	66.3
Milton Academy	15	76.3	77	58.7	63	76	43.7	59.3	69.3	82.3	52.3	55.3	55	58.3	65	78.7	64.7
Oshkosh High School	3	70	73.3	68.3	70	78.3	46.7	68.3	70	76.7	55	41.6	61.6	50	63.3	71.7	64.2

geographical areas such as most large urban and outlying rural school districts, new alternative routes to teaching have been opened up in most states that enable individuals to enter teaching with a supervised internship and varying and often minimal amounts of professional education (Feistritzer & Chester, 2000). Sometimes in situations where shortages are greatest, such as California, preservice teacher education occurs while teachers are already in the classroom full time as teachers of record. This is something that is not new in much of the world, but is relatively new to the United States. Some of these alternative programs are run by the school districts and states, and a number of them include only minimal involvement of college and university teacher educators (Zeichner & Schulte, 2001).

In this chapter, I discuss an aspect of the professionalization agenda in U.S. teacher education. Specifically, I focus on the near universal and often uncritical adoption of a performance-based approach to teacher education and teacher licensing and its implications for educating teachers for urban schools. Most scholars of the contemporary incarnation of performance-based teacher education (PBTE) trace the emergence of performance-based teacher education to the period immediately following the U.S. Department of Education's National Commission on Excellence in Education's publication of *A Nation at Risk* in 1983 and refer to the Carnegie Report and Holmes Reports, the work of the Interstate New Teacher Assessment and Support Consortium (INTASC), the National Commission on Teaching for America's Future, NCATE, and the NBPTS as the key aspects of this reform movement.

What is neglected in these accounts of the recent re-emergence of performance-based teacher education is the fact that what is going on today in most programs in the United States is not new. Performance-based teacher education was clearly the dominant movement in U.S. teacher education throughout the 1970s (Gage & Winne, 1975), and the broader social efficiency tradition, of which it is a part, has clearly been the dominant reform tradition in teacher education in the United States throughout the 20th century (Atkin & Raths, 1974; Liston & Zeichner, 1991). I could find only three instances in the current literature that acknowledge the link between what is going on now and previous incarnations of the same approach to educating teachers—a brief mention in a concept paper by Pearson (1994) that we are in the process of returning to something similar to the logic of the competency-based movement of the 1970s, and a brief but very informative paper published by the Association of Teacher Educators and written by Edelfelt and Raths (1999) that traces the history of standards in U.S. teacher education programs from the late 1800s to the end of the 20th century. Finally, Valli and Rennert-Ariev (2002) analyze the transformation of seven teacher education programs in one state to performance-based assessment and compare the degree to which these reforms resemble the narrow behavioristic competency-based teacher education (C/PBTE) of the 1970s and 1980s or the broader constructivist-based performance standards-based teacher education of the present (PSBTE). They compare C/PBTE and PSBTE along several dimensions—views of the role of the teacher, of the knowledge base for teaching, of the nature of teaching, and of assessment—and detect some "slippage" back to C/PBTE in the way in which some aspects of the program reforms have been enacted.

There have been several major developments in the performance-based teacher education movement in the United States during the last 75 years. I discuss two of them in this chapter and briefly address the question of what, if any, lessons can be learned from our experience with PBTE over time. The two historical moments that I discuss are the Commonwealth Teacher-Training Study published in 1929, and the period of the 1970s with its emphasis on C/PBTE.

THE COMMONWEALTH TEACHER-TRAINING STUDY

The first major standards development project in U.S. teacher education was the Commonwealth Teacher-Training Study, a 3-year study carried out between 1925 and 1928 by Charters and Waples of the University of Chicago with a $42,000 grant from the Commonwealth Fund (Charters & Waples, 1929). Ralph Tyler served as the statistician for the project that Saylor (1976) refers to as "an orgy of tabulation." The study was based on an assumption that the curriculum of teacher education programs needed to be radically reorganized because it often lacked a clear definition of objectives and logical plans of procedure. Applying the principles of scientific curriculum making that Charters had proposed in his book, *Curriculum Construction* (Charters, 1923), Charters and Waples and a team of over a hundred administrators who assisted in collecting data from several thousand teachers and others, sought to increase accuracy in the selection of the topics in the teacher education curriculum by obtaining a more exact knowledge of what the activities of teachers are in practice.

First, using the method of "consensus," the researchers determined the traits that characterize excellent teachers at the high school, junior high school, and intermediate grades, the kindergarten–primary grades, and teachers in rural schools. Parents, teachers, administrators, teacher union officials, professors of education, and students were interviewed to discover what they believed to be the traits most essential for success in teaching the various grade levels and in different types of communities. These nominations were then individually "translated" by 21 judges, and each of the 83 traits was defined by a series of indicators, not unlike what is going on today in many teacher education programs.

Here are a few examples of these traits and indicators. Some of them may seem silly today, but if you look closely enough at the ones that address the process of teaching, you can see very similar things in today's standards. Some of the traits have as many as 12 different "indicators":

- *Adaptability.* Does not dance or play cards if the community objects.
- *Alertness.* Reacts quickly to new trends of thought brought up by pupils.
- *Inspiration.* Encourages pupils to investigate problems themselves.
- *Leadership.* Develops a spirit of harmony and happiness in the group.
- *Tact.* Handles angry parents successfully.
- *Wittiness.* Gives a pleasant exchange of banter.
- *Calmness.* Does not try to cover up the noise of pupils by talking louder than they do.
- *Magnetism.* Creates a desire in pupils to be assigned to his room (Charters & Waples, 1929).

Following the identification of the traits of good teachers, Charters and Waples employed job analysis techniques and collected a comprehensive list of the activities of teachers by mailing surveys to teachers in 42 states. The final list of 1,001 activities was subdivided into seven major divisions such as instruction and classroom management. Over 200,000 statements were analyzed to get to this final list. Some of these activities get right to the heart of teaching and can be found in contemporary teacher standards such as the INTASC standards. For example, under instruction, one can find such activities as selecting types of instruction adapted to the needs of the class, selecting effective illustrations, and suggesting methods of overcoming pupil difficulties. Others, like the following example cited by Kliebard (1975), may not be found so explicitly stated in current standards, but may in fact be employed anyway:

> #788 Securing cordial relations with the superintendent.
> This involves being loyal to and respecting the superintendent. Becoming acquainted with the superintendent and working in harmony with him. Performing friendly acts for the superintendent; remembering the superintendent at Christmas; making designs and drawings for the superintendent; and making lampshades for the superintendent's wife. (p. 35)

The idea here was that teacher educators were to use the 83 traits and 1,001 activities to revise the existing courses and to develop new courses in their teacher education programs. Many examples are provided in the book of how to do both. For a variety of reasons, including the lack of capacity in teacher education institutions to implement such a complex and detailed system, the Commonwealth Teacher-Training Study did not have much influence on teacher education programs in the United States. What we can see here is the beginning of an attempt to construct the curriculum of teacher education programs on a scientific basis that is related to the realities that teachers face in schools. Although the procedures used to construct the standards for teacher education students were somewhat different from those used today, various aspects of the logic are similar, such as the belief that a student's completion of a teacher education program should be based on mastery of knowledge, skills, and dispositions that are associated with the work of good teachers. What was lacking in this early version of performance-based teacher education was the influence of systems theory that was used in later years in the design of assessment and management systems to monitor student-teacher progress on the standards.

PBTE IN THE 1970s

In 1969, the U.S. Office of Education funded, at a cost of $1.3 million, the development of 10 model performance-based teacher education (PBTE) programs in elementary education (Clarke, 1969), and, with the cooperation of the American Association of Colleges for Teacher Education (AACTE), conducted a massive public relations campaign promoting the development of performance-based teacher education programs. All of these model programs incorporated systems models into their designs (DeVault, 1973). All National Teacher Corps projects were also required to use a performance-based approach to assessment (Houston & Howsam, 1972). Teacher Corps was the largest federal investment in teacher education in the history of the United States and focused on improving education in urban and rural areas in schools attended primarily by students living in poverty, 1965–1980 (Weiner, 1993). For the next decade, performance-based teacher education dominated the literature in U.S. teacher education, although the actual extent of implementation of the approach was limited. Tyack and Cuban (1995) distinguish between "policy talk" (diagnosis of problems and the advocacy of solutions), and "policy action" (the adoption of reforms through state legislation) and implementation. With regard to PBTE in the 1970s, there was a lot of policy talk and action, but minimal implementation of full-scale performance-based programs.

It was estimated that full-scale implementation of performance-based programs occurred in only about 13% of teacher education institutions (Joyce, Howey, & Yarger, 1977; Sandefur & Nicklas, 1981). Gage and Winne (1975) concluded that in 1975 about 27 states had adopted or had plans to adopt a performance-based approach to teacher education as at least an acceptable option, and two states, New York and Texas, had adopted it as the only form of teacher education.

During this period, PBTE was contrasted with what was referred to as "experience or course-based" teacher education and arguments were made to change the licensing of teachers so that it would be based on demonstrated performance rather than on the completion of a set of required courses (Gage & Winne, 1975). Elam (1971) concisely defined PBTE as follows:

> In performance-based programs, performance goals are specified in rigorous detail in advance of instruction. The student must be able to demonstrate his ability to promote desirable learning or exhibit behaviors known to promote it. He will be held accountable, not for passing grades, but for attaining a given level of competency in performing the essential tasks of teaching. (p. 1)

In the 1970s version of PBTE, there was extensive use of behavioral psychology and systems theory that had been employed during and after WW II in training programs in industry and the military (McDonald, 1973). The models that were developed with federal funding included numerous competencies stated in behavioral terms and elaborate management systems for monitoring student teacher progress on mastering the competencies. One major criticism of PBTE at that time was the proliferation of long lists of competencies (the Michigan State model program had over 1,500). It was argued by those like Harry Broudy of the University of Illinois that this fragmentation of teaching into numerous micro competencies does not add up to the whole of teaching and limits our conception of teaching to teaching as telling (Broudy, 1973). Art Combs (1972) of the University of Florida argued, "Requiring a teacher education program to define precisely the behaviors it hopes to produce may be the surest way to destroy the effectiveness of its products" (p. 288). Another criticism of the long lists of competencies was their arbitrary nature. The competencies in each program were often very different from one another (Edelfelt & Raths, 1999). Because of the interconnection among all of the various pieces in a teacher education program within a systems design, many college and university teacher education faculty were also concerned about PBTE impinging on academic freedom and limiting their ability teach what they wanted to teach (Roth, 1976). A PBTE program also makes many more demands on faculty to be present and available to students, which conflicts with the culture of universities that devalues practice and teacher education.

A key assumption made by advocates of PBTE was that the competencies or performances that made up the teacher education curriculum were related to student learning. In Elam's (1971) words, "A student must either be able to demonstrate his ability to promote desirable learning or exhibit behaviors known to promote it" (p. 1). One of the major criticisms of PBTE in the 1970s was the lack of empirical validation for the competencies included in teacher education curricula. Heath and Nielson's (1974) comprehensive review of the research base for performance-based teacher education published in *The Review of Educational Research* was one among several major reviews of the research on teaching that concluded that there was not an empirical basis for the prescription of competencies in teacher education programs.

Another line of criticism of PBTE in the 1970s came from those such as Apple and others who criticized the conservative political tendencies that, they argued, were associated with the approach (Apple, 1972; Nash & Agne, 1971). By basing the specification of competencies on current conceptions of the teacher's role in a system that was felt to be in need of fundamental reform, it was argued that PBTE served to legitimate the status quo in schools and society. One response to these charges of conservatism and technicism by those teacher educators who espoused goals related to social reconstructionism was the development of competencies that addressed the teacher's role as a reformer. For example, Nash and Agne (1971) proposed:

> We shall have to include in our curricula competencies that will enable our students to innovate. For example, we might help students to assess the power structures in their buildings and communities, to understand and intervene in the political processes of administrators; to form alliances with like-minded teachers in order to transmit new ideas; to build an interpersonal support system in the school and community so that reformers are sustained by a vast nexus of psychological and practical assistance. (p. 154)

Another major criticism of PBTE, and probably the one most responsible for its disappearance for a couple of decades before reemerging again in the 1990s, was the high cost associated with developing and implementing a performance-based teacher education program. Hite (1973) estimated that PBTE is 150% more expensive than traditional experienced-based programs and that the cost of developing a single PBTE program in one institution is between $5 and $6 million. Whether one accepts these particular cost estimates or not, there is no denying the huge costs associated with the development and implementation of these programs. Even the AACTE (1974) Committee on Performance-based Teacher Education, which produced numerous publications on PBTE, admitted:

> The committee is [also] forced to recognize that the Achilles heel of PBTE may be that while sound in theory, it may be so difficult to implement in practice that its promise will never be realized in any significant degree. (p. 12)

Because of problems associated with the cost of implementing the approach, concerns about the narrowing of vision caused by the proliferation of long lists of behavioral competencies, the demands that PBTE would make on university faculty to be more present to student teachers, the alleged infringements on academic freedom, and concerns about the lack of empirical validity of the competencies, PBTE largely disappeared from the scene at least temporarily. As PBTE was fading out of view, state mandated teacher testing and the AACTE work on the development of the knowledge base for teaching were accelerating. PBTE came back into view in the 1990s with the reemergence of the professionalization movement following *A Nation at Risk*. It never entirely disappeared, though, because after the flurry of activity to convert all preservice programs to a performance base, Florida and Georgia continued developing and using performance-based assessment systems with beginning teachers, and a few individual institutions like Alverno College in Milwaukee, Wisconsin continued developing the C/PBTE programs that they had begun (Zeichner, 2000).

CURRENT FORMS OF PERFORMANCE-BASED TEACHER EDUCATION

In the current incarnation of PBTE, which has been referred to as performance standards-based teacher education (PSBTE; Valli & Rennert-Ariev, 2002), there is no longer a focus on the development of only behavioral competencies. Contemporary statements of standards and performances are broader and attend to the cognitive and dispositional aspects of teaching in addition to the technical aspects and are compatible with a view of teachers as reflective practitioners.[2] The standards of today are also fewer in number than the lists of hundreds of competencies that were common in C/PBTE programs in the 1970s. There also is no longer a preoccupation with the empirical validity of the standards as there was in the 1970s—that is, with whether research has established that the standards are related to student learning. This is accepted based on the judgment of panels of experts, and attention is given to scrutinizing the process used in the development of the standards.

We are closer today to the process used in the Commonwealth study, where a group of experts comes up with a set of standards about what represents good teaching at a particular career stage, than we are to the quest for the key to teaching effectiveness in process–product research of the 1970s. The technique of job analysis employed by Charters and Waples in a much cruder form in 1925–1928 was employed by the Educational Testing Service (ETS) in the development of Praxis III, their performance-based as-

---

[2]Whitty and Willmont (1991) define two major approaches to competency-based teacher education: a narrow skills-based approach and a wider definition that encompasses intellectual, cognitive, and attitudinal dimensions as well as performance. The narrower view is informed by behaviorist learning theories and the broader view is informed by cognitive and constructivist learning theories (Shepard, 2000).

sessment system for beginning teachers. In the development of Praxis III, large-scale national surveys were used in which teachers were asked in detail about the importance of specific tasks for their own teaching and the teaching of beginning teachers. Both INTASC and ETS relied heavily on the use of expert panels of teachers, school administrators, college and university faculty, and state education and teacher union officials in the development of their standards. These were then widely circulated to these same groups for comments (Porter, Youngs, & Odden, 2001). There has also been some attempt to have student teachers show directly that they can create pupil learning as part of the process of licensure, as in Oregon (e.g., Mcconney, Schalock, & Schalock, 1998).

In many ways other ways, PBTE in the 1990s and beyond has been a lot like what went on in the 1970s in terms of its high expense, its demands on the time and on the teaching autonomy of faculty, and so on. In some states like my own, teacher educators were given the option to develop their own teaching standards and to propose them to the state education department for approval. We did this at my university after spending about 3 years working out what the standards would be with all of the university faculty and cooperating teachers and school administrators. In some states, a set of standards was imposed on teacher educators and there was some resentment of who is setting the agenda. Even where teacher educators are given the option of charting their own course with regard to standard setting, little or nothing in the way of new resources has been provided to support the development of the elaborate assessment and management systems needed to run the programs.

In research universities, where there is already a tension between research and teaching and a big problem in finding faculty willing to work in teacher education programs (Goodlad, 1990), the reemergence of PBTE has intensified the distaste of some faculty for being involved in teacher education as they are asked to write performance indicators and rubrics and examine their courses to see if they are covering what will be included on the state content examinations. Both the lack of new financial resources needed to implement and monitor these programs and the lack of capacity of faculty to carry out the additional work needed to transform programs to a performance-based mode could mean that once again the failure to provide financial resources and human labor needed to implement a genuine performance-based program may lead to its demise or to superficial implementation. Even with the broader and more constructivist based standards that avoid the narrow, technical, and fragmented approach to teaching that was represented in the competencies of the 1970s and that was the focus of much criticism (Haberman & Stinnett, 1973), the implementation demands may be too great to handle in many institutions. Additionally, with declining resources in many states, the ability of state departments of education to adequately monitor the compliance of teacher education institutions with performance-based mandates may not be present.

One reason that the concept of PBTE keeps coming back on the scene is related to the low status of teacher education in the university culture and the chronic dissatisfaction expressed by teachers about the quality of their preparation for teaching in college and university-based programs. One purpose of the quest for the knowledge base for teaching over the last hundred years or more has been to legitimize the activity of teacher education within higher education. It has also been argued that full scale adoption of the professionalization agenda of performance-based teacher education, mandatory national accreditation of teacher education programs, National Board certification, and so on will lead to higher salaries and better working conditions for teachers. This remains to be seen. According to some indicators, the status and working conditions of teachers has declined across the world despite the increasing rhetoric about professionalization (UNESCO, 1998) Performance-based teacher education has also been used as a response to those external critics like Bestor, Koerner, and in today's arena, the friends of the Fordham Foundation, who argue that there is no necessary content in professional education that cannot be learned on the job in an apprenticeship (Bestor, 1953; Koerner, 1963; Kramer, 2000). Presenting a list of standards or performances that panels of experts say are needed to be a successful teacher contributes to a justification for professional education beyond a content major and contributes to the arguments against those alternative programs that do not provide any professional education content.

There is also a belief by many advocates of the idea of systemic standards-based reform that the alignment of the curriculum of teacher education programs with K–12 curriculum standards will create greater coherence in the educational system and more effective schools (see Diez, 1994; Dilworth & Brown, 2001).

Teacher educators like Diez and Hass (1997) at Alverno College have made the argument that performance-based assessment, done well, contributes to the development of prospective teachers and is much more than a way to determine if teacher candidates have met a set of standards:

> The experience of the assessment process can contribute to candidate development when candidates practice the abilities that will be demanded of them as teachers and when those responsible for preparation use assessment and feedback to help candidates develop. Assessment is a powerful guide to growth. In this way assessment becomes integral to learning. (p. 21)

It is also assumed by many other advocates of PSBTE that, in addition to overcoming the limitations of paper and pencil teacher tests and providing a more valid assessment of the abilities of prospective teachers (Wilson, 1994), performance assessment, portfolios, and so forth will enhance the quality of teaching and result in better prepared teachers. There has been very little study to date of the educative value of participating in performance-based assessment as part of a preservice teacher education program (e.g., Zeichner & Wray, 2001).

Where the current wave of performance-based assessment in preservice teacher education in the United States will end up is not clear at this early stage of implementation. We do know from past experience, though, that unless we are willing to invest the resources to enable teacher educators to design genuine performance-based programs, we will end up with superficial imitations that possess all of the structures that are required but have little substance. We will have standards, portfolios, rubrics, and all of the rest, but we will not have assessments that tell us very much about candidates' teaching or that will facilitate better teaching.

As Richardson (1994) warns:

> Teachers may begin to focus more time and energy on developing good portfolios, rather than developing portfolios that represent their teaching. Thus, we will have wonderful looking portfolios that do not represent what is going on in classrooms—a situation leading to inflated scores that decrease the validity of portfolio assessment. (p. 19)

"Assessment as learning," as Diez and her colleagues at Alverno College have described it and done it (Zeichner, 2000), is a complex and labor-intensive effort that requires making teacher education a high priority for many faculty. If it is not done right and the focus is put on the mechanics of the process and on producing "good looking" portfolios, there is a danger, Richardson (1994) warns, that not only will PSBTE fail to promote teacher learning in a positive sense, it will actually undermine teacher learning.

Another issue that arises in the current incarnation of PBTE with regard to urban schools is the adequacy of the standards used in teacher education programs for preparing teachers who can be successful in today's complicated and under-resourced urban school systems (see chap. 3). As I argued elsewhere (Zeichner, 2003), there is some feeling among urban teacher educators that the current standards, which are often based on the INTASC standards, fail to incorporate some of the key elements for the successful teaching of diverse students that have been identified in the literature on culturally responsive teaching (e.g., Gay, 2000; Ladson-Billings, 1994; Villegas & Lucas, 2002).

Finally, some form of performance-based teacher education has recently been put into place in a number of countries across the world. The United Kingdom was one of the first to move toward performance-based teacher education on a broad scale in the current ways of reforms (Furlong, Barton, Miles, Whiting, & Whitty, 2000). More and more countries in addition to the United States, such as Australia (Sachs & Groundwater-Smith, 1999), Chile (Ministry of Education, 2000), and South Africa (Robinson, 2001), have taken similar paths to what has gone on in the United Kingdom. There are many different explanations given for this nearly universal movement toward the implementation of performance-based assessments in teacher education programs across the world. Some have argued that this trend is part of the neoconservative and neoliberal agendas to prepare better workers for the global economy and to open up all aspects of education to market forces (Apple, 2001). Others have argued that PSBTE is aimed at addressing long-standing equity problems in schooling and is part of a social reconstructionist agenda (Dilworth & Brown, 2001). In addition to paying attention to the history of performance-based teacher education in the United States, there is a need to study the experience of other countries with this approach to reforming teacher education.

REFERENCES

American Association of Colleges for Teacher Education. (1974). *Achieving the potential of performance-based teacher education*. Washington, DC: Author.

Apple, M. (1972). Behaviorism and conservatism: The educational views in four system models of teacher education. In. B. Joyce & M. Weil (Eds.), *Perspectives for reform in teacher education* (pp. 237–262). Englewood Cliffs, NJ: Prentice Hall.

Apple, M. (2001). *Educating the "right" way: Markets, standards, God, and inequality.* New York: Routledge-Falmer.

Atkin, M., & Raths, J. (1974). *Changing patterns of teacher education in the U.S.* Paris: Organization for Economic Cooperation and Development.

Ballou, D., & Podgursky, M. (1998). The case against teacher certification. *The Public Interest, 132,* 17–29.

Ballou, D., & Podgursky, M. (2000). Reforming teacher preparation and licensing: What is the evidence? *Teachers College Record, 102*(1), 28–56.

Bestor, A. (1953). *Educational wastelands: The retreat from learning in our public schools.* Urbana: University of Illinois Press.

Broudy, H. (1973). *A critique of performance-based teacher education*. Washington, DC: American Association of Colleges of Teacher Education.

Charters, W. W. (1923). *Curriculum construction*. New York: Macmillan.

Charters, W. W., & Waples, D. (1929). *Commonwealth teacher training study*. Chicago: University of Chicago Press.

Clarke, S. C. T. (1969). The story of elementary teacher education models. *Journal of Teacher Education, 20*(3), 283–93.

Combs, A. (1972). Some basic concepts for teacher education. *Journal of Teacher Education, 22,* 286–90.

Darling-Hammond, L., & Snyder, J. (2000). Authentic assessment of teaching in context. *Teaching and Teacher Education, 16*(5–6), 523–545.

Darling-Hammond, L., Wise, A., & Klein, S. (1999). *A license to teach: Raising standards for teaching*. San Francisco: Jossey-Bass.

DeVault, M. V. (1973). Systems approach applications in designing teacher education programs. In D. Anderson (Ed.), *Competency-based teacher education* (Book 2, pp. 22–23). Berkeley, CA: McCutchan.

Diez, M. (1994). Relating standards to systemic reform. In M. Diez, V. Richardson, & P. D. Pearson (Eds.), *Setting standards and educating teachers: A national conversation* (pp. 1–14). Washington, DC: American Association of Colleges for Teacher Education.

Diez, M., & Hass, J. (1997). No more piecemeal reform: Using performance-based approaches to rethink teacher education. *Action in Teacher Education, 19*(2), 17–26.

Dilworth, M., & Brown, C. (2001). Consider the difference: Teaching and learning in culturally rich schools. In V. Richardson (Ed.), *Handbook of research on teaching* (4th ed., pp. 643–657). Washington, DC: American Educational Research Association.

Edelfelt, R., & Raths, J. (1999). *A brief history of standards in teacher education*. Reston, VA: Association of Teacher Educators.

Elam, S. (1971). *Performance based teacher education: What is the state of the Art?* (PBTE Series No. 1-36). Washington, DC: American Association of Colleges for Teacher Education.

Feistritzer, E., & Chester, D. T. (2000). *Alternative teacher certification: A state by state analysis, 2000*. Washington, DC: National Center for Education Information.

Furlong, J., Barton, L., Miles, S., Whiting, C., & Whitty, G. (2000). *Teacher education in transition: Re-forming professionalism*. Philadelphia: Open University Press.

Gage, N., & Winne, P. (1975). Performance-based teacher education. In K. Ryan (Ed.), *Teacher education* (pp. 146–172). Chicago: University of Chicago Press.

Garvin, P. (Ed.). (2003). *Developing knowledgeable teachers: A framework for standards-based teacher education supported by institutional collaboration*. Washington, DC: American Association of Colleges for Teacher Education.

Gay, G. (2000). *Culturally responsive teaching*. New York: Teachers College Press.

Goodlad, J. (1990). *Teachers for our nation's schools*. San Francisco: Jossey-Bass.

Haberman, M., & Stinnett, T. M. (1973). *Teacher education and the new profession of teaching*. Berkeley, CA: McCutchan.

Heath, R. W., & Nielson, M. (1974). The research base for performance-based teacher education. *Review of Educational Research, 44*(4), 463–84.

Hite, H. (1973). The cost of performance-based teacher education. *Journal of Teacher Education, 24*, 224.

Houston, W. R., & Howsam, R. (1972). *Competency based teacher education*. Chicago: Science Research Associates.

Joyce, B., Howey, K., & Yarger, S. (1977). *Preservice teacher education*. Palo Alto: Booksend Laboratory.

Kanstoroom, M., & Finn, C. (1999). *Better teachers and how to get more of them*. Washington, DC: The Fordham Foundation.

Kliebard, H. (1975). The rise of scientific curriculum making and its aftermath. *Curriculum Theory Network, 5*(1), 23–38.

Koerner, J. (1963). *The miseducation of American teachers*. Baltimore: Penguin Books.

Kramer, R. (Ed.). (2000). *School follies: The miseducation of America's teachers.* Lincoln, NE: Li.Universe.com

Ladson-Billings, G. (1994). *The dreamkeepers: Successful teachers of African-American children.* San Francisco: Jossey-Bass.

Liston, D., & Zeichner, K. (1991). *Teacher education and the social conditions of schooling.* New York: Routledge.

Mcconney, A., Schalock, M., & Schalock, D. (1998). Focusing improvement and quality assurance: Work samples as authentic performance measures of prospective teachers' effectiveness. *Journal of Personnel Evaluation in Education, 11*(4), 343–363.

McDonald, F. (1973). Behavior modification and teacher education. In C. Thoresen (Ed.), *Behavior modification in education* (pp. 41–76). Chicago: University of Chicago Press.

Ministry of Education. (2000, November). *Estandares de desempeno para la fomacion inicial de docents* [Standards of performance for the initial formation of docents]. Santiago de Chile: Ministerio de Educacion, Division de Educacion Superior.

Nash, R., & Agne, R. (1971). Competency in teacher education: A prop for the status quo. *Journal of Teacher Education, 22*(2), 147–156.

National Board for Professional Teaching Standards. (1994). *What teachers should know and be able to do.* Detroit: Author.

National Commission on Teaching and America's Future. (1996). *What matters most: Teaching for America's future.* New York: Author.

National Commission on Teaching and America's Future. (1997). *Doing what matters most: Investing in teaching.* New York: Author.

Pearson, P. D. (1994). Standards and teacher education: A policy perspective. In M. Diez, V. Richardson, & P. D. Pearson (Eds.), *Setting standards and educating teachers: A national conversation* (pp. 37–67). Washington, DC: American Association of Colleges for Teacher Education.

Porter, A., Youngs, P., & Odden, A. (2001). Advances in teacher assessments and their uses. In V. Richardson (Ed.), *Handbook of research on teaching* (4th ed., pp. 259–297). Washington, DC: American Educational Research Association.

Richardson, V. (1994). Standards and assessments: What is their educative potential? In M. Diez, V. Richardson, & P. D. Pearson (Eds.), *Setting standards and educating teachers* (pp. 15–36). Washington, DC: American Association of Colleges for Teacher Education.

Robinson, M. (2001, April). *Competence-based teacher education in South Africa: From policy to practice.* Paper presented at the annual meeting of the American Association of Colleges for Teacher Education, Seattle.

Roth, R. A. (1976). *A study of competency based teacher education: Philosophy, research, issues, and models.* Lansing, MI: Department of Education.

Sachs, J., & Groundwater-Smith, S. (1999). The changing landscape of teacher education in Australia. *Teaching and Teacher Education, 15*, 215–227.

Sandefur, J. T., & Nicklas, W. L. (1981). Competency-based teacher education in AACTE institutions. *Phi Delta Kappan, 62*, 747–48.

Saylor, J. G. (1976). *Antecedent developments in the movement to performance-based programs of teacher education.* Washington, DC: American Association of Colleges for Teacher Education.

Shepard, L. (2000). The role of assessment in a learning culture. *Educational Researcher, 29*(7), 4–14.

Tyack, D., & Cuban, L. (1995). *Tinkering toward utopia*. Cambridge, MA: Harvard University Press.

Valli, L., & Rennert-Ariev, P. (2002). New standards and assessments? Curriculum transformation in teacher education. *Journal of Curriculum Studies, 34*(2), 201–206.

UNESCO. (1998). *World education report: Teachers and teaching in a changing world*. Paris: Author.

Villegas, A. M., & Lucas, T. (2002). *Educating culturally responsive teachers: A coherent approach*. Albany: SUNY Press.

Weiner, L. (1993). *Preparing teachers for urban schools: Lessons from 30 years of reform*. New York: Teachers College Press.

Whitty, G., & Willmott, E. (1991). Competence-based teacher education: Approaches and issues. *Cambridge Journal of Education, 21*(3), 309–318.

Wilson, S. (1994). Performance-based assessment of teachers. In S. W. Soled (Ed.), *Assessment, testing and evaluation in teacher education* (pp. 189–219). Norwood, NJ: Ablex.

Examination of teachers. (1863). *Wisconsin Journal of Education, 7*, 19.

Zeichner, K. (2000). Ability-based teacher education at Alverno College. In L. Darling-Hammond (Ed.), *Studies of excellence in teacher education* (pp. 1–66). Washington, DC: American Association of Colleges for Teacher Education.

Zeichner, K. (2003). The adequacies and inadequacies of three current strategies to recruit, prepare, and retain the best teachers for all students. *Teachers College Record, 105*(3), 490–519.

Zeichner, K., & Schulte, A. (2001). What we know and don't know from peer-reviewed research about alternative teacher certification programs. *Journal of Teacher Education, 52*(4), 266–282.

Zeichner, K., & Wray, S. (2001). The teaching portfolio in U.S. teacher education programs: What we know and what we need to know. *Teaching and Teacher Education, 17*, 613–621.

Chapter 2

Foundations of a Sociocultural Perspective on Teacher Performance Assessment

Paul F. Conway
National University of Ireland, Cork

Alfredo J. Artiles
Arizona State University

In this chapter, we are concerned with the theories of learning underpinning models of assessment for preservice teachers in urban contexts. One fundamental premise in this chapter is that teacher performance assessment ought to document teacher learning. In outlining this perspective, we draw specifically on the sociocultural perspectives on learning and development that have grown primarily out of the work of Russian psychologists Vygotsky, Leont'ev, and Luria (Cole, 1996; Daniels, 2001; Tharp & Gallimore, 1988; Werstch, 1985b). A sociocultural perspective is our chosen stance on learning because it offers a socially just approach to learning and assessment, concurring with Oakes and Lipton's (1999) rationale that "sociocultural theories are important at the turn of the twenty-first century, because they shift the burden of low achievement from culturally and linguistically diverse groups ... to where it belongs: on schools and the larger society" (p. 78).

Unfortunately, more often than not, deficit thinking permeates the discourse around issues of instruction and assessment in urban settings (Tharp, 1997; Valencia, 1997). In adopting a sociocultural framework, we highlight the inequities with which practicing urban teachers and teacher

21

candidates must grapple in such settings—for example, dearth of resources, less qualified corps of teachers, a legacy of less-demanding instructional practices and curriculum materials (Anyon, 1980; Artiles, 1996; Darling-Hammond, 1994; Krei, 1998; Means, Chelemer, & Knapp, 1991; Oakes, 1986). As such, researchers and policymakers have drawn attention to the differences in teacher absenteeism, resource allocation, and teacher qualifications in urban settings to highlight the structural inequities underpinning teaching in urban schools and to unpack the cultural–historical precursors of pedagogical practices in such settings (Bruno, 2002; Kozol, 1992; Wayne, 2002). As Zeichner (chap. 1, this volume) illustrated, debate about teacher performance assessment has a long history in U.S. education. In a contemporary context, the public's concern about both teacher quality and teacher testing is reflected in the 2,100 articles published in *The New York Times* between 1996 and 2001 on these two topics (Cochran-Smith, 2001). Our focus, in this chapter, is how, in more recent times, learning theories have influenced models of teacher performance assessment, and how in turn these theories can be used to understand and reframe dominant teacher performance assessment approaches in the context of contemporary urban education.

A number of assumptions about teaching and teacher education guided us in writing this chapter. First, teacher assessment in urban schools needs to take into account the unique, complex, interactive challenges of urban contexts, as described by Peterman and Navarro (chaps. 3 & 8 respectively in this volume). Second, teacher assessment must be grounded in explicitly articulated visions of both teaching and teacher and student learning. Third, teacher assessment systems operate as powerful "message systems" with far-reaching influences on definitions of good teaching, resource allocation, professional development, perceptions of competence both individually and collectively by teachers, and instructional and curricular choices (Cochran-Smith, 2001).

We emphasize throughout the chapter a concern for issues of equity, as our work is situated in urban, multicultural contexts where disenfranchised groups of students are typically educated. Our goal is not to advance a detailed socio-cultural model of teacher assessment; instead, we outline the theoretical tenets of such an approach and discuss their implications. The chapter is divided into five sections. First, we emphasize the way equity pervades matters of curriculum, pedagogy, and assessment, and that the implications of the dominant teacher performance assessment systems have not been sufficiently examined in the context of urban teacher education. Second, we briefly address the limitations of influential approaches to teacher assessment, testing out their implicit theories of learning. That is, we examine the assumptions underpinning behavioral and cognitive approaches to assessment. Third, we provide an introduction to three assumptions of sociocultural learning theories: (a) the social origins of learning, (b) a situated view of teaching, and (c) a view of teacher performance assessment that examines the genesis and transformation of teaching performance. Fourth, based on these assumptions about learning, we identify and outline three implications for teacher performance assessment. Fifth, we describe a sociocultural approach to teacher performance assessment based on the work of the Center for Research in Education, Diversity and Excellence (CREDE), at the University of California, Santa Cruz (CREDE, 2002; Dalton, 1998). Finally, we identify three challenges in enacting a sociocultural-based teacher performance assessment system: the cost–benefit given the necessary investment, the complexities of engaging in intensely collaborative assessment processes, and the broader educational change agenda implied in a sociocultural approach to teacher performance assessment.

EQUITY ISSUES: SITUATING TEACHER PERFORMANCE ASSESSMENT IN THE IDEOLOGIES OF MESSAGE SYSTEMS

Equity issues pervade instruction, assessment, and curriculum practices in teacher education and can place teachers and teacher candidates in urban settings at an educational disadvantage. Moving beyond the immediate concern with preservice teacher performance assessment, the current accountability climate across the United States often results in a punitive stance toward urban schools. Nowhere is this more obvious than in the use of school report cards or league tables to compare schools' performance, as reflected in student test scores on annual state mandated tests (Conway, Goodell, & Carl, 2002). Such raw rankings and their simplistic interpretations now constitute a normative discourse in U.S. society, although they give a seriously distorted picture of the performance of teachers and students in urban settings (Amrein & Berliner, 2002). Largely forgotten in the public furor and the allied misuse of such high-stakes test results by the real-estate buyers and sellers, the media, and politicians is that students' performance is largely accounted for by socioeconomic background factors (e.g., family income, parents' education). The background factors have been evidenced in various value-added or multilevel analyses of student performance (Bryk & Raudenbush, 1992; Raudenbush, 1988, 1993). Furthermore, Zvoch and Stevens (2003) noted, based on a multilevel longitudinal analysis of urban middle schools, that

> … assessments of school performance depend on choices of how data are modeled and analyzed. In particular, the present study indicates that schools with low mean scores are not always "poor performing" schools. Use of student growth rates to evaluate school performance enables schools that would otherwise be deemed low performing to demonstrate positive effects on student achievement. (p. 38)

In a similar fashion, we are concerned that urban teacher education candidates may fall afoul of a normative discourse that is content to sideline issues of context, the social capital of their students, and vastly superior funding of suburban schools (Berliner & Biddle, 1996). In light of these equity concerns, we now examine curriculum, evaluation, and pedagogy as "message systems."

Bernstein (1971, 1973, 1977, 1982, 1996) has argued that curriculum, pedagogy, and evaluation mechanisms act as powerful "message systems" in education (Gipps, 1999). Each, in their own way, controls what and whose knowledge is valued and taught, how it is taught to particular groups, and most importantly, that "the education system … always works in the interests of particular dominant social groups" (Gipps, 1999, p. 362). Over the last decade in the United States, assessment has become *the* policy instrument of choice for many politicians and educational policy makers—that is, the message system (Delandshere & Petrosky, 2004). Although assessment has been used as a policy mechanism in one form or another for the last 50 years (Linn, 2000), teacher education in the 1990s can be labeled the decade of teacher evaluation (Porter, Youngs, & Odden, 2001). This is clearly evident in initiatives by various organizations such as the Interstate New Teacher Assessment and Support Consortium (INTASC), Educational Testing Service (ETS) through its PRAXIS exams and assessments, and the National Board for Professional Teaching Standards (NBPTS). Each organization, mainly responding to state legislature demands for teacher accountability, designed teacher assessment instruments supported by extensive validity and reliability studies (Porter et al., 2001). Contemporaneously, teacher assessment and evaluation has generated considerable debate in the last 15 years (Ambach, 1996; Cochran-Smith, 2001; Curry & Cruz, 2000; Darling-Hammond, 1997; Feiman-Nemser & Rosaen, 1997; Ladson-Billings, 1998; Pecheone & Stansbury, 1996; Shulman, 1987, 1988). What has been missing in this debate is an analysis of the assumptions that inform these policy initiatives. For instance, what assumptions about learning underpin various teacher performance assessment message systems? What are the images of the good teacher embedded in these message systems? To what extent do these assumptions about learning and images of the good teacher take into account the challenges of urban teaching?

MODELS OF LEARNING UNDERPINNING
TEACHER ASSESSMENT APPROACHES

Zeichner (chap. 1, this volume) traces the historical roots of teacher performance assessment and makes clear the complex political and social forces influencing its development. From the perspective of learning theory, over the last 40 years, three approaches to learning have underpinned systems of teacher assessment systems: the behavioral, the cognitive, and the sociocultural perspectives (see Table 2.1).

The assumptions about learning and development that underlie these theories have shaped[1] the nature of the assessment instruments, influenced the phase(s) of teaching chosen to assess (i.e., preactive, interactive, and postactive phases of teaching), guided the use of the instruments, and most importantly, conveyed powerful messages about the nature of both good teaching and, by implication, learning to teach (Conway, 2002).

Behavioral Perspective

The behavioral approach to learning depicts learning to teach as the accumulation of discrete behaviors that can be learned in a sequential and hierarchical fashion from simple to complex. This position assumes a building block model of learning to teach, where it is necessary to learn the simplest behaviors prior to the more complex. Consequently, from this perspective, complex teaching behaviors are best broken into their component parts, with the simplest being taught first and the complex skills best left until teachers have fully mastered the more rudimentary teaching skills. The beginning teacher (i.e., the learner) remains relatively passive as the environment—orchestrated by teacher educators—strengthens or weakens various stimulus–response pairings. Three flaws of this perspective are that, first, it presents learning to teach as something that can be broken into subcomponent elements; second, it uncouples the link between skill and context; and third, it depicts teaching as a collection of general pedagogical skills only. In terms of teacher assessment, rather than assessing teaching in a holistic fashion, the focus is on discrete behaviors. The reductionist nature of a behavioral approach to assessing teaching was particularly evident in its focus on only the interactive phase of teaching, as only overt behaviors were viewed as the target of assessment. Furthermore, because the link between skill and context was broken, assessors assumed that the observed teaching behaviors transferred across teaching contexts and across various content areas. Skills are seen as portable, abstracted from contexts in which they were learned. The behaviorist paradigm for teacher assessment results in rating scales focused on discrete and hierarchically sequenced teacher behaviors, such as those used in the Florida Beginning Teachers Assessment. Embodied in these scales was a vision of the good teacher as manager of

---

[1]We use preactive, interactive, and postactive phases of teaching, drawing on Jackson (1968). These terms have been useful to educational researchers in partitioning teaching temporally. Clark and Peterson (1986), in their extensive review of research on teacher thinking, adopted these categories and noted Jackson's use of this tripartite categorization.

TABLE 2.1
Behavioral and Cognitive Learning Theories and Teacher Assessment

Learning as …	*Behavioral* … change in behavior	*Cognitive & individual constructivist* … change in thinking
Teacher education pedagogy seeks to …	… make, strengthen, and then link discrete behaviors	… link new knowledge with old, … challenge misconceptions as teacher candidates in active construction of knowledge, … develop efficient and self-regulated information processing and decision making … reconstruct teacher beliefs
What is assessed?	Overt and discrete teaching behaviors	Teachers' schemas and constructions (including misconceptions) about teaching, subject matter, students and other aspects of teaching (i.e., teachers' "purposive action"/teacher behavior)
Nature of assessment instrument and use	Checklist of teacher behaviors divided into various domains of teaching competence with focus on frequency of observed behaviors	Checklist and/or open or focused observation notes; Formal and/or informal interview about teaching and related planning and evaluation
Phase(s) of teaching chosen to assess or target	Interactive phase of teaching	Preinteractive, interactive, and postinteractive phase
View of teaching and learning to teach	Teaching is a behavioral matter and learned as the accumulation of discrete behaviors across a variety of teaching domains	Development of efficient information processing, knowledge base for teaching, and/or construction of valid conceptions of teaching teacher behaviors/action in the classroom and underlying thinking.
Example in case of teacher assessment	Process product research (Good & Brophy, 1986)	Teacher Assessment Project (TAP) (Shulman 1987); PRAXIS III

environmental contingencies based on rules of reward and punishment (Clark, 1995; see Table 2.2).

Cognitive Perspective

In contrast to a behavioral perspective, the cognitive perspective on teacher assessment offers a more complex view of teaching as a demanding intellectual activity encompassing teacher candidates' performance, as well as their beliefs and knowledge about teaching, students, learning, subject matter, and a range

TABLE 2.2

Images of the Good Teacher in Theories of Learning

	Behavioral	*Cognitive*	*Sociocultural*
Image of the good teacher	Manager of environmental contingencies, that is, rewards and punishments	Executive decision maker and knowledge broker	Leading learner in a knowledge-building community of learners
Image of learning to teach	Developing skill in discrete and sequential hier-archical behaviors and rating scales congruent with these assumptions	Purposive action, involving preactive, interactive, and postactive phases of teaching	Activity system, becoming a member of a community, learning to participate in a community of practice
Advantages	Direct measure of teaching—not just a proxy	• Expands target of assessment, that is, beyond interactive • Attuned to link between skills and context (e.g., INTASC and NBPTS portfolio and case assessment exercises) • Encompasses general and domain specific teaching knowledge	• Assessment of solo and assisted performance → focus on potential not only achievement → does not conflate potential with achievement • Explicit meaning making focus where reflection is viewed as a social practice • Integrates social and individual dimensions of learning within the history of institutions
Problems and constraints	• Teaching can be broken into subcomponent elements • Uncouples link between skills and context • Teaching as only a collection of general pedagogical skills • Focus only on the interactive phase of teaching	Like behavioral, 'bounded individual' view of learner, privileging solo learner (e.g., INTASC, PRAXIS, and NBPTS view of teachers' own culture?)	• At odds with the dominant deficit- and punitive-focused approaches to assessing teachers and teaching (and students) in urban settings • Language and constructs of SC perspective sometimes seen as very abstract with unclear implications for the practice of assessment?

of other domains pertinent to teachers' thought processes and knowledge bases. The cognitive view of teaching encompasses both information processing and constructivist approaches to teaching. The target of assessment expands beyond but includes the interactive phase of teaching, encompassing the preactive (e.g., planning) and postactive (e.g., reflection, self-assessment) phases of teaching as valid domains for assessing teacher candidates' "purposive actions," knowledge, and beliefs. Commenting on the way cognitive approaches to learning pushed assessment beyond reductionist designs based on behavioral learning, Shepard (1991) notes that:

> Tests ought not to ask for demonstration of small, discrete skills practiced in isolation. They should be more ambitious instruments aimed at detecting what mental representations students hold of important ideas and what facility students have in bringing these understandings to bear in solving their problems. (p. 9)

The cognitive perspective presents a number of improvements on the behavioral perspective on assessment. First, it expands the scope of teaching phases that are the target of assessment to include the preactive and postactive, inasmuch as these additional dimensions of teaching are central in ascertaining the intellectual work of teachers. Second, the cognitive perspective links skills to context. For example, applying a cognitive view of teaching, INTASC and NBPTS designed portfolio and case assessment exercises to deliberately tap into the contextual dimension of teachers' work (Darling-Hammond & Snyder, 2000). Third, the cognitive view of teaching encompasses not just general pedagogical skills but knowledge specific to representations of content areas, including what Shulman (1986) terms pedagogical content knowledge, subject matter, and other knowledge domains. Finally, the cognitive model supports a range of assessment tasks designed to unveil the teacher candidate's thought processes and knowledge about teaching over time—for example, portfolios, cases, exhibitions of performance, and action research. A cognitive perspective on teacher performance assessment is, of course, concerned with teachers' behaviors, but is also attentive to the thought processes guiding these behaviors. As such, the focal concern of a cognitive perspective is "purposive action." The image of the good teacher embodied in the cognitive perspective is that of the executive decision maker and knowledge broker (Clark, 1995).

Frequently, the approach to teacher learning and development underpinning teacher assessment systems is insufficiently articulated. Porter et al. (2001), for example, analyze the conceptions of teaching and student learning underlying the INTASC, PRAXIS, and NBPTS assessments, but do not pay similar attention to conceptions of teacher learning underpinning each assessment. Porter et al. (2001) note that there are significant similarities among the three assessments despite the fact that the NBPTS standards refer to experienced teachers, INTASC focuses on preservice, and PRAXIS deals with early career teachers. We can see in these examples that a conception of the generality of teaching skills is still an important underpinning of teacher assessment.

Sociocultural Perspective

We argue that a sociocultural perspective offers a sound alternative to the behavioral or cognitive views as a foundation for urban teacher assessment because it integrates and systematically accounts for individual, social, and cultural–historical forces in learning. Indeed, a sociocultural model of teacher performance assessment can make a significant contribution to assessing the teacher in his or her cultural context. Unlike either behavioral or cognitive conceptions of learning, a sociocultural model is fundamentally social in nature (Cole, 1996; Daniels, 2001; Gipps, 1999; Wertsch, 1991). Such a perspective on teacher performance assessment explicitly attends to the constitutive relational and cultural nature of teaching. The emphasis on the social genesis of learning, thus, situates the learner in a sea of relationships and cultural symbols that shape and are shaped by the learner. From this perspective, while learning to teach, candidates draw not only on the knowledge, beliefs, and skills they have acquired, but also on the cultural and historical legacy of previous generations of teachers—that is, the knowledge embedded in their society's cultural tools and signs. For example, teachers rarely choose the physical layout of the school or classroom in which they teach, yet the architecture of teachers' workplace affords and constrains certain ways of teaching in its communication of particular thinking habits about what is knowledge and teacher–student relationships. In essence, the architecture of teachers' workplaces is a relational facet of an institutional epistemology, an observation that sociocultural theory affords, which is overlooked by both the behavioral and cognitive theories. Sociocultural theory also affords an expanded view of assessment as a cultural practice (Gipps, 1999, 2002) and is consistent with Moss' (1998) interpretive measurement model. Her interpretive model of measurement has, according to Porter et al. (2001), guided INTASC's portfolio scoring procedures.

Moss' (1998) hermeneutic approach "provides a means of combining information across multiple sources of evidence and of dealing with disabling biases that readers may bring" (p. 206). This hermeneutic approach involves a dual dialectic.[2] In a hermeneutic form of teacher assessment, evalu-

---

[2]The hermeneutic tradition as an approach to reading texts focuses on interpretation of the text in terms of an iterative process of focusing on the whole and then the parts. For example, in reading and understanding a sentence, one might focus on a specific word, then zoom out to focus on the whole sentence and maybe the entire paragraph and then back again to the word. The tension between the whole and parts constitutes a dialectic.   *(continued)*

ators keep two things in mind: First, the different facets of a teacher candidate's performance as well as the whole performance, and second, the teacher candidate's foreknowledge, preconceptions, and biases in the context of the teaching performance being evaluated. Finally, Moss's hermeneutic approach to assessment favors a dialectic and more reflexive stance by the teacher educators and others who evaluate teachers. These are particularly valuable qualities in the light of equity concerns we raised earlier in interrogating assessment as a powerful message system because it allows for ongoing dialogue that challenges inequities and makes visible the assumptions about teaching and learning that promote individual development within a complex, challenging setting.

TEACHING AS A CULTURAL ACTIVITY: A SOCIOCULTURAL PERSPECTIVE ON TEACHER PERFORMANCE ASSESSMENT

A sociocultural perspective defines teaching as a cultural activity embedded in the practices of local activity systems. This means teacher educators need to pay attention to the social contexts of teaching, to the ways teaching is mediated by the intellectual or ideational tools and material artifacts of a culture (e.g., the physical design of schools and classrooms, the format and content of textbooks, images of teaching as portrayed in the popular media and conversations between people in society, curricular documents, and the images of good teaching embedded in evaluation scales and assessment rubrics), and to the historical and institutional contexts of teaching practices.

A sociocultural perspective on teacher assessment offers a number of advantages over alternative perspectives grounded solely in behavioral or cognitive views of learning: (a) the emphasis on the potential rather than the limitations of learners, (b) the capacity to reflect and support learning to teach, and (c) the assumption that a human activity, such as teaching, is culturally embedded. In adopting a sociocultural approach on teacher assessment, we focus on the holistic assessment of teaching, a natural outgrowth of Vygotsky's concern for the holistic analysis of psychological activities.

Social Origins of Learning: Present and Potential Performance

Vygotsky's (1978) concept of the zone of proximal development (ZPD) is his most widely known contribution to a theory of human learning and development and has generated considerable research attention (Allal & Pelgrimes Ducrey, 2000; Brown & Ferrara, 1985; Tharp & Gallimore, 1989; Tudge,

---

[2](continued)   The dual dialectic here refers to Gadamer's (1987) advocacy of a particular stance he thought readers ought to adopt in reading any text; that is, simultaneously embracing the tension between the whole and the parts of the focal text, as well as the tension between their own frames and preconceptions as a reader and possible alternative frames.

1992; Tudge, Putnam, & Valsiner, 1996). The ZPD refers to the difference between what a person can do with and without the assistance of a more knowledgeable other or supportive external tool. The ZPD has implications for assessment especially in regard to learning as dynamic rather than static and for teaching as a support for learning. As such, the ZPD draws attention to the constraints of conventional assessments that rely on the evaluation of an individual's competence unaided by either a more knowledgeable other or external tools. Conventional assessments typically measure the lower bound of performance. In contrast, rather than focus on the limitations of learners in a solo or unassisted assessment scenario, a sociocultural approach to learning seeks to understand the potential of a learner in the context of assisted performance at the upper bound of the ZPD.

Sociocultural theory assumes that individuals learn to participate in cultural practices initially through the support of more knowledgeable others in goal-directed human activity—for example, learning to teach (Claxton & Wells, 2002). Eventually, as the person (e.g., student teacher or novice teacher) becomes more familiar with the expectations, routines, structures, and rituals of a given activity system (e.g., classrooms, schools), he or she takes on more responsibility. As such, learning in sociocultural theory can be seen as the transformation of participation. At the point where an individual (e.g., student teacher) begins to use the strategies, skills, and knowledge of the social context (e.g., school) in conventional and/or novel ways, one infers that he or she has appropriated the culture, that is, learned something. We use the term *activity system* here, drawing on the work of Finnish psychologist, Yrjö Engeström (1999), who defined an activity system as consisting of "object oriented, collective, and culturally mediated human activity" (p. 9). The adoption of the activity system as the unit of analysis is an important feature of the framework articulated in this chapter as it compels us to transcend the mind–society duality through an understanding of a person's performance as mediated by both individual and structural forces (Engeström, Miettinen, & Punamäki, 1999).

The assessment of changing participation, with and without assistance, in activity systems is the primary implication of the sociocultural perspective on learning for teacher assessment. According to Rogoff (1997), there are a number of strategies for evaluating changing participation. In terms of performance assessment of student, beginning, or experienced teachers, the assessment of changing participation might involve evaluation of the following:

- roles teachers play;
- changing purposes for involvement, commitment, to the endeavors and trust of the unknown aspects of it;
- flexibility and attitude toward change in involvement;

- interrelations of different contributions and contributors to the endeavor and readiness to switch;
- relation of participation in this activity and other activities;
- relation of change in the community's practice (Rogoff, 1997, p. 280).

When teacher educators pay attention to participation and its changing nature in activity systems, they are pressed to reframe their notions of thinking such that it is viewed as a collaborative undertaking rather than something that unfolds solely in the psyche of individuals. The essentially cultural nature of learning to teach and the adoption of an assessment approach congruent with this understanding is paramount. Relying solely on the thinking of teachers individually and outside of the social contexts, within which they engage professionally, more than likely masks and inhibits professional growth. Whereas most teacher education and assessment focuses on the individual learner, a sociocultural perspective elevates the social context as a focal assessment target.

The implications of sociocultural theory for teacher performance assessment in diverse cultural settings have been specified in detailed rubrics by the Center for Research on Education, Diversity, and Excellence (CREDE, http://www.crede.ucsc.edu/). Central to these rubrics are concepts based on an assisted performance conceptualization of learning (Tharp & Gallimore, 1988) that explicitly operationalize units of analysis beyond the individual teacher. Consistent with sociocultural theory, an emphasis on teachers' capacity to enact constructs such as joint productive activity deliberately focuses assessment toward teachers' and students' socially negotiated actions rather than teachers' discrete behaviors. We elaborate on CREDE's sociocultural-based "Standards for Effective Pedagogy" later in this chapter.

The ZPD and Ideal Form of Teaching

Shepel (1995) suggests that: "A child is from the very early stages two individuals—he himself and the other (the desired ideal of himself)" (p. 430). Shepel argues that the "relationship between individual 'ideal form' and cultural 'ideal form' is an abstract notion of the ZPD of a historical child" (p. 430). In terms of teacher performance assessment, his distinction between "individual ideal forms and cultural ideal forms" presents a challenge at two levels in efforts to enact what Cole (1996) has identified as "bringing the end point forward" (p. 183). Specifically, assessment should be based on an ideal view of teaching and thus, we should create conditions and situations of such an ideal state of affairs (i.e., we should bring the end point forward), not only to promote the formation of professional identity (i.e., teachers' cultural ideal) but also to assess their performance. This means teacher education programs should articulate a vision of what a socially just vision of teaching in urban schools should look like, as well as the roles teachers are expected to play in such a vision. It also means that preservice programs' curricula, pedagogy, and field experiences should be interrogated and reconstructed so that teacher candidates engage individually, as well as with the assistance of more capable others, in the use of those ideal forms of professional practice.

At the level of individual ideal forms, the challenge for teacher educators includes but reaches beyond engaging prospective teachers in interrogation of their beliefs to developing a vision of ideal forms. In addition, generative ideal forms must be construed in a manner that invites and inspires rather than solicits mere imitation. As such, images of good teaching in urban or educationally disadvantaged contexts, or what Shepel (1995) calls ideal forms, are a good example of the cultural and social mediation of teachers' conceptions of teaching.

A Situated View of Learning: The Mediation of Action Through Use of Artifacts

"… the central fact about our psychology is the fact of mediation" (Vygotsky, 1982, cited in Wertsch, 1985, p. 15). The belief in the cultural and social mediation of individual cognitive processes is the distinctive feature of Vygotskian theory (Cole & Wertsch, 1996; Wertsch, 1985a). For Vygotsky, our intellectual development takes place on the shoulders of previous generations (Bruner, 1986). The cultural tools, both material and psychological (e.g., speech, literacy, mathematics, art) that have been created over time reconfigure our nature as human beings. However, a conceptual challenge to Vygotsky's claim of the social origins of mental functions was that infants appear to have quite well developed powers of attention and perception. In addressing this anomaly, Vygotsky distinguished between lower psychological functions (LPF) and higher psychological functions (HPF). The former was unmediated and the latter culturally mediated.

Vygotsky's premise that higher psychological functions are culturally mediated draws our attention to how cultures mediate teaching, that is, how artifacts may mediate the internalization of cultural practices such as indicatory gestures, "doing school," or various teaching practices. Here, we again point to the preactive, interactive, and postactive phases of teaching and how each encompasses different components of reflective thinking. As most teacher education programs in the United States now espouse a reflective practitioner model of teacher education, even though the meaning of these may be considerably different from institution to institution, we turn to the ways in which reflection is mediated in teachers' development and, in turn, how it can be the focus of assessment.

From a teacher educator's viewpoint, the culturally mediated semiotic emphasis in Vygotsky's thinking, as the basis of preservice teachers' reflection, draws the teacher educator into a circle of meaning making with the prospective teacher. The teacher educator, in being attentive to the importance of the social context for learning, can seek to create contexts in which awareness and mastery of cultural tools (e.g., reflection) can take place (Hoffman-Kipp, Artiles, & López-Torres, in press; Moll, 1990). In this scenario, the role of reflection is twofold; it is both the goal of teacher education and the process itself:

> Reflection is the ability to make one's own behavior an object of study; to manage it via the ideal ability to regard oneself as the other. Reflection in this case works as an ideal artifact, a cultural tool, cardinally changing human consciousness. (Shepel, 1995, p. 434)

In seeking to promote reflection among teacher candidates, one can think of the work of teacher educators as "applied developmental work" (Nakkula & Ravitch, 1998). As such, student teacher reflections are seen as one basis for assessment, but also as a means of fostering teacher development. The teacher educator is challenged to identify and create social contexts—means of assistance—to support reflection. In doing so, teacher educators inevitably invite the student teacher into a conversation about his or her own development as a teacher (Conway & Clark, 2003):

> Reflection means asking basic questions of oneself. The basic and comprehensive question during reflection is "What am I doing and why?" ... On the other hand, to reflect means to stop acting, but at the same time, it is one of the most powerful actions ... reflection is a "becoming space" for the new thinking and imagining. (Shepel, 1995, p. 434)

In this conversation about the development of self as a teacher, "this slightly distorted self-evaluation," the centrality of meaning making is brought to the fore. Meaning making could be mediated by various data generation exercises encompassing portfolio artifacts, journal entries, or conversations among teacher candidates and others involved in teacher education (Hoffman-Kipp et al., in press).

Historical Analysis: Tracing the Genesis and Transformation of Performance

A third tenet, and key methodological insight, in Vygotskian theory is that human activity must be studied in transition for it to be understood; that is, the analysis of human development ought to focus on processes of change instead of an exclusive focus on outcomes (Artiles, Trent, Hoffman-Kipp, &

López-Torres, 2000). In this regard, Vygotsky was interested not only in the normal unfolding of activity but in its unfolding under conditions of disruption or interruption (Moll, 1990). An activity system perspective draws our attention to the social, historical, and political milieu within which assessments take place (Engeström et al., 1999; Leont'ev, 1981). Typically, teacher assessment involves the appraisal of an individual teacher's performance, thus, the spotlight is on the individual teacher. A sociocultural perspective shifts the unit of analysis from the individual to the activity setting. This shift from individual teacher to the activity system is a potentially valuable contribution to understanding teacher assessment systems because it offers a timely reminder that teaching and its assessment are embedded in the cultural and political contexts of social institutions. As such, the various tensions, contradictions, and conflicts as well as the patterns of resolutions, reinforcements, and accords that arise from this embeddedness are potentially instructive (D. Gibson, personal communication, 2001).

IMPLICATIONS FOR TEACHER PERFORMANCE ASSESSMENT IN URBAN SETTINGS

The three basic tenets of sociocultural theory summarized in the preceding section have explicit implications for teacher assessment. Integrating Moss' (1998) hermeneutic approach with a focus on its dual dialectic and sociocultural theory we have identified three principles for designing a teacher assessment system: (a) providing means for assisting performance; (b) evaluating changes in participation of teacher candidates over time; and (c) meaning-making processes as central to teacher assessment (see Table 2.3).

Provision of Means for Assisting Performance

The provision of means of assisting performance is a central implication of sociocultural theory as a means of both supporting learning and assessing the learner. A sociocultural approach is attentive to both solo and assisted performance, in contrast to the exclusive focus on solo performance in conventional assessment systems. In urban settings, the provision of means to assist performance inevitably raises questions of equity. These are likely to be raised by both teacher candidates and their assessors. This equity raising dividend of adopting assisted performance as a working principle is desirable and would help foster a "dual dialectic" (Gadamer, 1987), whereby teacher educators question their judgments and preconceptions in the light of local capacities. A frequent response to the challenges of teaching in urban settings is to dilute the quality of curriculum and pedagogy for students (Oakes & Lipton, 1999). From an equity stance, the frequent problem of curricular and pedagogical dilution in urban settings begs the question as

TABLE 2.3

Rubric Based on CREDE Standards for Effective Teaching and Learning—Standards I and IV

	Not Observed	Emerging	Developing	Enacting	Integrating
	The standard is not present.	The teacher designs and enacts activities ... where one or more elements of the standard are enacted.	... that demonstrate a partial enactment of the standard.	... that demonstrate a complete enactment of the standard.	The teacher designs, enacts, and collaborates in activities that demonstrate skillful integration of multiple standards simultaneously.
Standard I. Joint Productive Activity **Teacher and Students Producing**	Joint Productive Activity is not observed.	Students are seated with a partner or group, and (a) collaborate* and assist one another, or (b) are instructed in how to work in groups, or (c) contribute individual work, not requiring collaboration, to a joint product.*	Students collaborate on a joint product.	Students work in small group or fully inclusive whole-class activities in which teacher and students collaborate on a joint product.	The teacher designs, enacts, and collaborates in joint productive activities that demonstrate skillful integration* of multiple standards simultaneously.
Standard IV. Challenging Activities **Teaching Complex Thinking**	Challenging Activity is not observed.	The teacher (a) sets and presents standards for student performance, (b) accommodates students of varied ability levels, (c) connects instructional elements to academic concepts, or (d) provides students with feedback on their performance.	The teacher designs and enacts activities that advance student understanding to more complex levels,* or connects instructional elements to academic concepts.	The teacher presses, assists, and uses challenging standards to advance student understanding to more complex levels; connects instructional elements to academic concepts; and provides students with feedback on their performance.	The teacher designs, enacts, and collaborates in challenging activities that demonstrate skillful integration of multiple standards simultaneously.

Notes. Standards Performance Assessment Continuum (SPAC), Manual for Classroom Observation. Based on research funded by the OERI, NIERS, and USDOE funded research. Available online at: http://www.crede.ucsc.edu/ ; *See Appendix.

to how forms of assistance for student teachers can support more challenging curricular and pedagogical experiences for students in urban settings. Thus, in promoting mentoring, a form of assistance, teacher educators must attend to the quality of the mentoring in terms of its capacity to enhance equity. Furthermore, when assisting performance is taken seriously, assessment must support learning. Consequently, formative assessment ought to play a major role in a sociocultural-based teacher assessment system. The acknowledgment by school- and university-based teacher educators that what happens *between* people can either support or inhibit learning is a prerequisite if assisted performance is to be taken seriously in teacher education. However, we want to spell out in more detail what the actual assessment might look like, noting the implied tension between solo and assisted performance by addressing the implications of our views of learning and teaching.

Learning.   We must document both the precursors of individual performance during guided participation and the actual performance in subsequent activities. But the emphasis on the social origin of learning does not mean learning should not be assessed on an individual plane; we argue a cognitive perspective can be used to gauge the individual dimension of learning—that is, knowledge, beliefs. This means that sociocultural assessment models should document the tension that exists between the individual and social dimensions of learning, while accounting for the institutional dimension. In this vein, assessment must document how the institutional dimension mediates teacher performance. Thus, we must document how institutionally sanctioned rules, community expectations and goals, and the prescribed division of labor (i.e., roles) mediate teacher performance—attention to power issues within the division of labor is crucial (Artiles et al., 2000).

These ideas may translate in assessment activities that include: (a) continuous documentation of knowledge and beliefs, inasmuch as cultural models/schemas mediate performance (e.g., via concept maps and/or interviews; Trent & Artiles, 1998); (b) observation of teacher performance during guided participation in natural (e.g., team or collaborative teaching arrangements) and structured (e.g., demonstration lessons or analysis of videotaped teaching performance) contexts—this includes specification of the nature of guidance offered. For instance, assessment models could include sets of standardized tasks and assistance strategies (for examples of standardized tasks and strategies to "diagnose ZPDs," see Brown & Ferrara, 1985), and (c) documentation of solo performance in natural and structured contexts. Such observations provide access to the ZPD. Observations in "natural and structured contexts" can be conducted in the activity systems of planning, teaching, and postteaching reflection.

Teaching. The image of the teacher as leading learner in a knowledge-building community of learners is a starting point for the sociocultural assessment of teaching. From this perspective, we focus on the "social organization of learning" instead of "teaching" to stress the social and cultural roots of learning, and to shift the unit of analysis from the teacher to the group. Concrete examples of how to assess the social organization of learning is found in Englert, Tarrant, and Mariage's (1992) work. We think that a socioculturally-based teacher performance assessment system might utilize an assessment scale such as Englert et al.'s, as well as using more open ended and descriptive accounts of teaching performance (see also CREDE's web site for an alternative model http://www.crede.ucsc.edu).

Evaluating Changes in Participation of Teacher Candidates

From a sociocultural perspective, learning is viewed as change in participation, and as such, the variety of ways in which teacher candidates become involved in various professional relationships takes on central importance. Therefore, our focus turns to assessment over time, assessment based on an ideal view of professional practice, and changes in teachers' roles and professional identity. Thus, a sociocultural model attends to student teachers interactions, collaborative problem-solving skills, the development of teacher identity, and the structure, assets, and limitations of the cultural context of the school and community:

> Sociocultural theorists do not merely believe that culture influences learning, rather they believe that "learning and mental activities are cultural ... People cannot separate *how* thinking takes place from *what* knowledge is available in the place *where* learning happens. (Oakes & Lipton, 1999, p. 20, emphasis in original text)

As a complex and culturally embedded human activity, the assessment of learning to teach is not amenable to cursory engagement. Rather, a sociocultural approach highlights the importance of and impediments to paying attention to change and growth of teachers over time.

Meaning Making Central to Teacher Assessment

Drawing on both the centrality of semiotics in sociocultural theory and Moss' (1998) use of Gadamer's (1987) hermeneutic method, we think that meaning making ought to be a central feature in a teacher assessment system. Brown, Ash, Rutherford, Nakagawa, Gordon, and Campione (1993) discuss the notion of "mutual appropriation" and "negotiation" in the contexts of ZPDs. These notions highlight two aspects of assessment. First, we need to think about the process of assessment as a bidirectional process in which the teacher educator also learns (i.e., he or she sees himself or herself as a learner) during the assessment process not only about the novice teacher but also about himself or herself. This is indeed a neglected aspect in teacher assessment scholarship and in the entire teacher education literature. Second, the assessment process must be regarded as an eminently social and cultural process in which negotiation of meaning is paramount. If we accept meaning making as a central tenet of an assessment system, then teacher candidates and teacher educators are drawn into a hermeneutic circle. From this position, Moss' (1998) dual dialectic becomes a central feature of an assessment system. For instance, the issue of classroom management is often a central concern for novice teachers at both the preservice and early career stages (Veenman, 1984) and a particular concern for many teaching in urban settings. From the perspective of the dual dialectic, those assessing teachers must assess specific aspects of a teacher's actions in light of the teacher's overall actions in a given urban teaching context. For example, some novice teachers, in an effort to empathize with the often difficult life circumstances of their students, may set low expectations for students, which may contribute to poor academic engagement and class management problems. From an assessor's point of view, teacher candidates' understanding and urban students' life circumstances must be evaluated in terms of whether they do or do not set high academic expectations for students. This, then, is an example of how the part–whole dimension of teaching is important in performance assessment. In addition, those assessing teachers must pay attention to their own preconceptions about teacher expectations for urban students and how these ought to be enacted. The second part of Gadamer's (1987) dialectic puts an emphasis on the tension between their own frames and preconceptions as assessors and possible alternative frames. In terms of practice, teacher educators are challenged to continually press for new and alternative understandings of classroom management and teacher expectations in urban settings. We think that this fact can bring an important and generally neglected aspect of teacher assessment in urban settings to the fore, namely, teacher educators' own biases and cultural preconceptions.

Furthermore, self-assessment by teacher candidates becomes crucial as a stepping-stone toward holistic assessment. As such, paying attention to prospective teachers' prior knowledge and biography as learners is significant for teacher educators, evaluators, and those teachers being evaluated (Artiles, Gutierrez, & Rueda, 2002).

An Example: CREDE's "Five Standards of Effective Pedagogy"

The Center for Research on Education, Diversity, and Excellence (CREDE) at the University of California, Santa Cruz has developed a teaching assessment model based on sociocultural theories of learning (CREDE, 2002; Dalton, 1998; Doherty, Hilberg, Epaloose, & Tharp, 2002; Tharp, Estrada, Dalton, & Yamauchi, 2000). Based on CREDE's teacher assessment framework, schools serving diverse student populations are developing teacher performance assessment models based on these five standards. Such performance assessment models often rely on professional portfolios for teachers that are aligned with school and district requirements. CREDE's five standards for the assessment of effective pedagogy (see Dalton, 1998, pp. 43–47) are:

- Standard I: Joint productive activity (JPA)
- Standard II: Language and literacy development (LLD)
- Standard III: Meaning Making (MM)
- Standard IV: Complex Thinking (CT)
- Standard V: Instructional conversations (IC)

These five "Standards for Effective Pedagogy and Learning" were established through CREDE research, rooted in sociocultural theories of learning, and based on an extensive analysis of the research and development literature in education and diversity (Dalton, 1998). In the case of "joint productive activity" and other core constructs in the assessment system, CREDE (2002) acknowledges the sociocultural origins of these constructs (see Tharp & Gallimore, 1988):

> Learning occurs most effectively when experts and novices work together for a common product or goal, and are therefore motivated to assist one another. "Providing assistance" is the general definition of teaching; thus, joint productive activity (JPA) maximizes teaching and learning. Working together allows conversation, which teaches language, meaning, and values in the context of immediate issues. Teaching and learning through "joint productive activity" is cross-cultural, typically human, and probably "hard-wired."

The widespread appeal and emerging validity of the CREDE teacher assessment model in diverse urban and multiethnic contexts is evidenced in the proposed adoption of the CREDE standards by the International Reading Association (see www.reading.org/advocacy/standards/standards_instructions.html). As Dalton (1998) notes:

> The five pedagogy standards are joint productive activity (JPA), language and literacy development (LLD), meaning making (MM), complex thinking (CT), and instructional conversation (IC). These standards emerge from principles of practice that have proven successful with majority and minority at-risk students in a variety of teaching and learning settings

over several decades. Indicators are introduced for each standard, revealing action components of the standards and their functions in teaching and learning. (p. 4)

The proposal to adopt the CREDE "Standards of Effective Teaching and Learning" acknowledges their status as "basic general educational principles" (http://www.reading.org/pdf/1046.pdf, p. 3). Table 2.3 provides an example of Standards I and IV of CREDE's teacher assessment rubric.

Consistent with a sociocultural assumption about the potential learning dividend resulting from shared and collaborative undertaking of goals, Standard I, for example, focuses on the degree and nature of joint productive activity (JPA). As we noted at the outset of this chapter, a consistent feature of urban students' classroom experiences is the absence of both sufficiently challenging and supportive learning opportunities (Means, Chelemer, & Knapp, 1991). Consequently, Standard IV emphasizes the degree of challenge and nature of support provided by teachers in fostering complex thinking (CT).

CREDE has developed performance indicators in relation to the five standards. For example, in relation to Standard I, the indicators of joint productive activity are evidence that the teacher: (a) designs instructional activities requiring student collaboration to accomplish a joint product; (b) matches the demands of the joint productive activity to the time available for accomplishing them; (c) arranges classroom seating to accommodate students' individual and group needs to communicate and work jointly; (d) participates with students in joint productive activity; (e) organizes students in a variety of groupings, such as by friendship, mixed academic ability, language, project, or interests, to promote interaction; (f) plans with students how to work in groups and move from one activity to another, such as from large group introduction to small group activity, for clean-up, dismissal, and the like; (g) manages student and teacher access to materials and technology to facilitate joint productive activity; and (h) monitors and supports student collaboration in positive ways. In summary, CREDE's framework for teacher performance provides an empirically developed rubric (Doherty et al., 2002; Padron & Waxman, 1999) involving performance indicators across five standards rooted in sociocultural principles of learning.

CONCLUSION

In this chapter, we outlined the foundations of a sociocultural perspective on teacher assessment. We hope the broad principles sketched in this chapter will motivate teacher educators to develop context-specific adaptations to serve their unique needs. A number of issues arise out of our proposal for a sociocultural perspective on teacher performance assessment. We comment briefly on three challenges: (a) cost–benefit, (b) complexity of collaborative approaches to assessment, and (c) the educational change agenda inherent in a sociocultural perspective on teacher performance assessment.

First, the proposal for reframing the assessment of teachers from a sociocultural perspective poses many challenges, not least being the cost. Any effort to engage in systematic performance assessments is expensive. Furthermore, without sufficient professional development and induction for those involved, these efforts are likely to fail. As Mehrens (1992) noted:

> Because resources are always limited, the costs of performance assessments must be of great concern … this is not to suggest that we should not do performance assessments, but cost–benefit ratios must be considered. (p. 9)

Second, the inbuilt collaborative nature of a sociocultural perspective on assessment presents challenges not alone at a procedural level but also at the level of deeply held beliefs about teaching, learning, and assessment. In particular, Western notions of learning and assessment are deeply rooted in an individualist conception of the learner. Although a sociocultural perspective does not ignore the importance of solo performance as a valid and worthwhile target of assessment, it puts a particular emphasis on assessment in settings where assisted performance can be assessed with the dual purpose of both assessing and supporting learning.

Finally, the shift in perspective we advocate in this chapter implies significant educational change in terms of beliefs, methods, and resources. In underresourced urban settings, the challenge of accomplishing real change is particularly difficult and demands both resilience and creativity (Peterman, chap. 3, this volume). Nevertheless, we think the framing of teacher performance assessment within a sociocultural perspective will provide useful planning, implementation, and reflective tools for all those involved in teacher performance assessment in urban settings.

ACKNOWLEDGMENTS

We would like to acknowledge David Gibson's detailed feedback on an earlier draft of this paper. In addition, we thank members of UNITE's "Teacher Performance Assessment" subgroup for their comments, which influenced the shape of this chapter. Address for correspondence: Paul Conway, pconway@education.ucc.ie

The first author acknowledges the support of the University Office of Research and Economic Development (UORED) at Cleveland State University under New Faculty Grant # 0210-0511 awarded by the State of Ohio Department of Education. In addition, the first author acknowledges the support of the Education Department at the National University of Ireland, Cork.

The second author acknowledges the support of the National Center for Culturally Responsive Educational Systems (NCCREST) under grant # H326E020003 and the COMRISE Project (grant #H029J60006), both awarded by the U.S. Department of Education, Office of Special Education Programs.

APPENDIX: GLOSSARY OF TERMS FOR TABLE 2.3

Collaboration: joint activity that results in shared ownership, authorship, use, or responsibility for a product. It can also include division of labor for coordinated subsections.

Assistance: a two-part process in which the teacher first monitors current student performance capacity, and then provides tailored assistance that advances performance ability. Types of assistance may include: (a) modeling—providing a demonstration; (b) feeding back—providing information about student performance as compared with a standard; (c) contingency management—providing rewards or punishments contingent on student performance; (d) questioning—providing questions that guide the students to advance their understanding; (e) instructions—providing clear verbal directions for performance; (f) cognitive structuring—providing explanations or rules for proceeding; or (g) task structuring—providing assistance by segmenting or sequencing portions of the task.

Product: may be tangible or intangible. Examples of tangible products are: worksheet, essay, report, pottery, word-web, a math problem solved on the blackboard, play, skit, game, and debate. Intangible products include "story time," introductory lectures (the product is an accurate or elaborated understanding of a concept, procedure, idea), some instructional conversations, or some physical education activities (increased physical fitness is the product). The intangible products are an achieved physical, psychological, or social state that integrates a series of actions.

Complex thinking: activities that advance student understanding: (a) the "why" is addressed, not merely the "what" or the "how to"; (b) the activity requires that students generate knowledge or information, or use or elaborate on information provided (apply, interpret, categorize, order, evaluate, summarize, synthesize, analyze, explore, experiment, determine cause and effect, formulate and solve problems, explore patterns, make conjectures, generalize, justify, make judgments, interpret); (c) the teacher connects the specific content or activity to a broader concept or abstract idea to advance student understanding; or (d) the teacher provides instruction in critical thinking, or problem solving or metacognitive strategies.

Integrating: a single activity with two or more standards present at the enacting level.

Conversation (converse): is inclusive of topics familiar and interesting to students, is responsive to student contributions to the conversation, and includes joint participation structures that are responsive to students' interaction preferences. Conversation also includes sustained dialogue on a single topic and the asking of open-ended questions. A precondition or precursor of conversation is discourse between teacher and student(s) that is extended to at least two speech turns each, with each turn consisting of more than just providing an answer or providing a fact (responses to convergent teacher questions).

REFERENCES

Allal, L., & Pelgrimes Ducrey, G. (2000). Assessment of—or in—the zone of proximal development. *Learning & Instruction, 10*, 137–152.

Ambach, G. (1996). Standards for teachers: Potential for improving practice. *Phi Delta Kappan, 78*(3), 207–10.

Amrein, A. L., & Berliner, D. C. (2002, March 28). High-stakes testing, uncertainty, and student learning. *Educational Policy Analysis Archives, 10*(18). Retrieved July 3, 2003, from http://epaa.asu.edu/epaa/v10n18/

Anyon, J. (1980). Social class and the hidden curriculum. *Journal of Education, 168*, 61–80.

Artiles, A. J. (1996). Teacher thinking in urban schools: Toward a contextualized research agenda. In F. Ríos (Ed.), *Teacher thinking in cultural contexts* (pp. 23–52, 355–363). New York: SUNY Press.

Artiles, A. J., Gutierrez, K., & Rueda, R. (2002, April). *Teacher education in a culturally diverse inclusive era: Implications of a cultural historical vision for teacher learning research.* Paper presented at the annual meeting of the American Educational Research Association, New Orleans, LA.

Artiles, A. J., Trent, S. C., Hoffman-Kipp, P., & López-Torres, L. (2000). From individual acquisition to cultural–historical practices in multicultural teacher education. *Remedial and Special Education, 21*, 79–89.

Berliner, D. C., & Biddle, B. J. (1996). *The manufactured crisis: Myths, fraud, and the attack on America's public schools.* New York: Perseus Press.

Bernstein, B. (Ed.). (1971–1977). *Class, codes and control* (Vols. 1–3). London: Routledge & Kegan Paul.

Bernstein, B. (1982). *Codes, modalities and the processes of cultural production: A model.* London: Routledge & Kegan Paul.

Bernstein, B. (1996). *Pedagogy, symbolic control and identity.* London: Taylor & Francis.

Brown, A. L., & Ferrara, R. A. (1985). Diagnosing zones of proximal development. In J. Wertsch (Ed.), *Culture, communication and cognition* (pp. 272–305). New York: Cambridge University Press.

Brown, A. L., Ash, D., Rutherford, M., Nakagawa, K., Gordon, A., & Campione, J. C. (1993). Distributed expertise in the classroom. In G. Salomon (Ed.), *Distributed cognitions: Psychological and educational considerations* (pp. 188–228). Cambridge: Cambridge University Press.

Bruner, J. (1986). *Actual minds, possible worlds*. Cambridge, MA: Harvard University Press.

Bruno, J. E. (2002, July 26). The geographical distribution of teacher absenteeism in large urban school district settings: Implications for school reform efforts aimed at promoting equity and excellence in education. *Education Policy Analysis Archives, 10*(32). Retrieved July 3, 2003, from http://epaa.asu.edu/epaa/v10n32/

Bryk, A. S., & Raudenbush, S. W. (1992). *Hierarchical linear models: Applications and data analysis methods*. Newbury Park, CA: Sage.

Clark, C. M. (1995). *Thoughtful teaching*. New York: Teachers College Press.

Clark, C. M., & Peterson, P. L. (1986). Teachers' thought processes. In M. C. Wittock (Ed.), *Handbook of research on teaching* (3rd ed., pp. 255–296)). New York: Macmillan.

Claxton, G., & Wells, G. (Eds.). (2002). *Learning for life in the 21st century: Sociocultural perspectives on the future of education.* Oxford: Blackwell.

Cochran-Smith, M. (2001, April 2). Constructing outcomes in teacher education: Policy, practice and pitfalls. *Educational Policy Analysis Archives, 9*(11). Retrieved July 5, 2003 from http://epaa.asu.edu/epaa/v9n11.html

Cole, M. (1996). *Cultural psychology: A once and future discipline*. Cambridge, MA: Harvard University Press.

Cole, M., & Wertsch, J. V. (1996). Beyond the individual–social antimony in discussions of Piaget and Vygotsky. *Human Development, 39*(5), 250–256.

Conway, P. F. (2002). Learning in communities of practice: Rethinking teaching and learning in disadvantaged contexts. *Irish Educational Studies, 21*(3), 61–92.

Conway, P. F., & Clark, C. M. (2003). The journey inward and outward: A re-examination of Fuller's concerns-based model of teacher development. *Teaching and Teacher Education, 19*(5), 465–482.

Conway, P. F., Goodell, J., & Carl, J. (2002). Educational reform in the United States: Politics, purposes, and processes. In R. Griffin (Ed.), *Education in transition: International perspectives on the politics and processes of change* (pp. 83–108). London: Symposium Books.

CREDE. (2002, March). *Research evidence five standards for effective pedagogy and student outcomes*. (Technical Report No. G1). Center for Research on Education, Diversity & Excellence. http://www.crede.ucsc.edu/research/pdd/5stand_evidence.html

Curry, S., & Cruz, J. (2000). Portfolio-based teacher assessment. *Thrust for Educational Leadership, 29*(3), 34–37.

Dalton, S. S. (1998). *Pedagogy matters: Standards for effective teaching practice* (Research Rep. No. 4). Washington, DC & Santa Cruz, CA: Center for Research on Education, Diversity & Excellence. http://www.crede.ucsc.edu/products/print/reports.html

Daniels, H. (2001). *Vygotsky and pedagogy*. London: Routledge/Falmer.

Darling-Hammond, L. (1994). Who will speak for the children? How "Teach for America" hurts urban schools and students. *Phi Delta Kappan, 76*(1), 21–34.

Darling-Hammond, L. (1997). *Doing what matters most: Investing in quality teaching.* (ERIC Document Reproduction Service No. ED415183: 75)

Darling-Hammond, L., & Snyder, J. (2000). Authentic assessment of teaching in context. *Teaching and Teacher Education, 16*, 523–545.

Delandshere, G., & Petrosky, A. (2004). Political rationales and ideological stances of the standards-based reform of teacher education in the U.S. *Teaching and Teacher Education, 20*(1), 1–15.

Doherty, R. W., Hilberg, R. S., Epaloose, G., & Tharp, R. G. (2002). *Development and validation of the Standards Performance Continuum: A performance-based measure of the Standards for Effective Pedagogy.* Center for Research on Education, Diversity & Excellence. Manuscript submitted for publication.

Engeström, Y. (1999). Activity theory and individual and social transformation. In Y. Engeström, R. Miettinen, & R.-L. Punamäki (Eds.), *Perspectives on activity theory* (pp. 19–38). New York: Cambridge University Press.

Engeström, Y., Miettinen, R., & Punamäki, R.-L. (Eds.). (1999). *Perspectives on activity theory.* New York, NY: Cambridge University Press.

Englert, C. S., Tarrant, K. L., & Mariage, T. V. (1992). Defining and redefining instructional practice in special education: Perspectives on good teaching. *Teacher Education and Special Education, 15*(2), 62–86.

Feiman-Nemser, S., & Rosaen, C. (Eds.). (1997). *Guiding teacher learning: Insider studies of classroom work with prospective & practicing teachers.* (ERIC Document Reproduction Service No. ED408278: 113)

Gadamer, H. G. (1987). The problem of historical consciousness. In P. Rabinow & W. M. Sullivan (Eds.), *Interpretive social science: A second look* (pp. 82–140). Berkeley, CA: University of California Press. (Original work published 1963)

Gipps, C. V. (1999). Socio-cultural aspects of assessment. In A. Iran-Nejad & P. D. Pearson (Eds.), *Review of research in education* (pp. 335–392). Washington, DC: American Educational Research Association.

Gipps, C. V. (2002). Sociocultural perspectives on assessment. In G. Wells & G. Claxton (Eds.), *Learning for life in the 21st century* (pp. 73–83). Oxford: Blackwell.

Good, T. L., & Brophy, J. E. (1986). School effects. In M. C. Wittrock (Ed.), *Handbook of research on teaching* (3rd ed., pp. 570–602). New York: Macmillan.

Hoffman-Kipp, P., Artiles, A. J., & López-Torres, L. (in press). Beyond reflection: Teacher learning as praxis. *Theory into Practice.*

Jackson, P. W. (1968). *Life in classrooms.* New York: Holt, Rinehart & Winston.

Kozol, J. (1992). *Savage inequalities: Children in America's schools.* New York: HarperCollins.

Krei, M. S. (1998). Intensifying the barriers: The problem of inequitable teacher allocation in low-income urban schools. *Urban Education, 33*(1), 71–94.

Ladson-Billings, G. (1998). Teaching in dangerous times: Culturally relevant approaches to teacher assessment. *Journal of Negro Education, 67*(3), 255–67.

Leont'ev, A. N. (1981). The problem of activity in psychology. In J. V. Wertsch (Ed.), *The concept of activity in Soviet psychology* (pp. 37–71). Armonk, NY: M. E. Sharpe.

Linn, R. L. (2000). Assessments and accountability. *Educational Researcher, 29*(2), 4–16.

Means, B., Chelemer, C., & Knapp, M. S. (Eds.). (1991). *Teaching advanced skills to at-risk students: Views from research and practice*. San Francisco: Jossey-Bass.

Mehrens, W. A. (1992). Using performance assessment for accountability purposes. *Educational Measurement: Issues and Practice, 11*(1), 3–9, 20.

Moll, L. (Ed.). (1990). *Vygotsky and education: Instructional implications and applications of socio-historical psychology*. New York: Cambridge University Press.

Moss, P. A. (1998). Rethinking validity for the assessment of teaching. In N. Lyons (Ed.), *With portfolio in hand: Validating the new teacher professionalism* (pp. 202–219). New York: Teachers College Press.

Nakkula, M. J., & Ravitch, S. M. (1998). *Matters of interpretation: Reciprocal transformation in therapeutic and developmental relationships with youth*. San Francisco: Jossey-Bass.

Oakes, J. (1986). Tracking, inequality, and the rhetoric of school reform: Why schools don't change. *Journal of Education, 168*(1), 60–80.

Oakes, J., & Lipton, M. (1999). *Teaching to change the world*. Boston: McGraw-Hill College.

Padron, Y. N., & Waxman, H. C. (1999). Classroom observations of the five standards of effective teaching in urban classrooms with English language learners. *Teaching and Change, 7*(1), 79–100.

Pecheone, R. L., & Stansbury, K. (1996). Connecting teacher assessment and school reform. *Elementary School Journal, 97*(2), 163–77.

Porter, A. C., Youngs, P., & Odden, A. (2001). Advances in teacher assessments and their uses. In V. Richardson (Ed.), *Handbook of research on teaching* (4th ed., pp. 259–297). Washington, DC: American Educational Research Association.

Raudenbush, S. W. (1988). Educational applications of hierarchical linear models: A review. *Journal of Educational Statistics, 13*(2), 85–116.

Raudenbush, S. W. (1993). Hierarchical linear models and experimental design. In L. K. Edwards (Ed.), *Applied analysis of variance in behavioral science* (pp. 459–496). New York: Marcel Dekker.

Rogoff, B. (1997). Evaluating development in the process of participation: Theory, methods, and practice build on each other. In E. Amsel & K. A. E. Renninger (Eds.), *Change and development: Issues of theory, application, and method* (pp. 265–285). Mahwah, NJ: Lawrence Erlbaum Associates.

Shepard, L. (1991). Psycometrician's beliefs about teaching. *Educational Researcher, 20*(7), 2–16.

Shepel, E. N. L. (1995). Teacher self-identification in culture from Vygotsky's developmental perspective. *Anthropology and Education Quarterly, 26*, 425–442.

Shulman, L. S. (1986). Those who understand: Knowledge growth in teaching. *Educational Researcher, 15*(2), 4–14.

Shulman, L. S. (1987). Assessment for teaching: An initiative for the profession. *Phi Delta Kappan, 69*(1), 38–44.

Shulman, L. S. (1988). A union of insufficiencies: Strategies for teacher assessment in a period of educational reform. *Educational Leadership, 46*(3), 36–41.

Tharp, R. G. (1997). *From at-risk to excellence: Research, theory, and principles for practice*. Santa Cruz, CA: Center for Research on Education, Diversity, and Excellence.

Tharp, R. G., Estrada, P., Dalton, S. S., & Yamauchi, L. (2000). *Teaching transformed: Achieving excellence, fairness, inclusion, and harmony*. Boulder, CO: Westview Press.

Tharp, R. G., & Gallimore, R. (1988). *Rousing minds to life: Teaching, learning, and schooling in social context.* New York, NY: Cambridge University Press.

Tharp, R. G., & Gallimore, R. (1989). Rousing schools to life. *American Educator, 13*(2), 20–25, 46–52.

Trent, S. C., & Artiles, A. J. (Eds.). (1998). Multicultural teacher education in special and bilingual education: Exploring multiple measurement strategies to assess teacher learning [Special issue]. *Remedial and Special Education, 19*, 2–58.

Tudge, J. (1992). Vygotsky, the zone of proximal development, and peer collaboration: Implications for classroom practice. In L. C. Moll (Ed.), *Vygotsky and education: Instructional implications and applications of sociohistorical psychology* (155–172). New York, NY: Cambridge University Press.

Tudge, J., Putnam, S., & Valsiner, J. (1996). Culture and cognition in developmental perspective. In R. B. Cairns, G. H. J. Elder, & E. J. Costello (Eds.), *Developmental science* (190–222). New York, NY: Cambridge University Press.

Valencia, R. R. (1997). *The evolution of deficit thinking: educational thought and practice.* Washington, DC: Falmer Press.

Veenman, S. (1984). Perceived problems of beginning teachers. *Review of Educational Research, 54*(2), 143–78.

Vygotsky, L. S. (1978). *Mind in society: The development of higher psychological processes.* Cambridge, MA: Harvard University Press.

Wayne, A. J. (2002, June 13). Teacher inequality: New evidence on disparities in teachers' academic skills. *Education Policy Analysis Archives, 10*(30). Retrieved July 3, 2003 from http://epaa.asu.edu/epaa/v10n30/

Wertsch, J. V. (1985a). *Vygotsky and the social formation of mind.* Cambridge, MA: Harvard University Press.

Wertsch, J. V. (1985b). The semiotic mediation of mental life: L. S. Vygotsky & M. M. Bakhtin. In E. Mertz & R. J. Parmentier (Eds.), *Semiotic mediation: Sociocultural and psychological perspectives* (49–69). Orlando, FL: Academic Press.

Wertsch, J. V. (1991). *Voices of the mind: A sociocultural approach to mediated action.* Cambridge, MA: Harvard University Press.

Zvoch, K., & Stevens, J. J. (2003, July 8). A multi-level, longitudinal analysis of middle school math and language achievement. *Education Policy Analysis Archives, 11*(20). Retrieved July 9, 2003, from http://epaa.asu.edu/epaa/v11n20/

Chapter 3

Design Principles for Urban Teacher Assessment Systems

Francine P. Peterman
Cleveland State University

Teaching in an urban university affords me a close-up view of urban class-rooms and frequent interactions with urban educators. In one class, for instance, urban teachers and administrators discuss curriculum theory in light of their own daily experiences in inner city schools. Inevitably, in the midst of a hearty discourse about the work of John Dewey, Paulo Freire, bell hooks, Lisa Delpit, Gloria Ladson-Billings, Luis Moll, Ira Shor, and others, a teacher will ask, "But, what does this have to do with proficiency testing?" Thinking about culturally relevant teaching and liberatory pedagogy are engaging, they tell me ("It feels right"); such practices are contrary to cultural norms within their schools ("Other teachers don't do it.") and difficult to imagine amidst the competing demands placed on them ("I can't do it"). Culturally relevant and liberatory pedagogy become counterintuitive in teachers' situated realities of practice.

In light of daily reminders that scores on high-stakes, state-mandated tests matter from school administration, the local press, and the community, culturally relevant and liberatory pedagogy stirs the soul but remains impractical, to classroom teachers. "It won't work." "I have so much to cover before proficiency tests." "I don't have time to ask questions or to probe." "How would I be sure to cover all the content if I used students' questions to guide what I teach?" Truly competent, caring urban teachers respond honestly—with distress. Their daily lives in schools demand a practicality that supercedes the promise and relevance of sociocultural perspectives on teaching and learning, especially those that are liberatory. Although intrigued by the questioning, thinking, and reflecting at the heart of practices that are based on such theories, teachers often employ teacher-centered and directed practices. Such practices are reinforced by bureaucratic demands for higher test scores and supported by a smorgasbord of imported kits and texts that are not critically examined in light of the conceptions of teaching and learning on which they are based. Furthermore, grants that support the importation of such practices are implicitly grounded in political and theoretical assumptions that go unexamined as teachers in urban schools compete for additional funds, technology, and other resources (Freedman, 2000). The urban context itself challenges teachers to forego the intuitive and import the practical. The practicality ethic—continue to use what seems to work in this context (that is, easily managed and easily manages children)—often guides pedagogical decision making in urban settings (Doyle & Ponder, 1977).

To understand urban settings and their demands on successful teachers and to guide the development of performance assessment systems for urban teacher preparation, this chapter focuses on the complex features of urban settings and the distinguishing capacities of successful urban teachers. Furthermore, the author suggests how the complexities of urban schools and the traits of their best teachers define design principles for performance assessment systems for urban teacher preparation. Last, the author returns to how such design principles support the preparation of urban teachers who develop teaching practices that are culturally relevant, if not liberatory, and ultimately prepare students for success on high-stakes tests.

THE COMPLEXITY OF URBAN SCHOOLS

Urban settings entail a complex and demanding set of characteristics that inhibit critical reflection and inquiry and support teaching that is more reactive than reflective, more didactic than transformative. For instance, an increasing focus on high-stakes testing in an urban district may lead to administrators' implicitly supporting drill-and-skill activities rather than explicitly fostering advocacy for parents and children in ways that reduce inequities and promote learning. Furthermore, competing demands represented internally in administrative mandates and externally in the press, legislation, and RFPs (Requests for Proposals from foundations and other sponsors) drive teachers to ignore the intuitive (what they know might be best practice). Instead, they respond to implicit messages ("Drill and skill will improve test scores") without raising critical questions about the beliefs that underpin these texts and whether or not they are consistent with their personal, practical, and pedagogical content knowledge that is based on experience, research, and theory. Thus, complexities, demands, and limited resources, especially lack of time, often force teachers to act counterintuitively to what they know is best practice.

Hearing "Apply for grants, because we can use the resources to prepare students for the tests," a teacher dutifully applies for a technology grant, raising few questions about whether or not the outcomes of funded software match state standards. Hearing "Be sure your students are quiet and get right to work; they must pass the test," a group of teachers hurriedly prepare bell work using sample questions from high-stakes tests but without thinking about how the work connects to what students already know or will soon learn. Analyses of two such counterintuitive acts follow.

> An urban teacher, eager to increase the availability of technology and other resources in her classroom, applies for a grant. A company that creates supplementary computer programs for increasing students' mathematical problem-solving abilities sponsors this grant. The teacher follows the grant guidelines, receives the grant, and purchases the materials. With all good intentions, she uses the materials. The flashy, engaging, computer-based program requires that she place students into ability groups and promotes competition between individuals to increase their scores. Although she knows that cognitive coaching has been far more successful in promoting her students' understanding of concepts and problem solving, she did not think about this as she responded to the RFP. Happy to have children engaged by the computer program, to be able to track their progress, the teacher is content with the fruits of her effort. Her students' charted success on computer-generated quizzes prevents her from raising critical questions about what is actually being learned, who is not learning, and why. She is disappointed when the learning she believed was measured by the computer-generated quizzes is not replicated on her class scores on state-mandated proficiency tests. Her practicality ethic supports her sense of accomplishment   the innovation worked because her students learned and were well managed.

In urban settings, opportunities for resources often preclude a critical dialogue about teaching and learning and the theoretical underpinnings of imported solutions to classroom problems. Faced with competing demands for resources and success on high-stakes tests, practical and pedagogical content knowledge are laid aside for expediency and practicality. "We need the resources," the teacher may think in response to the administrator's "Let's get grants." Because the granted product seems to work—the children are quiet, engaged, and do well on program quizzes—there is no reason or time to question the content and process until the test scores are reported.

> "Keep children busy and quiet as soon as they enter the room," a principal announces at the opening faculty meeting. "We must improve test scores this year." In response, a small group of middle-grade teachers repro-

duces sets of worksheets, vocabulary lists, and problems to engage their students when the bell rings and attendance is recorded. This is known as "bell work" in many American schools. As the teachers meet, they recall what they remembered about last year's tests. One teacher gets online to review the state standards and finds several sample test items to use. Another gathers old test items from documents she borrowed from her sister-in-law in another school. From these items, the teachers generate a set of bell work activities to use during the first month of the school year. The students will be quiet as they busily engage in review activities for the proficiency test. Not a question is raised about how the bell work will relate to the units they had planned to teach that term or about how to embed the proficiency outcomes in rich content that is culturally relevant. When students' scores on proficiency tests improve slightly or do not improve at all, the teachers ask, "What's wrong with the test?" Worse still, "What's wrong with these children?"

As in this case, in urban American schools, sometimes bell work reflects teachers' response to an administrative mandate for taking time to prepare students for high-stakes testing. Often, bell work is simply a drill-and-skill task to keep children quiet, disconnected from what is to be learned and what has been learned. Although teachers often review standards that guide local high-stakes tests to prepare bell work, some may view the activity as distinctly different from the rest of the lesson. Despite what these teachers may know about their learning communities—the differences in culture, race, and language that are found there—they act expediently, sometimes dutifully, once again counterintuitively to what they have learned is best practice. Their practical knowledge—to bring students' backgrounds to the fore in planning—and their pedagogical content knowledge—to provide scaffolding for making meaningful connections—are abandoned in light of competing demands for using time, implementing prescribed practices such as bell work. In trying to use every moment to cover the content, the teacher misses the opportunity to connect children to learning and learning to children's experience. In effect, districts respond daily to external demands by issuing mandates that conflict with teachers' best pedagogical knowledge and sense of their own classroom communities. Faced with such dilemmas (competing demands and what they intuit is best for children), teachers may resort to the practicality ethic to guide their decision making.

Urban teachers hear conflicting messages: "Teach children to understand; be sure they can pass proficiency exams." "Use every minute to enhance learning; use bell work to keep children busy from the time they enter the room." "Use your head—ask questions; use others' ideas—without question." As illustrated in the previous examples, contradictions such as these illuminate the distinguishing characteristics of urban schools—bureaucratic and contradictory administrations; under-resourced institutions that serve communities distinguished by high levels of poverty; and diversity—that is, multicultural, multiracial, multiethnic, and multilinguistic learning communities.

These characteristics of urban settings may surely describe other settings —rural, innerring, suburban; however, they appear more intensely, in greater numbers, and in sets that interact deleteriously in the inner city environment. Moreover, they exist atop faltering infrastructures endemic to urban locales. Thus, regardless of increases in resources, transitions to innovative and responsive programs, curriculum and pedagogy, the political and physical structures on which urban schools are based erode the chances for long-term, positive effects. Needless to say, many urban schools face the challenges and thrive. Stories of urban settings and urban classrooms where communities engage in dialogue and invent practices that have enduring, positive effects abound. (See Delpit, 1995; Heckman, 1996; Hollingsworth, 1994; Ladson-Billings, 1994; Meier, 1995; Shirley, 1997; Wasley, Hampel, & Clark, 1997; Wilson & Corbett, 2001; Yeo, 1997.) Yet, few address the distinct capacities or knowledge, skills, and dispositions of highly successful urban teachers. Although Weiner (1993, 1999) has attempted to describe urban teaching and the best practices for preparing urban teachers, she stands among few teacher educators who focus their work on preparing teachers to face and overcome the fierce demands of urban settings. Nevertheless, all teacher educators who prepare urban teachers have a professional and moral obligation to prepare performance assessment systems that address the unique sets of characteristics that define urban schools. Such systems, built on a sociocultural framework as described in chapter 2 by Conway and Artiles, inevitably focus on issues of equity and excellence and challenge teachers, teacher educators, and other community members to rethink and redesign their beliefs and practices.

DISTINGUISHING CHARACTERISTICS OF URBAN SCHOOLS

Again, urban schools, in general, share common characteristics with schools in rural, inner-ring, and suburban districts. However, the intensity, complexity, and interactions of these characteristics atop faltering physical, economic, and political infrastructures further define urban schools as distinct challenges for new teachers. Basically, urban settings differ from others in that they are:

- *Bureaucratic and contradictory.* The size and organization of many urban districts inhibits significant change at the level of the school and the classroom. Many districts still operate as bureaucracies, where upper level administrators interpret laws and implement policies that conflict with the local knowledge and norms within their communities, their schools, and their classrooms. With competing demands created by legislated mandates taxing inadequate resources, districts sometimes resort to crisis-mode management, tangling urban teachers in bureaucratic red tape. Operating in a crisis mode while responding to legislated mandates and local demands with inadequate resources restricts administrators' and teachers' time for reflecting, planning, and choosing if, how, and when to respond to competing demands. Ensuing district policies and procedures sometimes stifle creativity and confound and complicate academic work, especially when resulting district mandates are enacted as practices whose underpinning beliefs remain in the minds of the creators and conflict with those of the teachers asked to implement them. Often these beliefs are contrary to what is known about how children learn and think, especially children coming together with a variety of differences in language and culture. Despite what has been learned about the difficulties in implementing innovations (e.g., Hargreaves, 1997; McLaughlin & Marsh, 1990), urgency or expediency rather than thoughtful reflection and analysis often dominates how and what decisions are made about practice. Often, but not in all cases, union contracts add to confusion. Thus, urban teachers receive a constant flow of mixed messages, messages that contradict their personal and professional knowledge.

• *Under-resourced.* Urban schools are traditionally under-resourced. Despite increased soft monies through grants and foundations, most urban districts heavily rely on inadequate state allocations and local tax dollars as their base budgets. Many urban schools are beyond repair, as the urban infrastructure crumbles. Time is a precious yet scant commodity. Underfunded legislation and local mandates tax depleted local dollars. Urban teachers struggle with competing demands for inadequate resources. The crisis-to-crisis mode of operation, supported by the bureaucracy, is heightened by a sense of need in the school and in the classroom. Urban teachers face dilemmas regarding how to assign homework when students do not receive individual textbooks or how to teach when administrators stress preparing for high-stakes testing through skill-and-drill strategies while sociolinguistic and cultural differences in the classroom may require alternative strategies. Furthermore, in responding to the underresourced nature of the district, school, and classroom by buying into what seems practical, educators ignore a critical view of their responses and solutions, reinforcing practices that maintain an inequitable status quo (Weiss & Fine, 2000; Yeo, 1997).

• *Poverty bound.* Distinguished by the number of families who live in poverty—a socioeconomic condition that is often reinforced by sociopolitical and educational practices that support and maintain the status quo rather than subvert it, urban settings create conditions that bind rather than liberate their constituents from poverty (Green, 2001;

Miron & St. John, 2003; Weiner, 2000, 2002; Weiss & Fine, 2000; Yeo, 1997). Although there are exemplars of urban schools where communities engage in liberatory practices (e.g., Ayers & Ford, 1996; Heckman, 1996; Heckman & Peterman, 1996; Middlebrooks, 1998; Yeo, 1997), urban teachers generally work in places that are ill prepared to confront inequities and prepare children and their parents for social and economic activism (Haberman & Post, 1998; Henig, Hula, Orr, & Pedescleaux, 2001; Knapp & Plecki, 2001). In some cases, then, poverty becomes a factor that defines students' ability to learn, rather than a condition that defines a new set of pedagogical practices that engages teachers and students in social activism (e.g., Oakes & Lipton, 2002; Payne, 2001). For instance, an urban teacher's labeling "these poor children" has quite a different impact from asking students to write about their homes and lives and reveling in the rich descriptions of where they live and dream. From a liberatory stance, the teacher confronts issues of race and class through dialogue both within the classroom (Freire, 1998; Shor & Pari, 1999) and community activism (Shirley, 1997). For example, literacy groups, where parents come to write and read in their own school communities, modeling the struggles and joys of learning for their own children, have provided rich models for community literacy building that combats the statistical position that poverty is directly related to low achievement (Ayers & Ford, 1996; Gallego & Hollingsworth, 2000; Heckman, 1996; Hollingsworth, 1994; Yeo, 1997).

• *Multicultural, multiracial, multiethnic, and multilinguistic.* Urban teachers work with students who differ across many lines, including but not limited to culture, class, race, language, and gender. Differences in culture and language usually multiply in urban settings, where students from many backgrounds reside. These differences often distinguish the students from their teachers, as many urban teachers are "teaching other people's children" (Delpit, 1995). In doing so, urban teachers may lack a general understanding of ways in which to assess and develop literacy, mathematical, and scientific knowledge. There may be significant gaps between how the teacher assesses knowledge and how the community members (especially students) value and express what and how they know and come to understand (Delpit, 1995; Gallego & Hollingsworth, 2000; Gamoran, Anderson, Quiroz, Secada, Williams, & Ashmann, 2003; Moll, 1990; Moll, Reyes, & Halcon, 2001). When teachers work with diverse populations, especially with parents and children whose cultures and languages differ from their own, they must develop intentional relationships that foster cultural understanding and create responsive conditions for learning and strategies for teaching (Delpit, 1995; Ladson-Billings, 1994; Noddings, 1992).

In general, but especially given these conditions, urban schools present complex problems for teachers, who must be resilient and committed as the foundations of their communities shift and falter.

URBAN TEACHERS AS RESPONSIVE PROBLEM SOLVERS

Successful urban teachers must invent transformative and responsive practices based on sociocultural theories of teaching and learning as described by Conway and Artiles (chap. 2 this volume) and others (e.g., Gallego & Hollingsworth, 2000; Moll, Reyes, & Halcon, 2001; Tharp, Estrada, Dalton, & Yamauchi, 2000). In times when high-stakes testing overshadows our schools, urban teachers must use highly developed personal, practical, and pedagogical content knowledge to guide their decision making. They must be prepared to use assessments of their students' learning to guide their own practice. In addition to having the prerequisite deep, strong content and pedagogical content knowledge, urban teachers must be creative problem solvers who are resourceful, resilient, and committed advocates for children and their families. At best, they engage in social activism that challenges the institutional structures that maintain socioeconomic and political inequities. Furthermore, urban teacher preparation programs must value and foster the development of these qualities in new teachers if they are to be successful in their urban classrooms and communities.

One might say, "Creativity, resourcefulness, resiliency, and advocacy—these capacities define the successful teacher in any setting." No doubt. However, the complexity and inconsistency of urban bureaucracies and the interactions of demands placed on the people who work there create challenges that exceed those in rural or innerring suburbs and tax severely impoverished resources. These conditions require specific attributes of urban teachers—attributes that are required, not simply defining. That is, quality teachers in any setting may be defined as creative, resourceful, resilient advocates for children and their families. However, to impact student learning as demonstrated, at least, on high-stakes testing, urban teachers are required to be creative, resourceful, resilient activists, or they will fail to overcome the bureaucratic, competing demands of their underresourced, complex settings, which reinforce counterintuitive practices that lead to student failure. Thus, urban teachers must be:

- *Creative problem solvers.* As creative problem solvers, urban teachers survey the landscape, identify the problems, name those problems, and determine a variety of solutions to those problems. Creative problem solvers are defined as those who can not only generate a variety of solutions to a problem but also can distinctly define the problem (Getzels & Csikszentmihalyi, 1967). In educational settings, such problem finding requires deep understanding not only of the content but of pedagogy and context. Urban teachers use these understandings to define the problem in terms of the setting, the learners and what they bring to the setting, the resources, the desired outcomes, and best practices (Starko, 2005). Problem solving becomes intuitive, as teachers use what they know to create learning communities where students achieve distinct learning outcomes, generally aligned with local, state, and national standards.

• *Resourceful.* Urban teachers know where and how to get what they need to teach—because they cannot often find all that they need within the schoolhouse gates. Furthermore, they look beyond the classroom as the center of learning in a child's life. They learn about their students and their communities of learning and knowing—their culture and language, what they bring to the classroom, how and what they learn inside and outside of school—in their homes and neighborhoods. Urban teachers begin to know the "community teachers"—those from whom their students learn (Moje, 2000; Moll, Reyes, & Halcon, 2001; Murrell, 2001)—and how to bring those teachers and/or their practices into the classroom.

• *Resilient and resistant.* Urban teachers may be discouraged by enforced practices and messages that are counterintuitive to what they know are best practices. To be successful, urban teachers learn to navigate complex systems that confront their self-efficacy and tax their stamina with resiliency. They resist competing demands, conflicting messages, and school cultures that force them to act counterintuitively to what they know is best and is right for urban schoolchildren. Urban teachers bounce back—daily, weekly, monthly, and annually, returning to places that subvert their efforts at advocacy and activism and remaining tolerant, while creatively addressing the challenges of intolerance, inadequacy, and inconsistency.

• *Activists for children, their parents, and their communities.* To help children learn and continue to learn, urban teachers develop a community of advocacy, drawing in resources that support their students' learning in and out of school. They proactively address issues of race, class, culture, and socioeconomic difference that continue to be used to sift and sort children rather than enrich their educational experiences. They engage in and support community activism.

Creativity, resourcefulness, resiliency, and advocacy define successful urban teachers who ride the wave of shifting foundations, increasing demands, and impoverished, often contradictory conditions.

DESIGN PRINCIPLES FOR URBAN
TEACHER ASSESSMENT SYSTEMS

Urban teacher preparation programs must not only value and prepare teachers with these characteristics but support their development with an assessment system that involves ongoing, multiple performances that capture the teacher candidates' capacities: (a) to creatively respond to complex, diverse settings; (b) to reflect on and learn from their social interactions with colleagues, parents, students, and others in their learning communities; (c) to serve as advocates for others in the learning community; and (d) to take an activist role to counteract social and bureaucratic injustices. In use, such assessment systems determine in which ways a teacher candidate is prepared to work in an urban setting—that is, how is and how has the teacher candidate become a reflective, professional, inquiring advocate. Thus, the assessment system must be sensitive not only to the candidates' capacities and performances but to the contexts in which they will work and the people with whom they will interact. Therefore, a sociocultural perspective on learning, teaching, and learning to teach (as described by Conway & Artiles, chap. 2, this volume) provides a practical framework for developing assessment systems for preparing urban educators. In such a system, learning is viewed as situated and assisted; thus, the assessment system becomes contextually bound and performance based, requiring ongoing dialogue and reflection. We recommend the following design principles for assessment systems for urban teacher preparation:

• *Situated and responsive.* The assessment system entails articulated, localized mission, vision, and/or goals and criteria that are consistent with and responsive to the complexity and politics of urban settings—in particular, the settings in which most candidates may find future employment. Such a situated mission or vision would be based on localized standards and aligned with state and national standards that guide teacher preparation. In addition, the mission or vision must be consistent with living in diverse settings, responsive to local conditions, and focused on addressing social, economic, and bureaucratic injustices. Assessment criteria must delineate the cultural, racial, ethnic, and linguistic diversity of the setting; require responsive teaching, learning, and assessing; and include indicators of creativity, resiliency, resistance, and commitment to advocacy and activism.

• *Longitudinal, reflective, in-action.* The assessment system must require a variety of representations of teacher candidate performance, including student work samples, over time and in multiple contexts. To develop and demonstrate the demanding capacities required of urban teachers, teacher candidates must engage in situated, complex tasks that mirror those with which they will be faced. These tasks—or assessments-in-action—would be designed not solely to evaluate a stagnant performance but to provide an opportunity for learning how to cope with and respond to counterintuitive, complicated, and competing demands. Such assessments-in-action would be assisted, that is, supported by peers and mentors whose own local pedagogical knowledge serves as scaffolding for the novice's professional growth. For instance, teacher candidates might be asked to develop and implement cooperative tasks that build learning communities and support literacy development. As they design, implement, and reflect on their tasks, the teacher candidates would engage in critical reflection on the activity with classmates, parents, teachers, faculty, and other community members who observe the teaching event and/or a video recording of it. The candidate would gather numerous artifacts reflecting the enactment of the task, its planning and implementation, and the reflections that guided revisions. Artifacts might include the written task, students' work created during and after the completion of the task, the candidate's evaluation of the task and lesson, videotaped lessons involved and reflective dialogues that followed, and journal entries that capture critical incidents and comments that supported professional growth.

Ideally, the same assessments-in-action would be situated in a variety of (at least two) urban settings and call for a sensitivity to the adults, children, resources, and others that define the context; include assistance in the form of reflective dialogue with peers, colleagues, and mentors to provide scaffolding and other forms of cognitive coaching; and require artifacts of the performance, reflection-on-action, and revision. Such professional performances may include implementing a unit plan, meeting with students and parents to create an action plan for a student's success, or coevaluating a student's work sample with a supervising teacher. Performances are represented in artifacts such as teachers' plans, reflective journals, or videotaped lessons as well as students' essays, problem solutions, projects, and experiments. These performances may be assisted through postobservation conferences, cognitive apprenticeships, informal conversations, or critical friends' dialogues. Using such representations and requiring individual and assisted reflection engages the teacher candidate in a professional practice that enhances professional growth.

• *Capacity building.* Assessments-in-action, when enacted in contextually rich, supportive environments, provide opportunities for capacity building, an important characteristic of urban assessment systems. Supported by appropriate scaffolding and embedded in rich circumstances and contextual incongruities, assessments-in-action allow the teacher candidate to come to know teaching and learning and to develop reflection-in-action through the engagement in real-life tasks. Through assisted performance, reflection, and dialogue, candidates unravel the roles of people and contexts in determining why and how a responsive educator might act under specific circumstances. Planned and informal discourse about professional practice within a supportive environment allows the candidate to name, rename, and rebuild professional understandings through action, reflection, and dialogue (Tharp & Gallimore, 1971). Teacher candidates and their mentors take ownership for their professional development, build capacity, and build resiliency. In such communities of inquiry, hope, and commitment teachers are transformed (Freire, 1970, 1998).

• *Activist.* Socioculturally based assessment systems promote advocacy and community activism simply because they require teacher candidates and others in their community to engage in critical and reflective dialogue about teaching, learning, and learning to teach. In such dialogue, as described by Conway and Artiles (chap. 2, this volume) and others (Hollingsworth, 1994; Weiss & Fine, 2000), the assessment system responds to the complexity and politics of the urban setting, providing opportunities for candidates to explore and use community resources to address situated concerns about such things as parental involvement, literacy, and student achievement. Such experiences and the reflection and dialogue required would inevitably lead to unearthing injustices and inequities that cannot be ignored—by the teachers, the teacher educators, and others. An activist system requires evidence of a teacher candidate's responding to injustice and inequity with reasoned, reflective actions that create caring classroom environments and promote students' learning and accruing social capital. The system requires urban teacher candidates to name the problems, develop a familiarity with the political networks employed to address them, and work with children, families, and communities to overcome institutional inequities.

These four design principles frame dynamic systems for assessing urban teacher candidates. Such systems must provide situated, longitudinal, and reflective assessments-in-action that allow for differences among urban settings and that support professional growth. As teacher educators set about the task of designing assessment systems for teacher candidates planning to work in urban settings, their inquiry might focus on questions like the following:

• *Situated and responsive.* What are the complexities, demands, and injustices of the urban setting? What defines the community? What are the implications of these characteristics for teaching, learning, and learning to teach? To what extent does the vision that guides the assessment system address these concerns? To what extent is this assessment system contextually responsive? What evidence of teacher candidates' reflective responses to crises and contradictions, diversity, poverty, and other contextually bound conditions are collected?

• *Longitudinal, reflective, in-action.* Which multiple representations of teacher candidate and student work samples are required? How do they represent the distinguishing characteristics, especially the complexity and competing demands, of the context? When, where, and how are these performances required and repeated? What forms of cognitive coaching, reflecting, scaffolding and revising are required to assist candidates in professional development? How do these change over time? How do the assessments-in-action support candidates' capacity building, especially in regard to creativity? Resourcefulness? Resiliency? Resistance? Activism?

• *Capacity building.* Who supports the candidates' professional growth? How? What types of planned and informal critical dialogue are provided for the candidate to recount successes and learn from mistakes, peers, parents, colleagues, mentors, and supervisors? How do candidates develop a sense of self-efficacy and ownership for professional growth? What are the differences among settings where the candidate will be assessed? How will these differences contribute to and enhance the candidate's professional growth? What opportunities are afforded for discussing capacity building and resiliency, both as professional strengths and responses to urban complexities?

• *Activist.* What evidence of advocacy for children and their families is required? How are political networks and community-based resources reflected in required performances and concomitant artifacts? How are teacher candidates' efforts documented? How and when are teacher candidates asked to discuss social and political inequities or address their impact on learners and their families? What evidence of advocacy and activism is required? At best, the assessment system requires evidence of social action to counteract societal and bureaucratic inequities.

Urban settings place a unique set of demands on new teachers. Not only must urban teachers be creative and resilient, have a positive sense of self-efficacy, and engage in advocacy and activism, they must ensure that their students score well on high-stakes testing. Thus, while responding to the complex, competing demands of the systems in which these teachers will work, the performance assessment systems we design for urban teacher preparation must provide opportunities for nurturing and further developing such capacities. Developing and implementing such systems is no easy task, as evidenced in the case studies that follow.

REFERENCES

Ayers, W. A., & Ford, P. (1996). *City kids, city teachers: Reports from the front row*. New York: New Press.

Delpit, L. (1995). *Other people's children: Cultural conflict in the classroom*. New York: New Press.

Doyle, W., & Ponder, G. A. (1977). The practicality ethic in teacher decision- making. *Interchange, 8*(3), 1–12.

Freedman, S. (2000). Teachers as grantseekers: The privatization of the urban public school teacher. *Teachers College Record, 102*, 398–441.

Freire, P. (1970). *Pedagogy of the oppressed*. New York: Seabury Press.

Freire, P. (1998). *Teachers as cultural workers: Letters to those who dare*. Boulder, CO: Westview Press.

Gallego, M. A., & Hollingsworth, S. (2000). *What counts as literacy: Challenging the school standard*. New York: Teachers College Press.

Gamoran, A., Anderson, C. W., Quiroz, P. A., Secada, W. G., Williams, T., & Ashmann, S. (2003). *Transforming teaching in math and science: How schools and districts can support change*. New York: Teachers College Press.

Getzels, J. W., & Csikszentmihalyi, M. (1967). Scientific creativity. *Science Journal, 3*(9), 80–84.

Green, C. (2001). *Manufacturing powerlessness in the Black diaspora: Inner-city youth and the new global frontier*. Walnut Creek, CA: Altamira Press.

Haberman, M., & Post, L. (1998). Teachers for multicultural schools: The power of selection. *Theory into Practice, 37*, 96–104.

Hargreaves, A. (1997). *Rethinking educational change with heart and mind*. Alexandria, VA: Association of Supervision and Curriculum Development.

Heckman, P. (1996). *The courage to change: Stories from successful school reform*.

Heckman, P., & Peterman, F. (1996). Indigenous invention: New promise for school reform. *Teachers College Record, 98*(2), 307–237.

Henig, J. R., Hula, R. C., Orr, M., & Pedescleaux, D. S. (2001). *The color of school reform: Race, politics, and the challenge of urban education*. Princeton, NJ: Princeton University Press.

Hollingsworth, S. (1994). *Teacher research and urban literacy education: Lessons and conversations in a feminist key*. New York: Teachers College Press.

Knapp, M., & Plecki, M. (2001). Investing in the renewal of urban science teaching. *Journal of Research in Science Teaching, 38*, 1089–1100.

Ladson-Billings, G. (1994). *The dreamkeepers: Successful teachers of African American children*. San Francisco, CA: Jossey-Bass.

McLaughlin, M. W., & March, D. D. (1990). Staff development and school change. In A. Lieberman (Ed.), *Schools as collaborative cultures: Creating the future now* (pp. 195–211). Bristol, PA: Falmer Press.

Meier, D. (1995). *The power of their ideas: Lessons for America from a small school in Harlem*. Boston, MA: Beacon Press.

Middlebrooks, S. (1998). *Getting to know city kids: Understanding their thinking, imagining, and socializing*. New York: Teachers College Press.

Miron, L. F., & St. John, E. P. (Eds.). (2003). *Reinterpreting urban school reform: Have urban schools failed, or has the reform movement failed urban schools?* Albany, NY: State University of New York Press.

Moje, E. B. (2000). To be part of the story: The literacy practices of gangsta adolescents. *Teachers College Record, 102*, 651–690.

Moll, L. (Ed.). (1990). *Vygotsky and education: Instructional implications and applications of sociohistorical psychology.* New York: Cambridge University Press.

Moll, L., Reyes, M. L., & Halcon, J. J. (Eds.). (2001). *The best for our children: Critical perspectives on literacy for Latino children.* New York: Teachers College Press.

Murrell, P. C. (2001). *The community teacher: A new framework for effective urban teaching.* New York: Teachers College Press.

Noddings, N. (1992). *The challenge of care to schools.* New York: Teachers College Press.

Oakes, J., & Lipton, M. (2002). *Teaching to change the world* (2nd ed.). Columbus, OH: McGraw-Hill.

Payne, R. (2001). *Framework for understanding poverty.* Highlands, TX: aha! Process.

Shirley, D. (1997). *Community organizing for urban school reform.* Austin, TX: University of Texas Press.

Shor, I., & Pari, C. (Eds.). (1999). *Education is politics: Critical teaching across differences, K–12.* Portsmouth, NH: Heinemann.

Starko, A. J. (2005). *Creativity in the classroom: Schools of curious delight (3rd Ed.).* Mahwah, NJ: Lawrence Erlbaum Associates.

Tharp, R. G., Estrada, P., Dalton, S. S., & Yamauchi, L. A. (2000). *Teaching transformed: Achieving excellence, fairness, inclusion, and harmony.* Boulder, CO: Westview Press.

Tharp, R. G., & Gallimore, R. (1971). *The instructional conversation: Teaching and learning in social activity.* A Report to the National Center for Research on Cultural Diversity and Second Language Learning, Santa Cruz, CA.

Wasley, P., Hampel, R. L., & Clark, R. W. (1997). *Kids and school reform.* San Francisco, CA: Jossey-Bass.

Weiner, L. (1993). *Preparing teachers for urban schools: Lessons from thirty years of school reform.* New York: Teachers College Press.

Weiner, L. (1999). *Urban teaching: The essentials.* New York: Teachers College Press.

Weiner, L. (2000). Research in the 90s: Implications for urban teacher preparation. *Review of Educational Research, 70*, 369–406.

Weiner, L. (2002). Evidence and inquiry in teacher education: What's needed for urban schools. *Journal of Teacher Education, 53*, 254–261.

Weiss, L., & Fine, M. (2000). *Construction sites: Excavating race class, and gender among urban youth.* New York: Teachers College Press.

Wilson, B. L., & Corbett, H. D. (2001). *Listening to urban kids: School reform and the teachers they want.* Albany, NY: State University of New York Press.

Yeo, F. L. (1997). *Inner-city schools, multiculturalism, and teacher education: A professional journey.* New York: Garland.

Part II

CASE STUDIES

Chapter 4

"Urban" Across Institutions: Portfolio Assessment at Cleveland State University

Kristien Marquez-Zenkov
Cleveland State University

In the 1990s U.S. state governments and universities could not develop alternative and compressed teaching certification options quickly enough to meet the nation's demand for new teachers (Olson, 2000). One of the most popular of these options was the graduate level certification program, which benefited myriad constituencies—universities, school districts, individual schools, potential teachers, and city kids—in innumerable ways (Darling-Hammond & Cobb, 1996). In startlingly brief turnaround times, masters certification programs (often called "Master of Arts in Teaching" or MAT programs) supplied universities with an entirely new population of students, furnished school districts with an additional resource for their growing demand for teachers, and delivered a more mature population of novice educators to school faculties already facing a dire need for new teachers (Mayer, Mullens, & Moore, 2000; Olson & Jerald, 1998).

Universities prized the lucrative nature of a full-time nonscholarship graduate student populace with high retention and degree completion rates, and MAT students valued the condensed path to licensure, as well as the supportive collegial character inherent in the cohort models used by many of the certification programs. All parties appreciated the public prestige associated with these intense degree programs. Colleges of education and their new audience of "nontraditional" students—older, returning, career-changers—were united by these programs' "basic training" regimens that yielded both a teaching license and a masters degree.

This chapter presents a case study of one example of this MAT trend, the development of the Master of Urban Secondary Teaching (MUST) program at Cleveland State University (CSU). Through its first 3 years of existence, MUST remained a MAT program in its infancy, where the conditions inherent in its founding had not yet allowed for the consistent implementation of many program components, including its portfolio assessment process. While the MUST program was an evolving quilt of elements, responsive assessments, and reactive decisions, these embryonic, responsive, and tenuous qualities were both something *other* and something *more* than the unique, short-lived features of this one program. More often than not, they are the inherent, *shared* attributes of urban universities and school districts, and the defining characteristics of urban settings and all of the educational institutions in them.

Peterman (chap. 3, this volume) details a specific set of conditions that are generally intensified in urban locales. Although the entire constellation of these circumstances may not be endemic to every K–12 urban district in the United States, one premise of this complete manuscript is that urban settings are commonly characterized by the existence of at least some of these conditions, in unique and particularly challenging combinations. As Peterman defines them, urban schools are intensely bureaucratic and contradictory, consistently underresourced and poverty-bound, and address the needs of populations that are especially diverse in culture, race, ethnicity, and language. Even a cursory glance at MUST and Cleveland State University reveals how these characteristics are core qualities of urban universities, as well. This study, then, first examines the parallels across one urban university and its partnering urban school districts, introducing the explicitly urban conditions faced by one masters licensure program and the effects these conditions have had on its nascent portfolio assessment system.

This focus reveals that related conditions in these apparently distinct organizations have exacerbated already challenging circumstances in both settings, and suggests that lessons for utilizing performance assessments in urban teacher education might be learned from a recognition of the interplay of these cross-institutional factors. The Conway and Artiles chapter that provides the theoretical foundation for this volume suggests that performance assessment systems for urban teacher education programs must be consciously grounded in sociocultural theory. But a recognition of the similarities across urban universities and urban schools reveals that such theory need be applied simultaneously—in and across *both* settings—if the most valid, responsive, and practical assessment systems are to be developed.

To be clear, this chapter is a study of the contexts of the birth and early years' evolution of a performance assessment system in an urban university setting, rather than a detailed portrayal of an actual portfolio assessment process in action or a definitive analysis of the impact of such a system on even a single cohort of future city teachers. Urban teacher educators nationwide would certainly benefit from "how to" lessons about implementing such an assessment system, and educators committed to these holistic systems require precise data about their impact on city teachers' practices and city students' achievement. But the challenges to such implementation and data collection appear at the foundational level of our urban institutions, and these trials must first be sufficiently acknowledged and understood. If urban teacher education programs are going to utilize these alternative assessments, then these systems must be developed with careful consideration of the factors that urban teacher educators and teachers encounter, in and across their university and school settings. If we are to achieve any lasting progress toward assessment systems that most effectively and equitably honor what city teachers should know and be able to do, then we must first candidly consider these details and the stories of the conditions that proscribe these systems' development.

METHODOLOGY

I utilized a case study methodology for researching the development of MUST's portfolio assessment system in its midsized, Midwestern city context. Such a methodological design allowed for the consideration and presentation of contextualized, in-depth understandings of a particular phenomenon with the expectation that appropriate details would allow readers to analyze the relevance of this study for their own use (Stake, 1995; Yin, 1994). As a new faculty member responsible for the implementation of the portfolio assessment system that is the focus of this chapter, I required such a concentrated, relational outlook in order to be responsible to both my researcher and teacher educator roles.

Although I have the opportunity to tell the story of this system's early development, and I am largely responsible for its current implementation and continued evolution, I was not heavily involved in its initial design and development. The primary authors of this system included CSU faculty members (Fran Peterman, Paul Conway, Marguerite Vanden Wyngaard, Joanne Goodell, Frank Johns, & Bram Hamovitch), program mentor teachers (Audrey Schneider & Karen Boyle), and at least one CSU doctoral student (Nona Burney). Consequently, data for this chapter came from multiple sources, including meeting minutes, draft program descriptions, extensive notes from interviews of current and former university faculty and administration, course syllabi, discussions of the portfolio assessment system's operation with early program coordinators and three cohorts of program participants, and supporting documents from the 6 years of this portfolio system's development and implementation. As with most types of qualitative research, I analyzed this data both during and after its collection (Creswell, 1994; Merriam & Simpson, 1995; Short, 1993).

Specifically, this case study highlights four features of the development of this portfolio assessment system: (a) the limitations placed on the MUST program by the complex administrative and often bureaucratic traditions of both Cleveland State and the urban school districts with which it partners; (b) the nature of the CSU faculty collaboration in the program design, portfolio assessment system design, and portfolio assessment implementation processes, concentrating briefly on my role in this collaboration as I facilitated the second, third, and fourth years of the portfolio assessment process; (c) the process of identifying performance criteria and assessments that address the program's unique urban, social justice mission; and (d) the relationship between the implementation of the MUST portfolio assessment process, and current, broad concepts of literacy (Gallego & Hollingsworth, 2000; Hull & Schultz, 2002; Moss, 1994). The first three features focus on the program's development and its first 2 years of implementation, and the fourth illustrates how such notions of literacy have found a permanent place in this program's portfolio assessment process. These four highlighted features are intimately related to each other, as well as to the urban characteristics by which all of the teacher education programs described in this volume are united.

Given the brevity of this case study, each of these characteristics is described in succinct terms, in a concise but useful snapshot. As is typical of such limited sample research, and like most attempts at formulating broad conclusions about the features of a complex setting, the findings of this study are tenuous and their generalizability and validity indeterminate. Naturally, only those readers who examine the findings shared here with an eye toward their own contexts will know their usefulness. Even with these limitations, this account of cross-institutional urban challenges may be enlightening for a range of constituents in urban colleges of education, urban school districts, and other institutions in urban settings.

Administrative Traditions and Bureaucracy

As evidenced throughout this volume, urban districts in the United States have long felt the brunt of the problems most school districts eventually face. Perhaps the most imposing challenge districts have faced in recent decades is a crisis-level shortage of qualified teachers. Tragically, some of the same conditions of urban school districts that have led to these teacher shortages also frequently conspire to make these city schools among the least responsive to this most urgent need. As Peterman (chap. 3) articulates, poor, city school districts often operate with an institutionalized "break even" mentality when it comes to predicting and addressing their crises. Whereas logic would suggest that these needs-rich and teacher-poor districts would be the first to successfully explore alternative certification avenues for new teachers, this has not often been the case. As an example, although districts in the Cleveland, Ohio area have been especially susceptible to this teacher deficit over the past decade, they have unsystematically appealed to local universities to assist with this shortage through a variety of alternative certification efforts. Thus, while Cleveland and its urban neighbors faced a teacher scarcity throughout the 1990s, these districts' administrations were slow to respond in effective ways.

An awareness of the Cleveland-area districts' teacher shortages and local institutions' marginally effective efforts at addressing them, combined with the nationwide trend toward masters and alternative certification programs, were noteworthy factors in Cleveland State University's development of its first masters certification program, the Master of Urban Secondary Teaching (MUST) program, in the late 1990s. Although this certification initiative offered to meet some of the most pressing needs of these districts, a history of decision making bogged down by bureaucracy and a tradition of failed cross-institutional collaborations delayed MUST's development and has served to inhibit the support of this program in both the university and the various district settings. Both in spite of and as a result of these traditions, the administrative pressures and initial energy among CSU faculty to design an innovative program were considerable.

MUST originated as a program chiefly because of an urgent call from the highest levels of the college hierarchy, rather than through a groundswell of support from effected constituencies. In December 1996, the Dean of the CSU College of Education appointed a committee of College of Education faculty, administration, and graduate students to develop a proposal for the University's first Master of Arts in Teaching certification program. These initial conversations moved along slowly until a faculty member and a school principal outlined a program design: The MUST program would focus on secondary teachers, specializing in math and science content areas, house students at one Cleveland high school with a Professional Development School (PDS) model (Abdul-Haqq, 1998; Darling-Hammond, 1994; Holmes Group, 1990; Johnson, 2000), and require two full-time faculty members to coordinate, teach, and supervise the students. At a later stage of these committee discussions, another faculty member introduced an alternative program outline, but by this time the exigency felt from the inception of the planning meetings extinguished any serious consideration of alternatives. A final MUST program plan was submitted to the Dean of the College of Education in June 1998; it was approved without significant modifications and officially formulated as a new masters program during the 1998–1999 academic year.

The adopted model called for MUST to be a selective, field-based graduate teacher education program. The program's goal was to graduate reflective, responsive teacher-leaders who would be prepared to address the effects of race, class, and gender on achievement and promote students' learning through responsive pedagogy (Ladson-Billings, 1998a). Admission requirements would include a bachelor's degree in mathematics, science, English, history, or a related field, above-average grades in that field, an articulated commitment to urban school and community renewal, and demonstrated competencies in communication, leadership, collaboration, and problem solving, in part evaluated during a group interview process. Students would be admitted as a cohort, taking classes together for the duration of the program. Prospective candidates would commit to a 14-month program, including a 9-month, unpaid, school-based internship, working side-by-side with their mentor teachers at an area urban high school. MUST graduates would earn a Masters of Education degree with a specialization in Curriculum and Instruction, and, on completion of state requirements, be certified or licensed to teach in Ohio. As exit requirements, students would complete a publishable classroom research project and a professional portfolio.

The nucleus of CSU faculty responsible for the MUST program's development recognized that a performance-based portfolio assessment system was not only a pedagogically credible feature, but also the only holistic assessment model consistent with the brevity of a MAT program (Barton & Collins, 1993; Darling-Hammond & Snyder, 2000; Lyons, 1998; Neill, Bursh, Schaeffer, Thall, Yohe, & Zappardino,1995; Reis & Villaume, 2002; Wolf, 1999). One of its founders described a portfolio as "an envelope of the mind" that is developed through an elaborate process, rather than "simply a set of outcomes and products." As well, several participants in these discussions believed that this portfolio system might encourage a revision in the employment portfolio that was then one of the few formal introductions to alternative assessment provided by the college's other teacher education programs. When the MUST program was pioneered, only the physical education program had done substantive work on a performance-based assessment system for a Cleveland State teacher certification program (Melograno, 1999). The MUST program design described an ongoing performance assessment system culminating in a professional teaching portfolio (Campbell, Cignetti, Melenyzer, Nettles, & Wyman, 1997; Diez & Hass, 1997; Martin, 1999; Murrell, 1998; Willis & Davies, 2002). Although it was understood that MUST students would complete a variety of both traditional and nontraditional assessments throughout their college and program coursework, it was expected that students would collect portfolio artifacts from all coursework and field experiences.

MUST university faculty and collaborating Cleveland-area school personnel approached each of the first two program years with the high ideals represented by the program admission requirements, program component descriptions, and the portfolio assessment system plan. But, much like the Cleveland Municipal School District with its insufficient teacher population, this fledgling program struggled to fill its available slots, for both applicants and university faculty. Although not synonymous with CSU or school district administrative incapacity, the cycle of bureaucratic lethargy followed by administrative urgency resulted in mandates for change that were underfunded, insufficiently supported, and incompletely outlined. In its first 3 years, this urgency took the form of frequent administrative inquiries into the status of the program, the top-down implementation of a hurriedly established program design, and the convulsive rather than developmental evolution of the portfolio assessment system. This urgent administrative implementation also played a role in limiting the amount and quality of faculty involvement in the overall program and its portfolio assessment system, which was intended as one of the program's unifying components.

Faculty Involvement

Just as most urban K–12 school settings face a complicated resource shortage, the MUST program and its development of a portfolio assessment system faced a similar reality: Faculty collaboration around such a program and one of its key components could not occur without the simple existence of a core group of interested faculty members. Because departments within the CSU College of Education had conducted several failed faculty searches in the late 1990s, the burden of developing a new masters certification program in a year's time placed intense pressure on already overworked personnel. Although several CSU faculty and high school faculty were involved with the program's early development (including Peterman, Conway, Goodell, Johns, Schneider, & Boyle), the overall faculty shortage resulted in a lack of significant involvement in the program's design and implementation, as well as a shifting of responsibility for this program to new faculty members (e.g., Hamovitch & Vanden Wyngaard). This shortage also played an important role in my being asked to teach in, and eventually coordinate a primary component of, the MUST program.

Based on decisions made about the selection of the program's first coordinators, this lack of faculty involvement might have been predicted. Late in the original MAT discussions, many of the committee's members argued that new faculty positions should be created for this program, rather than requiring existing faculty to take on the additional responsibility of administering it. During the 1998–1999 academic year, these positions were funded for the program's first year, posted, and filled. Although this added two new college personnel who were specifically committed to such a program, this decision eventually meant that a novel program would begin with brand new CSU faculty members who had not been involved with the program's generation and who had no previous relationship to each other. It was only natural that such faculty members, inundated by the responsibilities of new positions in an emerging program with established colleagues who were only peripherally involved, would not be able to facilitate collaboration. Consequently, as administrative and design decisions provided only an outline model for the portfolio system, incoming faculty members responsible for the system's use were provided few tools to further define the system's goals, operation, or rubrics.

In my research of the program's development and the implementation of its portfolio assessment system, one of the MUST founding committee members recalled how a wide range of faculty were invited to participate in discussions of the program's development but only a few attended these meetings consistently. Faculty discussed potential outcomes, artifacts, and methods to assess this new program's students. The real challenge appeared to be the personnel transition: It was understandably difficult to share the nature of these discussions with the program's new faculty, who almost immediately were in the throes of the program's first year of implementation.

During both of the program's first 2 years, MUST students took courses with faculty throughout the college, but few of these faculty participated in discussions of how they might localize, implement, and assess program-specific outcomes. Early in the fall semester of the program's first year (1999–2000), it became clear that the MUST content methods course instructors were each construing the practicum experience and the nature and significance of the portfolio development process differently. This meant that the artifacts students were able to gather for their portfolios varied so greatly that a clear programmatic consistency was not possible, and that the program's portfolio system had no grounds for a reliable assessment of these artifacts. Although the coordinators of the program had assembled a list of course projects from all of the college faculty who were teaching in the program, these lists were of little use in attempting to guide students or instructors toward a set of coherent portfolio artifact criteria.

During this first year, as well, one of the two new program coordinators was faced with a serious illness and eventually was forced to take a leave of absence during the second semester. With the burden of directing the program and all of its components on her shoulders, the remaining coordinator faced too large a learning curve and too many day-to-day duties to continue administering—let alone developing—this assessment system. During the second semester, oversight of the interns' portfolio development fell to one of the program's cofounders, who integrated the project into her MUST teacher research course using portfolio forms and review processes from the college's physical education certification program.

By the beginning of the program's second year in June 2000, a distinct tone had been established in the college: Existing faculty were increasingly protective of the time required to complete their current responsibilities and increasingly reluctant to attend meetings to discuss the MUST program and its portfolio assessment system. At the end of the second cohort's first summer session, one of the program's two coordinators abruptly resigned, leaving the program to be administered by the one remaining coordinator, who had not been healthy enough to participate in much of the first year's administration and had little professional interest in portfolio assessment. At the same time, the literacy area of the college was operating with less than half of its full-time faculty. In this context, I arrived at Cleveland State, agreed to teach the MUST program's required content literacy course as an overload, and, eventually, to take responsibility for further fashioning and managing the portfolio assessment system. Thus, for the second year of its existence, the MUST program again relied on a new faculty member to coordinate its portfolio assessment process. During this year, any possibility of increasing faculty collaboration around the MUST portfolio system often took a back seat to my introduction to the program and to my own professional acclimatization.

As an Assistant Professor of Literacy Education hired into my first academic position just as MUST was about to begin its second year, my own story is both inextricably woven into and illustrative of the complex, urban features of this MUST case study. Consistent with the experience of the program's first coordinators, I began my MUST experience in an already intensified urban work environment, in a program that was not housed in my own department. Faced with a sizable array of new duties as a novice professor, I did not have the time to initiate the collegial relationships from which a successful implementation of the MUST portfolio assessment system would result. But, given the conditions of the urban institutions across which I was working, the MUST portfolio assessment system very quickly became my own. This may be the primary result of teaching (teachers or K–12 students) in an urban setting: For better or worse, the qualities and often the very existence of novel programs depend on the efforts of a few well-meaning educators. In the case of MUST and its portfolio assessment system, its continued evolution fell to the chair of the department where the program was housed and to me.

Identification of Criteria

The MUST program was founded on the Cleveland State University College of Education model, encompassing a set of outcomes of which all faculty are at least cognizant. These criteria include such categories as "personal philosophy," "diversity," and "collaboration and professionalism" (see Appendix A). Through its portfolio assessment system, the program has also expected its students to demonstrate a commitment to a unique set of urban, social justice outcomes. The current (2003–2004) outcomes include the following ideals:

- *Social justice*. The MUST teacher candidate is a reflective, responsive teacher-leader who is prepared to effectively address the effects of race, class, and gender on student achievement.
- *Urban teaching*. The MUST teacher candidate promotes students' learning through responsive pedagogy and utilizes a variety of strategies to address the complex demands of urban schools.
- *Urban schooling and communities*. The MUST teacher candidate demonstrates a strong commitment to urban schooling and community renewal.
- *Resilience*. The MUST teacher candidate responds positively to challenges and changes, demonstrating resilience and an ethic of care in complex, demanding circumstances.

In the year leading up to MUST's first year of implementation, these outcomes were drafted by Peterman and Burney, and then revised significantly during the first year with considerable input from Vanden Wyngaard. One of the program's founding committee members recalls that two outcomes were initially selected in order to differentiate MUST from the other licensure programs in the College: "social justice" and "teacher research." In the program's first year, conversations among the coordinators and a few other faculty led to the addition of "culturally relevant pedagogy" and "urban schooling." During conversations that the program's department chair and I had during my first year at CSU, the addition of "resistance" was made to what had been "resiliency and persistence." "Caring" and "an ethic of care" were removed from the list of outcomes, but eventually returned as a point under "Resilience, Resistance, and Persistence" when the rubric was drafted in the program's third year.

In the program's first 2 years, an attempt was made to integrate the portfolio development process into other MUST coursework. Although this integration might have increased the relevance of the portfolio process, it also resulted in a disparate set of objectives that the MUST students were working toward and was met with faculty reluctance because of the additional time involved in coordinating such objectives across courses. This disparity was a direct result of both the urgent timeline on which the program was developed and the limited faculty collaboration around the portfolio process. This integration affixed additional deadline pressures that in some instances were merely traditional and expected norms within any as-

sessment process, but in numerous other ways seemed to be extraneous bureaucratic features that detracted from an authentic, naturally occurring
reflection process. At the end of the program's second year, it was clear that
the portfolio assessment system was perceived by many faculty as an organizational burden, rather than as a relevant tool for evaluating the MUST
students' knowledge and skills.

In the program's first two years, the portfolio requirement was introduced to students during the program's application process and the first
summer course sessions, but not reintroduced or addressed until well into
the students' second semester—halfway through the program. During the
first year, several staff events led to a series of reactive discussions that
shaped the portfolio assessment process. The remaining program coordinator, burdened by her health condition, was also burdened by her additional responsibilities to facilitating students' portfolio construction.
Consequently, what was intended to be a unique, urban, social, justice-ori-
ented teacher education assessment system rooted in the outcomes previously listed, relied instead on the standard College of Education outcomes
as assessment criteria and on a portfolio assessment method from a divergent field (physical education).

Based on this physical education framework and supported by discussion with the program's department chair, I developed an initial portfolio
assessment system with features unique to the MUST program. This system included three types of portfolios ("working," "presentation," and
"professional"), constructed across a program's experiences and com-
prised of portfolio artifacts, students' descriptions of these artifacts, students' reflections on the outcomes addressed by each artifact, and
conferences and reviews of all artifacts through which mentors, instructors, and other constituents of their schools assess these students' proficiency with particular outcomes (see Appendix B for details). The working
portfolio served as the "catch-all" for artifacts, reflections, conferences,
and reviews, and each of the other portfolios consisted of items gathered
from this collection.

In December of the program's first year and in January of the second
year, MUST students shared initial presentation portfolios with an audience of CSU students and faculty, mentor teachers, and area principals and
superintendents at campus showcases; students organized these presentations around metaphors that they believed represented their path to becoming professional, urban educators. For example, one student
compared her journey toward teaching certification to a chef concocting an
elaborate recipe, whereas another related his trek to teaching with playing a
game of "Pedagopoly." Then, over the final full (spring) semester and short
culminating summer sessions of the program's first 2 years, students con-

structed working portfolios of numerous artifacts from their student teaching experiences and courses. In the closing months of both of the first 2 years' spring semesters, students organized these artifacts into final presentation portfolios (publicly shared in May) and employment portfolios to be used during the job search process.

As noted previously, one of the primary results of the urgent early implementation of MUST and its portfolio assessment process had been the program's inability to assess artifacts using the MUST program outcomes. Although the program was a unique certification avenue within the college, during its first 2 years MUST students' portfolios were not formally evaluated using either these College of Education outcomes or the program-specific outcomes. Instead, because this assessment process was so novel in this setting, the college and program outcomes were only used to provide formative feedback to interns. Although the assessment process adopted from the Physical Education Department's system provided a means through which interns could reflect on their understanding of both sets of these outcomes, interns faced no consequences if these artifacts or their understandings were evaluated as failing to demonstrate proficiency with the college or program outcomes.

This inability—or reluctance—to use the MUST outcomes as part of a summative assessment process might have been the result of the often-isolated manner in which these criteria were determined. Although the College of Education and the founding MUST faculty outlined a program-specific set of outcomes, no rubric for assessing artifacts against these outcomes had been created. In the program's second year, I eventually had the responsibility for extending these outcomes into draft rubrics. Initially, I was not able to involve any wider range of faculty or program constituents in this elaboration, to invest sufficient time to be certain that these rubric criteria were valid, or to determine if our assessment process using these criteria was reliable.

In search of specific rubric details to guide my students' gathering and assessment of artifacts—including details that these students, their mentors, and I would honestly *own*—I turned to the notion of "multiple literacies" (Cope & Kalantzis, 2000; Gallego & Hollingsworth, 2000) in order to begin to translate the MUST outcomes into valid and assessable criteria. This multiliteracy framework was rooted in the subject matter of my content literacy course and it fit well with the responsive orientation of the program. It also supported the artifact gathering process involved in portfolio assessment and was consistent with the sociocultural theory grounding such an assessment system. And, although it was a framework that I initially used in isolation, after 3 years it has been established as a very useful foundation for assessing urban teachers' knowledge of the MUST program outcomes as they intersect with the lives of city students.

Multiple Literacies Orientation

Over a dozen years as a city teacher among cities in the Midwest and on the West Coast, I developed an assessment practice that relied on performances and portfolios, which was embedded in an application of a broad literacy framework. In the last two decades, "literacy" has grown to encompass one's proficiency with more than traditional texts—like textbooks and classic and contemporary literature (Gallego & Hollingsworth, 2000; Hicks, 2002; Hull & Schultz, 2002). It is now understood that high school students bring with them literacies in visual, electronic, and musical media, among myriad others. The sources for these literacies are students' community, school, family, emotional, interpersonal, intrapersonal, and spiritual experiences.

This "multiple literacies" theory suggests that students naturally acquire a range of abilities and knowledge that schools traditionally do not recognize (Barton & Hamilton, 1998; Cope & Kalantzis, 2000; Cushman, 1998; Knobel, 1999). It also posits that, particularly in diverse urban settings, educators must intentionally study and continually come to know their students and their experiences, strengths, and needs, so that they might appeal to these abilities as foundations for the development of traditional, school-oriented literacies such as reading, writing, speaking, and listening (Beaufort, 1999; Muspratt, Luke, & Freebody, 1997; Street, 1993). When I began working with the MUST program's portfolio assessment system, I recognized that a multiple literacies approach was consistent with its artifact orientation, as well as supportive of the myriad abilities, languages, and needs that urban K–12 students naturally bring to their school settings. And I hoped that by sharing this literacy framework with my MUST students— groups of novice teacher candidates very much in need of teaching tools to meet the diverse needs and interests of urban students—I would provide them with both a culturally relevant pedagogical and assessment framework (Irvine, 1997; Irvine & York, 2001; Ladson-Billings, 1998b, 1994) and some day-to-day tools to find "ways in" with their urban students.

As a part of the content literacy course I have taught for the MUST program in each of the last 3 years, I have called on student teachers to document the myriad literacies their students possess, by constructing a series of "literacy maps." Each set of maps has asked the MUST program's future teachers to consider the environments, resources, buildings, homes, and institutions of their students' communities, schools, and classrooms as "texts" that contribute to the "literacies" that these city students possess. The literacy map assignments have called on MUST students to document these items by completing brief ethnographies of their fieldwork classrooms, schools, and communities, and to complement these written descriptions with visual documentation of what they encountered in these settings, using both digital and 35mm photography.

Based on these multiliteracy inspired inquiries, the MUST interns have documented and described a range of the literacies for the students, families, teachers, and community members that they encountered in these urban communities, schools, and classrooms. Although many of these examples might seem like destructive capacities, I am careful to emphasize that documenting literacy does not invoke a judgment. It is merely an attempt at an honest observation of what people know how to do, out of habit and tradition, as a result of conscious intents and sincere desires, sometimes based on a self-aware wisdom and other times on a seemingly complete ignorance.

These student teachers have recognized community literacies such as spirituality and religion, community involvement, racism and discrimination, drug use and alcohol abuse, and violence and death. They have noted school and classroom literacies in social cliques and adolescent romance, academic failure and success, apathy, painfully low teacher and student expectations, and the ability to balance school requirements and family and personal financial and employment needs. Through these literacy maps and ethnographies, my students have begun to learn early on just how complicated the lives of urban students, families, and teachers are—and the issues that they (future teachers) will have to accept *and* integrate, if they are going to have any chance at helping their students find success in city schools.

Following on this integration of a multiple literacies perspective into the program, during the program's third year (my second year of directing its portfolio assessment system), Peterman and I co-taught EST 595, "Integrating Theory and Practice," which up until that point had concentrated on interns' teacher research projects. We decided to incorporate the portfolio assessment process into this course, reviewing artifacts frequently in class and expanding on what had been only a rudimentary rubric for the program outcomes. The interns in this almost magical third year cohort recognized that the outcomes were far too ambiguous to be used as assessable criteria. Thus, while we were attempting to assess interns' artifacts and understandings of the program outcomes, we also asked interns to help us—and sometimes lead us—in articulating specific rubric details.

One of the cohort leaders in this process was Michael Naffziger, who is now an award-winning science teacher in Chicago. In my conversations with him about this rubric development process, he recalled how he and other interns worked extensively on fleshing out "words or levels of assessment concerning the outcomes of MUST." He also shared how the interns, Peterman, and I collaboratively "worked on ways to clarify what qualified an artifact to be a mirror of a particular MUST outcome." Naffziger, Christine Royhab, Patricia Wolanski, and Andratesha Munn played significant roles in the evolution of the portfolio assessment system and the articulation of specific rubric criteria. In recent e-mail correspondence, Naffziger described how his own high school science assessment rubrics evolve often, and how he is happy to have been a part of the initial stages of portfolio assessment in MUST and to have been "a deckhand on the ship that is pushing these waters of social justice."

The experience of the most recent cohort of students to complete the MUST program has provided the best examples of the useful relationship between this multiple literacies approach and the program's portfolio assessment system. This multiliteracies method has provided specific criteria and strategies through which the MUST students have been able to begin to understand the cultures of their urban students, as well as some initial pedagogical tactics to use in coming to know specific, individual students. Evidence from their initial lesson plans (completed in my literacy course at the start of the MUST program) and from their final portfolio assessment conferences (completed with me at the end of their program) both suggest that they adopted the inquiry orientation provided by this broad literacy notion as a foundational practice of their teaching and their engagement in the program's portfolio assessment process. Given this study's emphasis, I focus here only on the relationship between this multiple literacies method and the program's portfolio assessment system. Specifically, I concentrate on a few examples of the artifacts individual students presented in their recent, final portfolio conferences.

When one future science teacher (I'll call her "Nichole") considered the MUST outcome of "urban teaching," she identified a conductivity meter she had constructed as the best evidence of her understanding of "promoting students' learning through responsive pedagogy." The conductivity meter was a tool that she needed for a chemistry lab class, but that the school did not have. With the assistance of another MUST student, Nichole went to a local electrical supply shop and purchased the film canisters, batteries, and LED lights to construct a model for her students. She then had her students construct their own meters and used these in the lab.

For Nichole, this artifact—gathered from what had previously been rather obscure resources in the school community—represented not only her ability to respond to a supply shortage and her students' need for tactile lessons, but also modeled for these city students, and then required them to demonstrate, the "real world" problem-solving skills that they would require in their lives after school. She understood that "responsive pedagogy" could take the form of something as simple and everyday as relying on the businesses in the students' neighborhood. In the portfolio assessment process, these businesses were examples of students' culture and lives beyond school; in the literacy mapping with which we had begun the program, these businesses were examples of the resources and institutions MUST students had documented.

Another MUST student—a future English teacher I'll call "Richard"— selected a videotape of a professional development seminar he and other

MUST students at his city high school had planned and implemented in February of his program year for all of the preservice teachers, mentors, and other teachers from the program's partner schools. The event focused on "building positive classroom communities" and was attended by approximately 75 current and future teachers. Richard understood that this videotape and the event it documented was evidence of his proficiency with the MUST outcome of "social justice," which called on him to be a "teacher-leader" who "is prepared to effectively address the effects of race, class, and gender on student achievement."

Richard explained that in the presentation that he and his MUST cohort members organized, they tried to "use situations that reflected the different backgrounds of students in the classroom … [including] problems between students of different races, fights between boys, girls, and boys versus girls." Their presentation considered the effects class differences can have on group assignments, and, in his words, "showed a willingness to learn from students by having [them] present." Although any savvy teacher would recognize such tensions and differences—in and among students of various races, classes, genders, and languages—not many teachers know how to actively consider these differences in the urban classroom. This one event was clearly not sufficient evidence of the complexity of Richard's responsive classroom practice, but it was ideal evidence of his teacher-leadership. As well, like Nichole's example, Richard's awareness of students' literacies in their own races, classes, genders, and languages echoed the literacy mapping efforts from our program's beginning.

Finally, a MUST student I'll call "Juan" selected a technology petition as evidence of his proficiency with the MUST outcome of "resilience." This outcome calls on MUST students to "respond positively to challenges and changes, demonstrating resilience and an ethic of care in complex, demanding circumstances." In the middle of a social studies lesson on the Luddites and their views on technology, Juan and his students were unceremoniously informed that they would have to vacate their classroom—*that day and that period*—to make room for the renovation of the space into a computer lab. Although Juan and his mentor had been informed some months prior that they would eventually have to move, they had been given no warning that day, or even that week, that such a shift was going to occur so soon.

Juan responded to this challenge by continuing his lesson and asking his students to construct petitions that reflected a critical view of technology in their lives. Although his students generally agreed that technology benefited their lives, this event revealed some of the complexities of a society—and a school and a single class—as they deal with the expansion of technology in their lives. Juan recognized this event as one of many teaching challenges he and other urban teachers face that, if approached with the appropriate resilience, could provide unique benefits and serve as important learning experiences. One of the compelling effects of this event was how Juan was forced to respond to it: Because his class was required to meet in an open library space for the final month of his student teaching experience, with the untold interruptions that such a setting involves, he met with students nearly every day after school for the rest of the year, to compensate for lost instructional time. And, of course, when meeting and working with students in this less formal context, he could not help but continue to learn about their lives and literacies beyond school.

CONCLUSION

This case study has provided an initial sketch of one urban university's attempt at developing and implementing a portfolio assessment system for future city teachers. Admittedly, this depiction is only a starting point for a complete analysis of the uses of alternative assessments in this urban context. Given the youth of this program and the shifting factors in its implementation, it is not yet possible to determine the relationship between this assessment system and the preparation of urban teachers. Also, the very nature of portfolio assessment calls on us to remember that no single experience—or perhaps no single assessment mechanism—can completely and accurately develop or assess the knowledge and dispositions toward which programs like MUST work (Moss, Schutz, & Collins, 1998; Wolf & Diez, 1998).

Through its first 2 years, the MUST portfolio assessment system at Cleveland State was an administratively energized program whose development, and as a result its content, were driven by the urgencies faced by the urban institutions it was meant to serve. Over its short existence, the skeletal nature of this system has gradually been fleshed out, but it remains an assessment mechanism that is developed and facilitated by a few individual faculty, rather than across all program experiences with the full participation of responsible instructors and staff. As the program outcomes have evolved into something more than guidelines—often as the result of input from the program's students—they have become specific, legitimate criteria for assessing MUST students' portfolio development (see Appendix C for the latest, 2002–2003, version of the MUST outcomes and rubric).

Like any new program, MUST will ultimately require several years to develop practices and traditions to answer its original design. In many cases, the program's CSU faculty and school-based personnel have recognized ambiguities in the program's original design descriptions as opportunities to develop responsive implementations (see Appendix D for a current overview of the system's operation). Yet, the outline form of several key aspects of the MUST program has presented as many dilemmas as possibilities. Initiating the program with only a portfolio assessment framework allowed for the greatest sensitivity to teacher candidates' needs and to individual faculty interests, but it also meant that many portfolio assessment administrative decisions have been made spontaneously.

If urban teacher education programs are going to utilize such assessment methods—as they should—then the rich, complex, and often contradictory circumstances of urban universities and schools need to be candidly understood and completely considered. The primary insight of this study's analysis pertains to the complexity of the contexts in which such alternative assessments are developed: The events described in this study illustrate the intrinsic resistance to the development of sociocultural systems of teacher assessment that the conditions and traditions of urban universities and schools present. The very nature of sociocultural theory reminds us that the development of a performance assessment system for an urban teacher education program cannot be detached from the urban context where the university administering the program resides.

While understanding that a university setting shares many features with a school district context may not be a comfortable awareness for many university personnel, it might be an even less comfortable acknowledgment for the teacher candidates completing programs at the university level. Arriving at CSU at the end of the school day, the MUST students have certainly longed to escape the intense, underresourced, and administratively heavy systems they have experienced in their school settings; ironically, recognizing and accepting the similarities across these institutions, and responding to them with resilience, might be the best evidence of their abilities as urban educators. Similarly, in making the transition from urban classroom teacher to urban teacher educator, I did not expect to face the same sorts of challenges in my university setting that I had dealt with for years in my city schools. Like my students, responding with resilience to the realities described in this essay may be the best evidence of my capacity as an urban teacher educator.

Urban teacher education demands an assessment system that calls for teacher candidates, as well as teacher educators, who do not compartmentalize the skills required to be successful in urban settings. Rather, urban teacher candidates must act with the tools and awareness required for teaching their urban students as they engage in their own learning as urban teachers, across the urban institutions in which they are working. The urban features and the resilient responses required of teacher candidates and teacher educators in these settings may not be the temporary conditions of a new MAT program and its portfolio assessment system; they may be the permanent conditions for which urban educators, across school and university settings, must be prepared and according to which they must be holistically assessed. Responding to these characteristics may need to become part of the definition of teaching in these urban settings and across the professional lives of educators in these settings.

APPENDIX A: CLEVELAND STATE UNIVERSITY— COLLEGE OF EDUCATION OUTCOMES

1. **Personal Philosophy:** The CSU teacher education student articulates a personal philosophy of teaching and learning that is grounded in theory and practice.
2. **Social Foundations:** The CSU teacher education student possesses knowledge and understanding of the social, political, and economic factors that influence education and shape the worlds in which we live.
3. **Knowledge of Subject Matter and Inquiry:** The CSU teacher education student understands content, disciplinary concepts, and tools of inquiry related to the development of an educated person.
4. **Knowledge of Development and Learning:** The CSU teacher education student understands how individuals learn and develop and that students enter the learning setting with prior experiences that give meaning to the construction of new knowledge.
5. **Diversity:** The CSU teacher education student understands how individuals differ in their backgrounds and approaches to learning and incorporates and accounts for such diversity in teaching and learning.
6. **Learning Environment:** The CSU teacher education student uses an understanding of individual and group motivation to promote positive social interaction, active engagement in learning, and self-motivation.
7. **Communication:** The CSU teacher education student uses knowledge of effective verbal, nonverbal, and media communication techniques to foster inquiry, collaboration, and engagement in learning environments.
8. **Instructional Strategies:** The CSU teacher education student plans and implements a variety of developmentally appropriate instructional strategies to develop performance skills, critical thinking, and problem solving, as well as to foster social, emotional, creative, and physical development.
9. **Assessment:** The CSU teacher education student understands, selects, and uses a range of assessment strategies to foster physical, cognitive, social, and emotional development of learners and gives accounts of students' learning to the outside world.
10. **Technology:** The CSU teacher education student understands and uses up-to-date technology to enhance the learning environment across the full range of learner needs.
11. **Professional Development:** The CSU teacher education student is a reflective practitioner who evaluates his or her interactions with others (e.g., learners, parents/guardians, colleagues and professionals in the community) and seeks opportunities to grow professionally.

12. **Collaboration and Professionalism:** The CSU teacher education student fosters relationships with colleagues, parents and guardians, community agencies, and colleges/universities to support students' growth and well-being.

APPENDIX B: MUST PORTFOLIO TYPES AND KEY TERMS

Artifact: Any document or object that represents at least one feature of a person's development. Sources for artifacts include, but are not limited to, course/field experiences, lesson/unit plans, videotaped lessons, teacher research components, reflective journals, response papers, photographs, relevant articles, syllabi, university transcripts, teaching evaluations, event/conference programs, and student work samples.

Description: A detailed written sketch depicting the primary features of an artifact.

Reflection: A written analysis addressing ways an artifact demonstrates a person's proficiency with a given outcome; each reflection details and evaluates a MUST student's professional development in light of MUST and College of Education outcomes.

Conference/Review: An analysis written by a student's peer, instructor, mentor teacher, student, advisor, or other, that serves as either a formative or summative evaluation of an artifact in light of a chosen outcome.

Working Portfolio: Gathered across all of a student's Cleveland State coursework, school efforts, and community interactions, the working portfolio is a collection of artifacts that represents a student's development as a professional urban educator. From each school, university, and community experience, students gather examples of the ideas they have encountered, the beliefs with which they began the program and which they have developed, the curriculum and strategies they have learned and used in their own teaching, and the strengths and needs of the urban students, teachers, MUST colleagues, and schools with which they have worked. Each artifact in the working portfolio must be accompanied by a description and a reflection.

Presentation Portfolio: A collection of artifacts, descriptions, reflections, and reviews organized in a creative manner to express who the urban educator is, how she or he has become a professional urban educator, and how she or he will become the urban educator she or he hopes to become;

requires a person to creatively use multiple literacies to represent growth and awareness of growth.

Professional Portfolio: A collection of artifacts and descriptions organized intentionally to secure employment; includes representations of distinguishing characteristics and talents of the professional urban educator; portrays the accomplishments and plans of the potential employee.

Showcase: Events where the MUST community honors its students' accomplishments and MUST students exhibit their demonstrated proficiency with MUST and College outcomes.

APPENDIX C: MUST PROGRAM OUTCOMES AND RUBRIC

Masters in Urban Secondary Teaching (MUST) Outcomes Rubric (Revised in June, 2003)

MUST Outcomes:	Social Justice	Urban Teaching	Urban Schooling & Communities	Resilience, Resistance, & Persistence
Assessment:	The MUST intern is a reflective, responsive teacher-leader who successfully addresses the effects of race, class, gender, and linguistic difference on student achievement.	The MUST intern promotes students' learning by utilizing culturally relevant and responsive pedagogy.	The MUST intern demonstrates a strong commitment to urban schooling and community renewal.	The MUST intern addresses the complexities and demands of urban settings by responding appropriately with resilience, resistance, and persistence.
Unacceptable: As demonstrated by this artifact and her or his reflection, the MUST intern:	1. Is unable or unwilling to reflect on and address effects of race, class, gender, linguistic difference, and sexual orientation on student achievement. 2. Is reluctant or resistant to learning from and about students. 3. Discriminates against individuals or groups. 4. Considers no personal, community, or school literacies. 5. Is unwilling to consider any personal or professional risks. 6. Is unwilling or unable to encourage students to actively participate in creating and governing their learning environment.	1. Is unwilling or unable to adjust teaching to meet student needs. 2. Is unwilling or unable to respond to students needing additional content instruction. 3. Uses very few and limited range of resources, relying on published curricula. 4. Uses almost exclusively teacher-centered strategies and/or ones that are unsuccessful. 5. Demonstrates no ability or interest in reflecting on student achievement and pedagogical practices. 6. Is unwilling or unable to encourage students to actively participate in creating their own learning experience.	1. Is unwilling to spend time in urban community. 2. Makes no attempt at instructing students in citizenship skills. 3. Demonstrates no ability or interest in teaching lessons that are relevant to conditions of students' lives, including family concerns, transience, and violent events. 4. Makes no connection between students' school and community experiences. 5. Utilizes few if any authentic activities and assessments. 6. Does not reflect on relationship between community, classroom practices, and student achievement.	1. Is unwilling or unable to provide alternative solutions to challenges, particularly those related to student achievement. 2. Enacts unoriginal solutions to problems. 3. Is unwilling to invest any personal resources or time to supplement lack of school resources. 4. Ignores or avoids challenges and changes. 5. Fails to exhibit ethic of care.

Emerging: As demonstrated by this artifact and her or his reflection, the MUST intern:			
	1. Is moderately willing and able to reflect on and address effects of race, class, gender, linguistic difference, and sexual orientation on student achievement. 2. Is open to learning from and about students. 3. Treats all students similarly, rather than considering individual needs. 4. Addresses limited number or range of personal, community, or school literacies. 5. Encourages limited range or number of personal and professional risks. 6. Occasionally encourages students to actively participate in creating and governing their learning environment.	1. Is moderately willing and able to adjust teaching to meet student needs. 2. Is beginning to respond to students who need additional content instruction. 3. Uses available resources in limited ways and begins to develop own curricula. 4. Utilizes mostly teacher-centered strategies and/or ones that are marginally successful in urban context. 5. Is beginning to reflect on student achievement and pedagogical practices. 6. Occasionally encourages students to actively participate in creating their own learning experience.	1. Spends limited amount of time in urban community. 2. Occasionally instructs students in skills required to be active, democratic citizens. 3. Develops and teaches lessons that are marginally relevant to conditions of students' lives, including family concerns, transience, and violent events. 4. Makes limited number of connections between students' school and community experiences. 5. Utilizes limited number of authentic activities and assessments. 6. Is beginning to reflect on relationship between community needs, classroom practices, and student achievement.	1. Transforms some challenges related to student achievement into learning experiences. 2. Enacts marginally creative and relevant solutions to problems. 3. Minimally invests personal resources or time to supplement lack of school resources. 4. Occasionally reflects on and addresses challenges and changes. 5. Occasionally exhibits ethic of care.

(continued)

Appendix C *(continued)*

MUST Outcomes:	Social Justice	Urban Teaching	Urban Schooling & Communities	Resilience, Resistance, & Persistence
Assessment:	The MUST intern is a reflective, responsive teacher-leader who successfully addresses the effects of race, class, gender, and linguistic difference on student achievement.	The MUST intern promotes students' learning by utilizing culturally relevant and responsive pedagogy.	The MUST intern demonstrates a strong commitment to urban schooling and community renewal.	The MUST intern addresses the complexities and demands of urban settings by responding appropriately with resilience, resistance, and persistence.
Proficient: As demonstrated by this artifact and her or his reflection, the MUST intern:	1. Is willing and able to reflect on and address effects of race, class, gender, linguistic difference, and sexual orientation on student achievement. 2. Actively learns from and about students. 3. Considers students' experiences with issues of race, class, and gender in classroom practice. 4. Addresses a range of personal, community, or school literacies. 5. Encourages well-defined personal and professional risks. 6. Encourages students to actively participate in creating and governing their learning environment.	1. Adjusts teaching to meet student needs. 2. Responds to students who need additional content instruction. 3. Thoughtfully and creatively uses available resources, and develops range of own curricula. 4. Utilizes a range of unique strategies, including hands-on, learner-centered, and teamwork-oriented techniques. 5. Reflects on student achievement and pedagogical practices, describing their responsive nature. 6. Encourages students to actively participate in creating their own learning experiences.	1. Spends substantial time in the urban community. 2. Effectively instructs students in skills required to be active, democratic citizens. 3. Develops and teaches lessons that are explicitly relevant to conditions of students' lives (including family concerns, transience, and violent events), and incorporates artifacts from their lives into her or his teaching. 4. Makes consistent connections between students' school and community experiences. 5. Utilizes authentic activities and assessments. 6. Consistently reflects on relationship between community needs, classroom practices, and student achievement.	1. Transforms challenges related to student achievement into learning experiences. 2. Enacts creative, relevant solutions to problems. 3. Uses personal resources and time to respond to lack of school resources. 4. Consistently reflects on and addresses challenges and changes. 5. Consistently exhibits ethic of care.

Exemplary:

As demonstrated by this artifact and her or his reflection, the MUST intern: Note: Intern's understanding can only be assessed as "exemplary" after she or he has demonstrated a "proficient" understanding over time, through all previous reviews.

1. Reflected on and addressed effects of race, class, gender, linguistic difference, and sexual orientation on student achievement.
2. Demonstrated willingness to learn from and about students.
3. Incorporated students' experiences with issues of race, class, gender into classroom practice.
4. Utilized wide range of personal, community, and cultural literacies.
5. Encouraged well-defined personal and professional risks.
6. Encouraged students to actively participate in creating and governing their learning environment.

1. Adjusted teaching to meet student needs.
2. Responded to students who need additional content instruction.
3. Utilized a range of unique strategies, including hands-on, learner-centered, and teamwork-oriented techniques.
4. Thoughtfully and creatively used available resources.
5. Reflected on student achievement and pedagogical practices, describing their responsive nature.
6. Encouraged students to actively participate in creating their own learning experiences.

1. Spent substantial time in the urban community.
2. Effectively instructed students in skills required to be active, democratic citizens.
3. Developed and taught lessons that are explicitly relevant to conditions of students' lives (including family concerns, transience, and violent events), and incorporated artifacts from their lives into her or his teaching.
4. Made consistent connections between students' school and community experiences.
5. Utilized authentic activities and assessments.
6. Consistently reflected on relationship between community needs and her or his classroom practices

1. Transformed any challenge related to student achievement into a professional learning experience.
2. Enacted creative, relevant solutions to problems.
3. Used personal resources and time to respond to lack of school resources.
4. Consistently reflected on and addressed challenges and changes.
5. Consistently exhibited ethic of care.

APPENDIX D: MUST PORTFOLIO SYSTEM OVERVIEW

Rationale

One of the primary goals of the MUST program is to prepare future urban teachers to provide their students with the greatest range of opportunities to show what they know. As well, the MUST program is committed to helping teachers to think in the broadest terms possible about how they can demonstrate their proficiency as educators. A portfolio assessment system—for students and teachers at any level—allows for such a demonstration of knowledge. To help MUST interns understand how such a system operates—in the assessment of students and teachers, the program requires interns to engage in a portfolio construction process during their MUST year.

Description

While in the MUST program, each intern constructs a "working portfolio" of artifacts gathered from the year's courses, field experiences, workshops, and events. Each semester (Summer I, Fall, Spring, Summer II) interns gather artifacts representative of their experiences, and assess these artifacts as evidence of their proficiency with the MUST and College outcomes. To ensure that the construction of the working portfolio is an ongoing process, interns should bring at least one artifact and one conference form to each practicum and student teaching seminar. In general, artifacts gathered during the first summer should focus on community contexts, artifacts from the fall semester should focus on school settings, and artifacts from the spring semester should focus on classroom contexts. All of these artifacts should reflect interns' proficiency with the MUST and College outcomes and represent a constructive impact on student learning. Each intern is responsible for selecting and presenting for review a minimum of four artifacts each semester that collectively demonstrate the intern's proficiency with the MUST outcomes. Interns also document their proficiency with the College outcomes by selecting and describing a minimum of four additional artifacts and describing these on the College Outcomes Chart.

During each semester interns engage in a formative assessment process around the artifacts they have chosen to address the MUST outcomes. For each of these selected artifacts, interns conduct a minimum of three conferences (with community, school, classroom, and university constituents), using the specific rubric for each MUST outcome. As well, near the end of each semester interns participate in a cohort portfolio review where they are again formatively assessed by their MUST peers. At the end of each semester, interns engage in a final formative assessment process at the university (during the Summer), at their fieldwork school (during the Fall), or in their individual classroom (in the Spring). At each of these events, interns' artifacts are reviewed by panels of community, school, classroom, and university constituents.

In late summer, the university review and coordinator review will take place on the Cleveland State campus. In mid-December, the school review will take place in the interns' schools, while the coordinator review will take place on the CSU campus. In early May, the classroom review will take place in the intern's classroom and will include interns' students, students' parents and families, mentor teacher, and university supervisor, while the coordinator review will take place at CSU.

All of these formative assessment events (conferences, cohort reviews, and university, school, and classroom reviews) are intended to prepare interns for the final, summative assessment by the MUST University Coordinator at the end of each semester. At the conclusion of each of these three summative, coordinator reviews, each intern must be assessed as "proficient" with each of the four MUST outcomes. If interns are assessed at any point as having only an "emerging" or "unacceptable" understanding of any MUST outcomes, she or he will have one opportunity to revise this artifact and its presentation, followed by one formal appeal of its assessment. After this revision and appeal, if an intern is not assessed as proficient with all four MUST outcomes in any semester, she or he will not be allowed to continue in the MUST program the following semester.

For the final, culminating component of the MUST portfolio assessment process, each intern will develop a presentation portfolio to be shared in a public event at the MUST Portfolio Showcase in late May. This portfolio will highlight the "best" artifacts from the working portfolio collection, organized around a theme and into a visual display of the intern's design. As well, each intern will receive assistance in developing an employment portfolio that will also be developed from the collection of artifacts in the working portfolio. Finally, interns will also be required to construct a final, electronic version of this employment portfolio.

Semester	Products/Events
Summer I	Working portfolio construction begins College outcomes chart describing minimum 4 original artifacts demonstrating proficiency with 12 College outcomes due at end of semester 4 original artifacts representing proficiency with MUST outcomes 3 conferences minimum with each of selected MUST artifacts (12 minimum) Cohort review of MUST artifacts (formative) University review of MUST artifacts (formative) Coordinator review of MUST artifacts (summative)
Fall	Working portfolio construction continues Employment and electronic portfolio construction begins College outcomes chart describing minimum 4 original artifacts demonstrating proficiency with 12 College outcomes due at end of semester 4 original artifacts representing proficiency with MUST outcomes 3 conferences minimum with each of selected MUST artifacts (12 minimum) Cohort review of MUST artifacts (formative) School review of MUST artifacts (formative) Coordinator review of MUST artifacts (summative)
Spring	Working portfolio construction continues Employment and electronic portfolio construction continues College outcomes chart describing minimum 4 original artifacts demonstrating proficiency with 12 College outcomes due at end of semester 4 original artifacts representing proficiency with MUST outcomes 3 conferences minimum with each of selected MUST artifacts (12 minimum) Cohort review of MUST artifacts (formative) Classroom review of MUST artifacts (formative) Coordinator review of MUST artifacts (summative)
Summer II	Employment and electronic portfolio construction concludes Presentation portfolio constructed and presented at Portfolio Showcase Final assessment of interns' proficiency with MUST outcomes (summative, with "exemplary" now an option)

REFERENCES

Abdul-Haqq, I. (1998). *Professional development schools: Weighing the evidence.* Thousand Oaks, CA: Corwin Press.

Barton, D., & Hamilton, M. (1998). *Local literacies: Reading and writing in one community.* London: Routledge.

Barton, J., & Collins, A. (1993). Portfolios in teacher education. *Journal of Teacher Education, 44*(3), 200–210.

Beaufort, A. (1999). *Writing in the real world: Making the transition from school to work.* New York: Teachers College Press.

Campbell, D., Cignetti, P., Melenyzer, B., Nettles, D., & Wyman, R. (1997). *How to develop a professional portfolio: A manual for teachers.* Boston: Allyn & Bacon.

Cope, B., & Kalantzis, M. (Eds.). (2000). *Multiliteracies: Literacy learning and the design of social futures.* London: Routledge.

Creswell, J. W. (1994). *Research design: Qualitative and quantitative approaches.* Thousand Oaks, CA: Sage.

Cushman, E. (1998). *The struggle and the tools: Oral and literate strategies in an inner city community.* Albany: State University of New York Press.

Darling-Hammond, L. (Ed.). (1994). *Professional development schools: Schools for developing a profession.* New York: Teachers College Press.

Darling-Hammond, L., & Cobb, V. L. (1996). The changing context of teacher education. In F. B. Murray (Ed.), *The teacher educator's handbook: Building a knowledge base for the preparation of teachers* (pp. 14–62). San Francisco, CA: Jossey-Bass.

Darling-Hammond, L., & Snyder, J. (2000). Authentic assessment of teaching in context. *Teaching and Teacher Education, 16*(5–6), 523–545.

Diez, M., & Hass, J. M. (1997). No more piecemeal reform: Using performance-based approaches to rethink teacher education. *Action in Teacher Education, 19*(2), 17–26.

Gallego, M. A., & Hollingsworth, S. (Eds.). (2000). *What counts as literacy?: Challenging the school standard.* New York: Teachers College Press.

Hicks, D. (2002). *Reading lives: Working-class children and literacy learning.* New York: Teachers College Press.

Holmes Group. (1990). *Tomorrow's schools: Principles for the design of professional development schools.* East Lansing, MI: Author.

Hull, G., & Schultz, K. (2002). *School's out: Bridging out-of-school literacies with classroom practice.* New York: Teachers College Press.

Irvine, J. J. (Ed.). (1997). *Critical knowledge for diverse teachers and learners.* Washington, DC: American Association of Colleges for Teacher Education.

Irvine, J. J., & York, D. E. (2001). Learning styles and culturally diverse students: A literature review. In J. A. Banks (Ed.), *Handbook of research on multicultural education* (pp. 484–497). San Francisco, CA: Jossey-Bass.

Johnson, M. (Ed.). (2000). *Collaborative reform and other improbable dreams: The challenges of professional development schools.* Albany, NY: State University of New York Press.

Knobel, M. (1999). *Everyday literacies: Students, discourse, and social practice.* New York: Peter Lang.

Ladson-Billings, G. (1994). *The dreamkeepers: Successful teachers of African American children.* San Francisco, CA: Jossey-Bass.

Ladson-Billings, G. (1998a). Teaching in dangerous times: Culturally relevant approaches to teacher assessment. *Journal of Negro Education, 67*(3), 255–267.

Ladson-Billings, G. (1998b). Toward a theory of culturally relevant pedagogy. In L. Beyer & M. W. Apple (Eds.), *The curriculum: Problems, politics, and possibilities* (pp. 201–229). Albany, NY: State University of New York Press.

Lyons, N. (Ed.). (1998). *With portfolio in hand: Validating the new teacher professionalism*. New York: Teachers College Press.

Martin, D. (1999). *The portfolio planner: Making professional portfolios work for you*. Columbus, OH: Merrill.

Mayer, D. P., Mullens, J. E., & Moore, M. T. (2000, December). *Monitoring school quality: An indicators report* (Report No. NCES 2001-030). Washington, DC: U.S. Department of Education.

Melograno, V. J. (1999). *Preservice professional portfolio system*. Reston, VA: National Association for Sport and Physical Education.

Merriam, S. B., & Simpson, E. L. (1995). *A guide to research for educators and trainers of adults*. Malabar, FL: Krieger.

Moss, B. J. (Ed.). (1994). *Literacy across communities*. Cresskill, NJ: Hampton Press.

Moss, P. A., Schutz, A. M., & Collins, K. M. (1998). An integrative approach to portfolio evaluation for teacher licensure. *Journal of Personnel Evaluation in Education, 12*(2), 139–161.

Murrell, P. (1998). *Like stone soup: The role of the professional development school in the renewal of urban schools*. Washington, DC: American Association of Colleges of Teacher Education.

Muspratt, S., Luke, A., & Freebody, P. (Eds.). (1997). *Constructing critical literacies: Teaching and learning textual practice*. Cresskill, NJ: Hampton.

Neill, M., Bursh, P., Schaeffer, B., Thall, C., Yohe, M., & Zappardino, P. (1995). *Implementing performance assessments: A guide to classroom, school and system reform*. Cambridge, MA: FairTest.

Olson, L. (2000, January). Taking a different road to teaching. *Education Week on the WEB: Quality Counts 2000: Who Should Teach?* [On-line serial], Special Report. Available: http://www.edweek.org/sreports/qc00/templates/article.cfm?slug=different.htm

Olson, L., & Jerald, C. D. (1998, January). The challenges: The teaching challenge. *Education Week on the WEB: Quality Counts '98: The Urban Challenge* [On-line special report]. Available: http://www.edweek.org/sreports/qc98/challenges/teach/te-n.htm

Reis, N. K., & Villaume, S. K. (2002). The benefits, tensions, and visions of portfolios as a wide-scale assessment for teacher education. *Action in Teacher Education, 23*(4), 10–17.

Short, K. (1993). Teacher research for teacher educators. In L. Patterson, C. M. Santa, K. Short, & K. Smith (Eds.), *Teachers are researchers: Reflection and action* (pp. 155–159). Newark, DE: International Reading Association.

Stake, R. (1995). *The art of case study research*. Thousand Oaks, CA: Sage.

Street, B. V. (1993). *Cross-cultural approaches to literacy*. New York: Cambridge University Press.

Willis, E. M., & Davies, M. A. (2002). Promise and practice of professional portfolios. *Action in Teacher Education, 23*(4), 18–27.

Wolf, K. (1999). *Leading the professional portfolio process for change*. Arlington Heights, IL: Skylight Professional Development.

Wolf, K., & Diez, M. (1998). Teaching portfolios: Purposes and possibilities. *Teacher Education Quarterly, 25*(1), 9–22.

Yin, R. (1994). *Case study research: Design and methods* (2nd ed.). Thousand Oaks, CA: Sage.

Chapter 5

The Assessment of Urban Teaching in a Not-So-Urban Setting

Michele Genor
Columbia University

In the mission of its elementary teacher education program, the University of Wisconsin–Madison emphasizes a social reconstructionist tradition. In theory, this orientation implies a deliberate commitment by teacher educators to work for social change and is based on the belief that it is absolutely necessary for "beginning teachers to adopt a critical consciousness … if they are to become educators who are willing and able to address the growing inequities in our schools and wider society" (Frykholm, 1997, p. 57). At its core, social reconstructionism "emphasizes the ability of teachers to examine the social and political implications of their practice and the contexts in which they work for their contribution to greater equity and justice in schooling and society" (Zeichner, 1994a, p. 30). This orientation toward reflective and activist teaching is relevant to all educational settings, but absolutely imperative if we are ever to rectify the inequities that exist in this country's urban schools and to sustain teachers who will advocate for change.

There are countless strategies teacher educators at the University of Wisconsin–Madison employ in attempts to develop reflective and activist habits in their preservice teachers. These include: the use of teaching stories (Gomez, 1994), field experiences in culturally diverse settings with supported seminar discussions (Zeichner & Hoeft, 1996), action research projects (Gore, 1991), performance-based portfolios (Booth, 2000), and participation in Professional Development School partnerships (Zeichner & Miller,

1997). The efforts that appear to be most empowering and successful "nurture students' confidence in the worth of their ideas while also encouraging them to reflect on and rethink their views" (Wade, 1994, p. 240).

This chapter provides a case study of the Professional Development School program (PDS) at the University of Wisconsin–Madison. Throughout my 4 years of doctoral study at the university, I supervised preservice teachers in this program and acted as the university liaison to the PDS. The Madison PDS described in this case is constantly changing to more effectively respond to the needs of all those who participate. Particularly, school and university-based teacher educators actively seek ways in which they might more successfully sustain the preservice teachers' commitment to teach in urban schools. In this chapter, I present my experience as a teacher educator in the PDS from 1997–2001. I also call on the experiences of the preservice teachers who participated in the program during that time.

In the Madison PDS program, direct attempts are made to prepare preservice teachers to develop the "attitudes, knowledge, skills, and dispositions necessary to work effectively with a diverse student population" (Zeichner, 1996, p. 183). To support this growth, PDS preservice teachers have multiple opportunities throughout their preparation to reflect on the beliefs they bring with them to the preservice program and the practices they engage in during their field experiences. PDS teacher educators facilitate ongoing written and oral discussions in which preservice teachers are able to make connections between their university course work—*the theory*—and the work they do in schools—*the practice*. I make this distinction very intentionally because, despite my desire as a teacher educator to blur these conceptions, our students continually describe their need for us to make the connections more explicit. In chapter 2 (this volume), Conway and Artiles describe the need for this type of cognitive preparation model, one that "supports a range of assessment tasks designed to unveil the teacher candidates thought processes and knowledge over time." This is not to say that the divide between practice and theory fails to exist with this kind of long-term collaborative support. It absolutely still exists. But in their cohorts, preservice teachers and teacher educators have multiple opportunities to make valuable connections and they have a greater sense of shared and contextual understanding to grapple with the ideas and questions about the dichotomy.

PDS preservice teachers are ultimately required to demonstrate the extent to which they have grown and developed throughout their preparation in a reflective portfolio process of assessment. Typically, that has meant that preservice teachers have collected and then presented representative examples of their teaching that help to articulate who they are as a teacher. Until recently, there was no systematic format for the collection or evaluation of the portfolio. This case study presents the ways in which Madison's approach has grown to include both.

UW–Madison, like all teacher education programs, has found that a preservice teacher's reflective growth is challenging to document and their sustainability in urban settings, even more so. As a former supervisor in the PDS program, I found that it was particularly difficult to support and nurture preservice teachers in their reflective growth while at the same time attempting to foster a more critical approach to teaching. To encourage reflection, PDS teacher educators/supervisors engage the preservice teachers in both critical and collaborative reflection and make attempts to bridge the two more seamlessly. Preservice teachers consistently communicate with their supervisor through dialogic journals; by engaging in ongoing action research that focuses on the school community requiring them to seek insight from outside resources as they attempt to make sense of their teaching questions; and by actively participating in an inquiry-based seminar that meets in the schools on a weekly basis. Although in all of these reflective exercises, it is essential to "honor students perspectives as legitimate and valuable" (Wade, 1994, p. 232), it is equally imperative for the supervisor to encourage the critique of ideas and opinions. Novice educators must have the opportunity to rethink, reimagine, and rework their beliefs about culture and teaching, so they can move to position themselves as agents for change by transforming and constructing curriculum and instruction that is appropriately responsive to issues of race, class, and culture. As a supervisor, I knew that I had to continuously investigate ways in which I could support this process of understanding and transformation. Successfully responding to how we assess this process is something even more elusive.

THE PROFESSIONAL DEVELOPMENT SCHOOL PROGRAM: SPECIFIC CONTEXT FOR THIS WORK

The Professional Development School (PDS) Program at the University of Wisconsin–Madison is a formalized commitment to prepare preservice teachers for diverse classrooms. It is a partnership between the University of Wisconsin–Madison, three elementary schools, and one middle school in the Madison Public School District (MPSD). Recently, a Madison public high school also joined the PDS partnership with support from various secondary education departments at the university. Although this chapter provides a generalized description of the Madison PDS, it focuses on the particular settings where I formerly worked as a supervisor in the elementary education preservice preparation program and as a site-based liaison to the middle school.

The elementary/middle grades PDS program at the University of Wisconsin–Madison (for those interested in being certified for Grades 1–9) operates alongside the regular elementary teacher education program and, because of size limitations, is offered as an option for practicum and student teaching field placements to only a small group of undergraduates. The Professional Development School program recruits preservice teachers from the regular program who express an interest in working in a smaller cohort setting throughout three semesters of their program, wish to be placed in diverse paired PDS schools, and are open to attending their weekly seminars in the schools where they are placed to student teach. In contrast, the regular program places preservice teachers in three different schools for each of their placements and randomly groups the students for larger, more decontextualized university-based seminars. In the application process for the PDS program, candidates also share their commitment to teach diverse learners and their motivation for participating in a program of this kind. Most of the applicants share their aspirations of teaching in urban settings after graduation and all express an interest in engaging in critical conversations about equitable and socially just teaching.

Goodwin (1994) states that multicultural education only really begins with teachers becoming more aware of their beliefs about "culture" and the relationship these understandings have to teaching practices. In the PDS, we believe that this process must begin with a thorough self-examination. Participants are aware of this focus when they join the PDS program and therefore have some willingness to engage in this self-analysis. However, in an already rigorous program of study, it is not uncommon to hear that preservice teachers feel as if they are "reflecting to death" and are overwhelmed by the demands placed on them. Thus, it is more important than ever for teacher educators to both model the reflective process and explicitly state all purposes.

The teacher educators who participate in the PDS work to nurture a sense of community within the cohort of approximately 15 students through team building and relational exercises. Each seminar begins with opportunities for participants to share personal life experiences. For example, in an introductory "*bag speech*," preservice teachers bring in five to seven artifacts that best represent who they are as individuals. Although participants make valuable connections across shared experiences and backgrounds, this activity and others like it are clearly structured to support preservice teachers as they examine their experiences in relation to the assumptions they may have about learning, schools, and children. As the semester progresses, the preservice teachers are encouraged to share their questions about teaching in their current placements while colleagues respond and offer insight. Ideally, this heightened state of collegial support provides a context where preservice teachers feel safe to explore sensitive issues related to their emerging teaching identities and to address the conflicts that arise as they negotiate their identity with what they may see practiced in schools.

The preservice teachers in the Madison PDS are typically representative of the larger teacher education population in the United States. They are primarily White, middle-class females who attended suburban or rural schools. Although the PDS program also attracts a small number of nontraditional preservice teachers, the participants are typically placed in schools very different, in terms of demographics (race, class, ability, culture) from the schools they themselves attended (Zeichner, 1996). One strategy that is intended to support the PDS students as they think more critically about these differences asks them to reflect on their own learning experiences. They think about ways in which their education was/is similar to, as well as different from, the students they will teach in urban settings. In this early draft of an educational philosophy and autobiographical analysis, the preservice teachers deeply analyze their own educational experiences. In many instances, it is through this reflection that preservice teachers come to realize the inherent privileges of their own upbringing. In many cases, it is the first time they have questioned the inequities that existed for some of their classmates and those they will teach:

> I read this book about tracking and the powerful effects that it can have on a student's potential to succeed. First of all, I had never even realized that tracking existed in my elementary school. Somehow, I imagined that my teachers could never have engaged in practices that might somehow limit "our" potential. The thing that I didn't realize that it wasn't necessarily my potential that was being limited. I was quite a reader in elementary school—a member of the sunflower reading group. I was constantly challenged and allowed to explore all kinds of texts. A group of students were dandelions. I remember that the dandelions really never had any choice or independence in what they read and the stories just never seemed very interesting. I knew that I was happy to be a sunflower, but I didn't really ever stop to think about what it meant to be a dandelion. Imagine that … the sunflowers and the dandelions! How offensive is that! I am realizing that I have taken so much for granted. Most importantly, I have a much greater awareness of the power of language. (LJ, 2000)

Although that is a powerful realization, this preservice teacher still has a limited understanding of an educational practice that is often unchallenged in today's classrooms. First, although it was perhaps important in the reflective process for her to receive an affirmative and formal acknowledgment of this realization, it was also essential that this preservice teacher be encouraged to interrogate her ideas more critically. These comments demonstrate how easy it is to condemn a practice or a person's role in that practice without more carefully analyzing the situation. This preservice teacher/writer was clearly experiencing some disruption to her own memories as a student when she realized that her teachers had engaged in practices she was now defining as inequitable. Although it may very well be an appropriate conclusion, it is absolutely essential that the preservice teacher gain a greater understanding of the sociocultural influences and the ways in which teachers sometimes both consciously and unconsciously respond to these influences. In this particular case, through an ongoing series of questions and dialogue, this preservice teacher continued to challenge her own conceptions of tracking and was then able to utilize this broader conception to examine her current teaching context and practices:

> It really struck me the other day when my supervisor asked how I had divided the class into work groups. I had all kinds of reasons for putting so and so with so and so, but when it came down to it and my supervisor continued to ask me questions about the way in which I was differentiating instruction for my student's individual needs—I realized that I wasn't doing anything different than dividing the dandelions from the sunflowers. It seemed so blatant when it was in somebody else's practice. I needed help to see it in my own. Now, I need help to rethink the way in which I work with all of my students to meet their needs—all of their needs. (LJ, 2000)

This type of systematic examination supports the sociocultural framework outlined in chapter 2 by Conway and Artiles because it recognizes how teaching and learning "integrates and systematically accounts for the individual, social, and cultural–historical forces in learning." Preservice teachers begin to appreciate the powerful influences of their own histories, but also to examine the greater external influences on a child's learning, their success in school, and a teacher's ability to confront these influences. Often, it is through this sharing and analysis that preservice teachers begin to realize the limitations of their preconceived visions of teaching and the assumptions they have about children and learning. In the supportive setting of their preparation, they are able to embrace a sense of ambiguity and contradiction that will no doubt be present in the urban teaching contexts in which they may teach. In chapter 3, when outlining how urban schools are different from others, Peterman describes how "urban teachers receive a constant flow of mixed messages, messages that contradict their personal and professional knowledge." It is for this reason that preservice teachers must be given the tools to successfully negotiate these contradictory conditions in their preparation to become successful urban teachers.

The work to prepare critically reflective teachers who are committed to teach in urban settings is difficult and sometimes painful. Even when candidates, in rhetoric, support the social reconstructionist approach, they sometimes resist the efforts that disrupt some of their ingrained notions and experiences of schooling and children. Through Conway and Artiles' (chap. 2, this volume) sociocultural lens of learning to teach, the University of Wisconsin–Madison "pays attention to the social contexts of teaching and to the ways teaching is mediated by the intellectual or ideational tools and material artifacts of a culture." The Madison program "articulates a vision of what a socially just vision of teaching in urban schools should look like as well as the roles teachers are expected to play in such a vision." They see and read about effective models and honestly discuss the challenges of implementation. Preservice teachers participate both individually and collaboratively with more experienced teachers in various forms of inquiry-based professional practice. One particular example is the way in which they study their teaching practice through action research. Each semester, preservice students generate a series of questions related to their teaching. Together with their cooperating teacher, they choose a particular focus, generate ways in which they might collect data, and actively engage in a process of inquiry. They come to the weekly seminar prepared to participate in a discussion about their question, and peers are able to suggest possible approaches and data collecting strategies. Not surprisingly, questions tend to focus on issues and areas of teaching where preservice teachers feel less confident. Often preservice teachers have concerns about meeting the individual needs of students in their classrooms, particularly when working in inclusive settings where the range of abilities and languages is diverse. Through engagement in the inquiry process, preservice teachers are supported in adopting a sociocultural perspective, one in which they are encouraged to gain a greater understanding of the classroom and instructional setting and those elements that actively influence the teaching and learning that takes place.

As described throughout this chapter, there are efforts made by school and university-based teacher educators to model empowering professional development. This occurs both in ongoing pedagogic discussions regarding field experiences and in enacting more progressive models of curriculum. However, in light of these issues, the Madison PDS program has begun to examine their assessment procedures. Most importantly, they ask whether the performance-based system that has recently been implemented authentically represents and documents the growth and development of preservice teachers, particularly as they engage in critical reflection on issues of equity and social justice.

In response to these questions, Conway and Artiles (chap. 2, this volume) remind us how important it is for teacher education programs to begin focusing on ways in which preservice teacher assessment can be "grounded in explicitly articulated visions of both teaching and teacher and student learning." They warn that teacher educators must also carefully consider the "images of good teaching that are embedded" in teacher education programs and examine how ideas of urban teaching are incorporated within preparation and assessment systems. The Madison PDS collaborations and partnerships are important because the conversations that take place across these settings help preservice teachers to create powerful models of instruction and creative visions of urban classrooms.

PREPARING TO TEACH IN DIVERSE SETTINGS— WHAT DOES MADISON HAVE TO OFFER?

All of the PDS schools in Madison serve communities of students with diverse cultural, socioeconomic, linguistic, emotional, and learning needs. Obviously, the Madison schools do not provide the same kind of "culturally different" or urban experience of schools in Milwaukee, Chicago, New York, or in other larger cities. However, that said, the "diversity" experience in the Madison Professional Development School program specifically refers to working in local schools that are the most culturally and socioeconomically diverse in the district. In the two PDS schools where I supervised, approximately 42% of the students qualify for free or reduced lunch (used as an indicator of poverty), approximately 50% are students of color, and 20% are not native speakers of English. Ten different languages are represented between the two schools, and students are supported in an English as a Second Language (ESL) program when appropriate.

In chapter 3, Peterman provides a discussion of how urban settings differ from other school contexts. She describes urban schools as often being challenged by the fact that they are bureaucratic and contradictory, under-resourced while poverty bound, and multicultural, multiracial, multiethnic, and multilinguistic. The Madison PDS schools may indeed be described by these characteristics, but I would hesitate to argue the extent to which these schools should be classified as "urban." Clearly, most urban schools elicit the characteristics that Peterman (this volume) presents much more intensely, not to mention the fact that the increased "intensity, complexity, and interactions of these characteristics atop faltering physical infrastructures further define urban schools as distinct challenges for new teachers."

In any case, the University of Wisconsin–Madison's Professional Development School Program does not propose to have "the" most effective way to prepare teachers for inner city teaching or for a highly diverse student population. In fact, Madison professor Ladson-Billings (1994) points out that as the need for culturally relevant pedagogy continues to grow, the task of preparing teachers effectively for a diverse school population remains an unmet challenge. Still, the PDS program is committed to confronting the challenges and complexities of urban teaching. Teacher educators in the PDS program actively seek out opportunities to discuss and practice socially just teaching and continue to explore strategies that might more effectively address the questions and concerns related to these issues. In weekly seminars, discussions around real-life teaching cases help preservice teachers translate this kind of theory into practice. By sharing their experiences in their field placements and concerns they have over practices that may fail to represent equitable practices, preservice teachers are given guidance and support from both teacher educators and their peers. This practice in negotiation helps them conceive of ways they might reenvision circumstances.

"When I think about making my teaching more culturally relevant for my students, I realize how difficult that really is for someone like me—that is, someone who knows very little about other cultures" (SP, 2000). This statement made in seminar created a tremendous amount of discussion. There were many preservice teachers in the cohort who felt they had struggled with this issue themselves and were seeking out ways in which they could actively promote a culturally relevant way of teaching and learning. This preservice teacher was especially interested in the idea of engaging her students more actively in the discussion of what it means to value diverse cultures in their classroom and why it was important to do so. In seminar, the preservice teacher was able to elicit her peers' insights and possible facilitation strategies. The next week, she shared her progress of powerfully engaging her students in class discussions and in providing them with a greater sense of community and curricular ownership.

I have found that preservice teachers are more likely to engage in a more critical dialogue and be challenged to explore highly personal and sometimes painful issues when they feel safe, respected, and understood by the colleagues and supervisors who support them. I am often reminded that "for one's knowledge to be useful, one must feel free to examine it, to acknowledge one's confusions, and to appreciate one's own ways of seeing, exploring, and of working through to a more satisfactory level" (Duckworth, 1997, p. 2). It is for these reasons that building and nurturing this kind of environment became an essential role for me as the Professional Development School program supervisor.

Besides attending the weekly seminars within the school settings, the PDS preservice teachers participate in numerous strategies intended to foster inquiry around issues related to diversity. As I alluded to earlier, they participate in an ongoing community-based action research project in which they seek to understand questions they have about children and teaching by seeking out insight from the community. Preservice teachers are also encouraged to actively promote closer coordination between the university, the public school staff, and the local community. They attend and reflect on their participation in parent–teacher conferences, school and community meetings, and other interactions that inform their work in the schools. These experiences, discussions across institutional settings, and field experiences within diverse schools help to support the development of "greater cultural knowledge, cultural sensitivity, and intercultural teaching competence" (Zeichner & Hoeft, 1996, p. 541). Of course, this assumes once again that all parties involved in this process are equally invested in this sense of collaborative meaning making and understanding. I have found that when this investment fails to exist or preservice teachers are unable to process their understanding with colleagues in a critical way, negative assumptions and stereotypes can actually be reinforced. This realization often goes unrecognized until a particular teaching event illuminates the issue or when a stereotypical notion goes unchallenged within a seminar discussion. As discouraging as these moments might be, they are important turning points in that they glaringly represent the work of teacher education.

Collaborative and critical support systems are important as preservice teachers confront difficulties and attempt to balance their emerging social conscience and identity with the multiple and competing demands of the daily realities of classroom life as a novice teacher. As Peterman (chap. 3, this volume) points out, for preservice teachers often "liberatory pedagogy becomes counterintuitive in their situated realities of practice." Therefore, teacher educators must ensure that preservice teachers recognize and critically analyze how their lives in schools can, and often already do, reflect the promise and relevance of a sociocultural and social reconstructionist perspective of teaching and learning. This is most successful when cooperating teachers are identified as models who represent "the distinct capacities of knowledge and skills, and dispositions of highly successful urban teachers" (Peterman, this volume). This modeling allows preservice teachers to begin their own teaching with the professional and moral motivation, hopefully, to become activist teachers who confront the current state of urban schools.

PORTFOLIOS AS A TOOL
TO ARTICULATE TEACHING PRACTICE

As participants in the PDS program at the University of Wisconsin–Madison, preservice teachers have always (over 10 years) been required to develop some kind of portfolio to serve as a self-reflective assessment tool. Until very recently, this portfolio primarily focused on their final student teaching semester. This meant that they struggled with the reflective purpose of the portfolio. They expressed frustration that their lives were overburdened and that the program made them "reflect to death" (DJ, 2000). Understandably, preservice teachers are usually consumed by questions of future employment. This has meant that the preservice teachers typically look at the portfolio as an employment tool. We contended that by documenting their learning, they would be better able to articulate who they were as teachers. It was particularly difficult for some of the preservice teachers to see the bigger picture or what we perceived to be the deeper, more reflective motivation:

> I have always been the type of person that needs a purpose. I guess that
> there is a purpose here, but to be honest—for me—it's more about getting
> a job at this point. It's hard for me to imagine that all this work is really go-
> ing to help me. We all know that principals don't have time to look at our
> portfolios when they hire us. And this whole thing about meeting the stan-
> dards … I feel like we are jumping through a bunch of hoops with these
> standards. (AT, 2000)

It is clearly the role of the teacher educator to articulate and demonstrate
the value of the portfolio process. Still, when competing with the realities of
their lives as new teachers, this is always a hard sell, especially when all of the
focus for them was on their last semester of student teaching.

More recently, as the Madison PDS teacher education program moved
into performance standards-based assessment, the portfolio has instead
become a place where preservice teachers are required to document the
growth and development of their practice over time. Teacher educators
are now supporting the preservice teachers in a developmental reflective
portfolio that demonstrates their growth throughout all of their formal
university preparation. This shift toward "continuous documentation of
knowledge and beliefs" (Conway & Artiles, chap. 2, this volume) demonstrate at least an attempt to integrate a sociocultural perspective of teaching and learning into the assessment of a preservice teacher's
preparation. However, it has not necessarily been embraced by all students as the reflective tool one might hope it would be:

> I am just not convinced that this process is as authentic as you all tell us it
> is. It seems artificial and definitely imposed. I find it very difficult to cap-
> ture what I am about as a teacher in this way—on paper and in the portfo-
> lio. It is such a limited look at what I can do with kids. You have to see me
> teach to understand what I am all about. The process is so frustrating for
> me because of those reasons. (SR, 2000)

Zeichner points out (in chap. 1, this volume) that the shift to performance-based assessment is not necessarily new to teacher education. In
fact, he provides evidence to demonstrate that throughout the 20th century, there have been various movements in each decade in which assessment has represented a performance-based focus. The more recent
changes in the University of Wisconsin–Madison teacher education program and its adoption of performance standards-based assessment has basically come from two fronts, one political and one technological. First, the
Department of Public Instruction of Wisconsin (DPI) demanded that
schools of education in Wisconsin either create their own teacher education
standards or have a standardized version imposed on them. The University
of Wisconsin–Madison chose to create its own version and, after 3 years of

collaboration between faculty in all education departments at the university and cooperating teachers in the Madison Metropolitan School District, the standards for teacher education were developed. The standards as statements were completed in 1998 (see Appendix A). Since then, various components have been added.

The PDS program has been in the forefront in piloting the use of the University of Wisconsin–Madison Teacher Education Standards, particularly in developing ways to document evidence of addressing the standards. In PDS seminars and supervisory discussions, the standards have been used to generate discussions about quality teaching, especially in the diverse contexts in which the preservice teachers are placed. Many seminar discussions focus on the meaning of the standards and on sharing specific ways in which preservice teachers can demonstrate and provide evidence of successfully addressing each standard. More recently, performance indicators (see Appendix B for an example) for each of the 15 standards were added to the document and help to define the meaning of the standards by providing more explicit language and delineated examples.

Assessment rubrics for each of the performance indicators were under development when I left the university. The purpose of these rubrics is to document a preservice teacher's progress over time and in a more objective manner. Preservice teachers gather evidence of addressing the standards in their teaching during their practicum and student teaching placements and throughout their university coursework. One interpretation of this performance standards-based approach might be to conclude that the standards are driving the work of teacher education in the Madison program. Actually, Zeichner (chap. 1, this volume) presents what I believe to be a more accurate interpretation. He states, "Contemporary statements of standards and performances are broader and attend to the cognitive and dispositional aspects of teaching in addition to the technical aspects that are compatible with the view of teachers as reflective practitioners" (p. __). The additional framework that the standards provide is intended to offer a lens for the preservice teachers to view their teaching practices through.

Although preservice teachers often begin the portfolio with a certain amount of resistance, in most cases, they begin to see their teaching articulated in the standards and use the language to present their work to others:

> You probably remember when I began this program—I had this really strong reaction against the standards. I thought to myself—well, I also said it out loud—here we go again. We can't just think about what is important for us to learn, we have to have someone tell us about it in a standard. And the worst part was that in my experience, when you had a standard, there was always a standardized test that followed. It just went against everything I believed about good teaching and especially ran up against my own experiences as a student … The interesting thing is that once I was

able to get beyond some of this resistance, I began to realize that the
teacher education standards did actually represent what I believed good
teaching should look or sound like. So, the standards took on a whole different purpose for me. They gave me a way to talk about what I thought
good teaching was. Before, I just kind of knew it when I saw it. Now, I can
actually talk about it. I guess that I have come to realize how important
that is—finally, right! (DB, 2000)

Many preservice teachers initially resist the portfolio process primarily
because of the work involved. However, this was especially the case with the
adoption of the standards and when they were required to provide documentation as evidence of meeting the standards. The preservice teachers
resented the abstract language used within the standards document and
failed to understand their meaning, let alone appreciate their purpose.
This meant they were less likely to find value in the process of documentation and failed to recognize it as an opportunity to critically reflect on their
learning to teach. The preservice teachers did not understand the portfolio
process as an interpretive model of assessment and instead identified the
collection of evidence as just another set of hoops to jump through in their
formal preparation to become teachers. As one preservice teacher wrote:

I think you have to psychologically get through peoples' blocks (about
the standards) because I think standards are often associated mostly with
do's and don'ts ... too simplistic. Some of the standards on the district
level are so cut and dry ... like as a teacher your students need to know
the dates of all the major wars ... These teacher education standards are
not those kinds of standards. I think people become more open when
they realize that the standards are all about what we believe in as teachers. It's nothing that restricts you ... they are actually really cool standards ... I think you really have to start out and try from the beginning to
translate them. Then, actually help us see what they really mean in our
practice. (JD, 2000)

Sensing and being told outright of this early resistance to the standards,
supervisors actively provided opportunities for the preservice teachers to
more directly connect their teaching practices to the standards. Time was
spent in seminars trying to help them find examples of ways that their own
teaching and learning represented the ideals and models of practice that
were outlined in the standards. This allowed the preservice teachers to see
the standards as a way of putting language around quality teaching practices. Gradually, it is this on-going documentation of evidence that becomes
the substance of the preservice teachers' portfolios. Preservice teachers
eventually find that with the standards, they now have a framework in which
to place their experiences. For example, one student wrote:

> Putting together the portfolio has helped me to focus my beliefs about
> teaching and then demonstrate how I actually behave as a teacher. It is
> more than just evidence of my reflection, which I think I do a lot of. It
> shows my growth as a teacher and who I really am. I have accepted that this
> portfolio is only a piece of me and that is ok. The portfolio is a good tool
> for reflection because it also helped me think about ways that I can im-
> prove on my weaknesses. Most importantly, it has helped me put language
> around who I am as a teacher. (BG, 2000)

Whereas the portfolio has become a tool for teacher educators to assess
preservice teachers' abilities in the teacher education standards, preservice
teachers describe how it is the portfolio process that has in turn become the
tool with which to critically reflect on their practice, allowing them to document growth and performance over the time they spend in their formal
preparation:

> The whole thing about doing this [portfolio] process and the way we have
> been taught in this education program is that we are not just being taught
> to be technicians. We are supposed to be professional people who know
> what we are doing and why. Doing a portfolio reinforces that. It makes you
> responsible for your learning, what you will teach, and what you believe. It
> puts it in your hands by reinforcing the whole idea of ownership—this is
> my teaching. As bad as it maybe is to admit, there are times I don't even re-
> alize that I am engaged in really problematic practices. This system—if
> that is what it's called—of critical reflection really has become a process
> that I actively engage in to keep my practices in check. It forces me to con-
> front why it is that I'm doing what I'm doing. If I can't find a way to articu-
> late my purpose and then represent it in some way—I have more
> examining to do. (JD, 2000)

THE PORTFOLIO AS A PLACE TO EXPLORE
URBAN TEACHING ISSUES

As discussed at great length earlier in this chapter, a crucial part of teacher
education must be to assist students as they unpack their "prior experiences
to better understand what they believe and how they came to believe it"
(Gore & Zeichner, 1991). In the portfolio process, preservice teachers become better able to construct their own meaning of their situated practices
and eventually understand what it means to be a teacher and how race, class,
gender, sexual orientation, religion, ability, and so forth influence those belief systems. Rarely, before entering the program, have preservice teachers
been asked to confront their unquestioned assumptions. This means that
typically "the beginning teacher is an outsider looking through the lens in
order to identify with the experiences of students from different cultural,

ethnic, and economic backgrounds" (Frykholm, 1997, p. 51). In many cases, it is a matter of a preservice teacher confronting two very different realities and the meaning making that occurs as they negotiate between the two. This confrontation is then "not only a sign of growth, it is foundational to the growth" (Meyer et. al., 1998, p. 24).

In their portfolio, preservice teachers articulate their own teaching philosophies, the beliefs they have about teaching, and what it means to teach in a diverse setting:

> The strongest practical benefit is that it [the portfolio] made me think about my philosophy. It made me think about how I connected what I had actually done, to my beliefs about teaching. The thing is that I want to be someone who thinks about multicultural teaching. I want to be able to tell others about how this actually looks in my teaching. When I looked through my collection of lessons, I began to realize how much that way of teaching is a part of me. It's evident in my planning, not just in my instruction. By choosing things to represent me as a teacher and then writing something to support it, I kept thinking about it and then I was able to connect it with something physical. This process makes it more strongly embedded. It is in me now. It's a part of me where as before it was sort of way out there in theory. Once that connection happens, then it's so much easier to talk about. (JD, 2000)

It is not the portfolio process per se that leads a Madison PDS preservice teacher to think about teaching in an urban and/or diverse setting, but it is, most definitely, the social reconstructionist focus of the teacher education program and the process of addressing the particular standards that emphasize cultural diversity, varied instructional strategies, and effective/relevant pedagogy for all students. The portfolio provides the preservice teachers the opportunity to document and reflect more deeply on multicultural issues and their own experiences and feelings about teaching in diverse settings. One preservice teacher explained the process in this way:

> I chose to become a part of PDS because I eventually want to teach in a diverse classroom—hopefully in an urban setting. I had heard about the portfolio requirement, but it didn't scare me. I knew that I needed a lot of help—not necessarily with the portfolio, but because my background is probably so different from the students I hope to teach—I was going to need help thinking about teaching differently than I was taught. This program has supported me in my learning and thinking through of these issues. I know that some people complain. They get tired of the agenda that the professors seem to have. I just don't get that. We are here—we chose to be teachers. To me that choice means that we have to think about these issues. I just appreciate the fact that I have a format like the portfolio to express my views. It is definitely about expression—I am now able to

communicate what I think about multicultural teaching, but it's also about showing something. In the portfolio you see the evidence. (DJ, 2000)

As preservice teachers examine the standards and compile evidence of their practice for the portfolios, they must further explore their own beliefs and philosophies about teaching in a diverse setting. For example, when preservice teachers collect evidence to address Standard Six, they must emphasize their knowledge of community cultures and resources, as it states:

> Standard Six: Connects School and Community: Teachers use the knowledge and abilities necessary for collaboration with individuals, groups, and agencies within the school and community. They base instruction of students on an understanding of curricular goals, subject matter, and the community, and help the students make connections between community-based knowledge and school knowledge. (University of Wisconsin–Madison, 1998)

Evidence of meeting this standard might include documentation from journal entries about specific efforts that the preservice teacher has made to establish respectful and productive relationships with parents, guardians, and community members from diverse home and community environments. Detailed descriptions of these efforts must also illustrate how these relationships helped to support student learning in the classroom. One preservice teacher included a unit on *voting rights* in her portfolio. In the reflective piece that accompanied her evidence, she explained how she became a voter registrar and took her class to one of the neighborhoods within the school community to have the students help register people in their community to vote:

> As a class we confronted all types of questions. For example, why is it that minority communities, especially those with serious socioeconomic challenges tend to have less registered voters? And, how is it as children, not yet allowed to vote, can we participate in the process of active citizenship? It wasn't just about getting out there and doing some kind of community service—not that community service is bad or anything, but this project really came from the kids learning about their community and deciding how they could address some of the needs of the community. It wasn't this really neat and tidy project—instead the children engaged in some powerful examination of inequities that exist for them and their families, things they now feel they have a voice in changing. (JB, 2001)

An important piece in documenting these kinds of experiences is the reflective component that must accompany the evidence. Through this reflection, the preservice teacher is actually able to articulate his or her growth and performance. If this articulation is absent, it is impossible to assess any real development of understanding.

In chapter 3, Peterman asserts that successful urban teachers must be creative problem solvers, resourceful, resilient and resistant, and advocates for children and their parents. In the PDS portfolios, preservice teachers are supported throughout their preparation to engage in inquiry-based projects that elicit growth and performance in these four areas. As mentioned earlier, the preservice teachers conduct community-based action research projects by seeking out school and community resources as insights into the contexts (academic and/or social) that may yield students' success. Preservice teachers make these valuable resource connections, and their peers provide a cohort model of support. Preservice teachers state that the collaborative model of support informs the types of collective professional development they will seek out as teachers:

> I wonder a lot about whether the teachers that I had as a student were ever collaborating and supporting one another like we do here in seminar, through this portfolio process, and in our action research projects. It's very powerful to see my cooperating teacher and her colleagues work together this way. It just seemed like teachers used to do their own thing—close the door—live and teach in isolation. I actually imagined that's how teaching would be. I was so wrong. It was intimidating at first—not having that sense of control over my own work, but I can't tell you how much I have learned from the other people in my cohort and the teachers in my school. They really push me to think about what I'm doing. They have helped me develop a little inner voice. I even hear them when they aren't there—kind of spooky, but I know that I will seek people out when I get my own classroom—people who think like me, but also people who challenge me. My students deserve that kind of teaching. (SR, 2000)

Although it is impossible to guarantee that all cooperating teachers working with our preservice teachers support this type of professional development, the relationships that are nurtured as a result of the Professional Development School partnership might make this more likely. This collaborative engagement is not necessarily a unique way of thinking about teacher preparation. Most programs represent similar social learning perspectives. However, the key to teacher sustainability, especially in urban settings, is whether this preparation translates into their ongoing professional development as novice teachers. This professional development must offer opportunities for teachers to demonstrate that they are creative problem solvers, resourceful and resilient (Peterman, chap. 3, this volume). Ultimately, it is these kinds of teachers or those who exhibit these qualities who are able to respond through their teaching as advocates for children, parents, and the community.

MOVEMENT TOWARD ELECTRONIC PORTFOLIOS

As state requirements continue to change, graduation from teacher education programs and certification will ultimately be determined by successful
performance on standards-based assessments. This increased emphasis on
standards has translated into various concerns and movements across the
University of Wisconsin–Madison campus. Specifically, the university has
explored how this movement will influence both undergraduate liberal arts
and teacher education coursework. There are also questions about how the
preservice program will support both the content and logistics of portfolio
development.

Traditionally, the portfolio documentation was assigned to the final field
component of teacher education, and evaluation was in the hands of that semester's supervisor. Now, faculty and staff are investigating ways to document the preservice teachers' ability to address the standards over time
within both the formal course work and in all field settings. This coordination is proving to be a daunting task.

In response to these issues, faculty began considering an electronic
portfolio format. For a number of reasons, electronic portfolios were
thought to be attractive alternatives to the more traditional paper portfolios because electronic portfolios can be accessed by a number of people,
in a variety of settings, and can be stored more efficiently. Also, in response to criticism that technology instruction was lacking in the formal
teaching preparation program at the University of Wisconsin–Madison,
electronic portfolios were seen as possible opportunities to engage the
preservice teachers in technology learning. This initiative, of course, also
assumes a significant amount of technology learning for the teacher education faculty as well.

Since the spring of 2000, preservice teachers in the PDS have been offered the opportunity to develop an electronic portfolio on a secured
website. Recently, the electronic portfolio has become the preferred format. The Web-based electronic template is a series of six folders that allows
a preservice teacher to accumulate evidence of his or her ability to teach and
meet the teacher education standards. The preservice teachers can share
their materials visually in a variety of ways. The capability of linking pages
in one folder together with other sections in the portfolio is seen as an especially powerful tool in the electronic portfolio. In a more traditional paper
format, it is often difficult to make the link between skills of teaching and
the contexts within which a preservice teacher is working. Making these
connections becomes easier with the linking capability:

> It was easier for me to see *it* when I was able to link or maybe it was all about
> making connections—something I was trying to do as I created my portfo-

lio. The electronic format provided me with flexibility that I didn't think I would have with the old scrap book/paper format. (JB, 2001)

Also available in the electronic template is the capacity to connect to outside Web sites. Preservice teachers can provide a link to the University of Wisconsin–Madison's Professional Development School Web site as well as to individual schools within the partnership. They can also provide access to sites that have acted as instructional resources.

The six folders provided in the template offer flexibility in how preservice teachers examine their practice and ways in which they might address the teacher education standards. The folder titles are: *Teaching Philosophy*, *Teaching and Learning*, *School and Community*, *Technology*, *My Story*, and *Standards*. For example, some preservice teachers put the paper they are required to write up of their community action research experience in the *School and Community* folder, others put it in *My Story*, and others saw that their action research should be placed in the *Teaching and Learning* folder. Another preservice teacher demonstrated the flexible nature of the electronic portfolio folders by taking a video production project that he used with a group of below-grade-level readers. He used the project as a representation of what he had become as a teacher and was able to use pieces of his teaching within the project across all six folders. Having been assigned a reading group early in the semester, he was given flexibility to design curriculum and implement new practices. He shared a sense of hope for this group that seemed to be lost by other teachers. Ultimately, he was able to support these students in new ways, and they were able to reconstruct their ideas about school and finally experience success. The way in which he shared the project throughout the portfolio allowed him to represent his ability to teach (particularly reading), motivate students, and break barriers of previous failures. He was not only able to link his project across many of the pages/folders within the portfolio template, but more importantly, he was able to demonstrate interesting links between the standards:

> I was so excited when my organizational structure came to me—and one day it really just came to me. Obviously, we had the template to use that definitely provided the structure I like to have, but I really couldn't figure out how to organize it all. I decided to use this unit that I really felt represented what I was all about as a teacher. Now, my supervisor was leery about whether I could actually represent my growth and development in the program—basically just using my final student teaching semester—and even just a piece of that. I knew I could do it and she trusted me … she pushed a bit which was great, but basically what I needed to do was to articulate how this work in the unit represented the growth that had taken place—it really did. (WP, 2001)

This ability to link is clearly important as it allows preservice teachers to provide a more descriptive discussion of their context as they talk about their practice. Overall, the electronic format was definitely a novelty when I was working in the Madison PDS program. It was easy to become overwhelmed by the visually attractive representation instead of focusing on the content. Perhaps, through time and with widespread adoption, the novelty wears off and addressing the problematic issues and potential of this format takes precedence.

CHALLENGES OF ELECTRONIC PORTFOLIOS

This innovative transition to electronic portfolios has generated excitement across the program. In spite of this excitement, some key issues challenge preservice teachers and faculty. First, preservice teachers and those supporting them in the field and in courses struggle with the technology learning curve, such as: accessing a Web site, adding documents through a Web editing program, scanning pictures, creating links, utilizing the terminology, and embracing the complexity of the process itself. In many cases, large cohorts of students and professors are learning this together. Conceivably, this could be a very powerful example of collaborative learning. Instead, it tends to be a logistical nightmare. It is imperative, but somewhat difficult, to provide the kind of individual technical support that is necessary for preservice teachers to successfully create their electronic portfolios.

Currently, efforts are underway to provide a structure for this kind of consistent and long-term technical support. For example, a number of electronic portfolio sessions are held on campus each semester and technical staff is available for assistance. However, it is important to note that this technical staff does not usually represent appropriate content resources. These support individuals are seldom familiar with teacher education and are obviously more focused on providing technical assistance. This can sometimes undermine our notion of reflective practice. In addition, it has become glaringly clear that university faculty and staff also need professional development as they are required to incorporate this electronic portfolio process into their course work. This has translated into professors inviting individuals into their courses to provide the technical support necessary for the project. Professors will ask that their students come prepared with the content, but will wait for the technology assistance before they support their students to represent the work in the electronic portfolio. This division of tasks would not necessarily be the case in a more traditional paper portfolio format. At this point, the process seems more seamless. It is for these reasons that the electronic format elicits anxiety. For the students, it has to do with the creation:

When I first heard that we were moving to the electronic portfolio I really got nervous. I definitely have some of the technology skills that we need, but there are just so many things that can go wrong when you are dependent on computers. That has been really obvious in some of these training meetings. I just sometimes wish that we could go back to the old system—for me that would have meant laying out everything on my bedroom floor and getting creative. I know that some people are able to get really creative with the electronic process, but for me it's harder. I just don't see it as easily and I feel as if I'm way too focused on the technical stuff—that can't be what they want. (LJ, 2000)

For the university faculty, their frustration seems to have more to do with the preparation, ongoing support, and whether or not the electronic format is actually serving a purpose:

I am not uncomfortable with the fact that my students know more about technology than I do or that they are all at different levels of their knowledge and abilities. It's a perfect lesson in differentiated curriculum. However, the reality is that this project seems to be consuming my class. I do appreciate the ongoing nature of this type of assessment and I have no resentment in the fact that I am being asked to participate in that assessment—it makes perfect sense. I do wonder if we are a bit wowed by the electronic presentation. We need to make sure that what we are seeing is as impressive as how it's presented! (GM, 2000)

In the PDS program, an attempt has been made to negotiate this anxiety, but according to some, not without cost. When I was working in the PDS program, at least two seminars each semester were dedicated to providing the preservice teachers with exemplar models and technical support to guide them through the electronic process. In addition, there were many more discussions that focused on what the preservice teachers should include as content. Preservice teachers worked in smaller groups with technical staff to set up their own folder system, and together they learned how to negotiate the process. After these formal sessions, preservice teachers were responsible for setting up work sessions with the technical support staff assigned to the PDS group. Preservice teachers were required periodically, throughout the three semesters, to share pieces of their electronic portfolio in the cohort seminar, and they received feedback from their peers and supervisors. It was in these discussions that preservice teachers were asked to reflect more specifically on the piece that they shared and what they thought it said about their ability to teach in urban settings:

I may not have done it the first time ... in fact, I would bet that I didn't, but eventually, when it was my time to share my work I knew someone would ask that question. I knew that I would have to make the connection—to be able to talk about what I was sharing—in a way that addressed diversity. (BJ, 2000)

At the end of their final student-teaching semester, preservice teachers must formally present their portfolios to an audience of their peers, invited guests, experienced teachers, and university faculty and supervisors. This presentation is an opportunity to not only celebrate their accomplishments, but also demonstrate and articulate their teaching philosophy. There are some teacher educators at Madison who would like to see this presentation become more rigorous and evaluative in nature. In any case, these presentations focus on what the preservice teacher has learned about teaching in a diverse setting and what their students have, in turn, taught them about teaching. It is a relatively short presentation, followed by questions from the audience. Typically, these conversations are more celebratory rather than any sort of critical commentary:

> When I walked into this classroom my teacher told me, "You will never be-
> lieve that you are in seventh grade—that group of kids over there barely
> read at a 3rd grade level." I began to think about what that really meant—
> how education had really failed this group of kids. While I understand all
> of the pressures that teachers face, the reality is that these kids were fail-
> ing, but more importantly "we" were failing—failing to hold ourselves ac-
> countable. I also wondered about something—why was it that this group
> of students were the students of color—is that part of why we were willing
> to place the blame on others? I guess it sort of became my mission. I knew
> that I wanted to try something with this group of kids, so my cooperating
> teacher basically just handed them over. I think the most powerful thing
> about my work with these kids, which I will now show you, is that I helped
> them believe that they *could* be students. They have self-confidence that
> was really missing before and people around the school say that it really
> shows—they are starting to excel—especially for them—in other things.
> (WP, 2001)

This introduction to the portfolio piece that he shared was definitely celebratory, but there are elements of critical reflection in which he explains the inequities that existed for this particular group of children and his sense of advocacy for them. A challenge is that it is very difficult to engage in any powerful dialogue when the purpose of the presentation is yet unclear.

After the presentation, supervisors review the completed portfolio more comprehensively and respond with extensive written feedback. Currently, this feedback is subjective in nature and still generally comes at the end of the whole process. Although the supervisors witness the periodic sharing and enter into the online portfolios at various points in the semester, that feedback is more dialogical and reflective. Supervisors then make a recommendation for revisions or pass along news of the "passing" to the department. This is the extent to which the process was formalized when I left the program. However, assessment rubrics are being designed to make the feedback process more objective, thorough, consistent, and ongoing through various checkpoints. Eventually, these rubrics will be used by methods instructors, advisors, supervisors, cooperating teachers, and the preservice teachers themselves to self assess their progress.

Whether or not a portfolio, electronic or not, can successfully assess a preservice teacher's ability to teach in an urban setting is yet to be seen. Madison PDS preservice teachers are definitely able to focus their portfolio to represent themselves as urban teachers. The electronic format seems to have potential in providing further flexibility, which means that perhaps it is better able to represent the complexity of teaching and the intimate connection that practice has to context—an aspect perhaps more relevant to urban teaching.

CONCLUDING REMARKS

Historically, learning to teach has meant that the university has provided the preservice teacher with knowledge about teaching through course work in theory and sometimes specific skills to utilize in the classroom. The schools have provided the field setting where knowledge can be practiced (Britzman, 1991). This positivist tradition of teacher education decontextualizes schooling and fails to recognize the inherent beliefs and experiences that preservice teachers bring to their teacher education. The literature on learning to teach is abundant with accounts of innovative efforts that exist among programs representing a more progressive and social conception of teacher preparation. What is known is that successful teacher education initiatives need to "build upon the beliefs of preservice teachers and feature systematic and consistent long-term support in a collaborative setting" (Wideen, Mayer-Smith, & Moon, 1998, p. 160).

In the Professional Development School Program at the University of Wisconsin–Madison, relationships with preservice teachers are developed over time. There is a comfort level nurtured that allows the group to confront challenging teaching questions. Once this comfort is established, a sense of empowerment can be cultivated so that preservice teachers "take ownership and responsibility for their learning and become involved in a process that enables them to express, define, address, and resolve problems by creating appropriate changes" (Saavedra, 1996, p. 273). The intent of the portfolio is to represent this process and provide an opportunity for the preservice teacher to reflect on his or her development with tangible evidence of that growth:

> [The portfolio] represents me as a professional who sees the importance of doing quality work with students. It shows that I am aware of standards

based education and that I can articulate my philosophy about teaching and learning. Most importantly, the entire [portfolio] process shows that I am a reflective teacher—that I learn from each lesson and strive to make myself a better teacher. I would say that I am still learning how to define my teaching and how to represent myself. I hope that I will never stop questioning my philosophy. (SP, 2000)

Perhaps the most important aspect of the PDS cohort model is that it provides a valuable opportunity for preservice teachers to reflect on multicultural issues in a safe collegial setting. This reflective dialogue can promote resourcefulness, resiliency, tolerance, and creativity necessary to work in diverse settings (Peterman, chap. 3, this volume). Clearly, it is necessary for preservice teachers ultimately to demonstrate how they have translated their increased awareness of diversity into teaching behaviors and strategies that meet the needs of a diverse student population, ideally in an urban setting. This translation of multicultural knowledge into practice eventually provides preservice teachers with the necessary skills to recognize cultural relevance and bias in their planning, instruction, and assessment (Davidman, 1990). The cohort model assumes that this translation occurs more successfully when there is a collaborative sense of purpose and advocacy.

Portfolios in the PDS program can probably only represent a limited sense of the translation of preservice teachers' multicultural knowledge into contextually responsive practices. Still, it allows teaching to become situated and assisted (Wenger, 1998), partly because of the collaborative support provided by the PDS cohort model.

This chapter discussed the somewhat recent trend toward a performance standards-based system of assessment at the University of Wisconsin–Madison. As a partial case study, it responds to the ways in which the Madison PDS program and portfolios represent the design principles presented in Peterman's earlier chapter in this text. That is the extent to which the Madison model is: situated and responsive; longitudinal, reflective, in action; capacity building; and advocacy based.

Whether or not an electronic portfolio provides a more effective means of assessment, particularly in addressing specific aspects unique to urban teacher preparation is an important investigation. Also worthy of further study are the many questions and challenges that present themselves when a program considers the ramifications of attempting to prepare teachers for urban teaching in a not so urban setting.

ACKNOWLEDGMENTS

The author would like to thank Nancy Booth for contributions she made to an earlier draft of this case study. Nancy continues to work with preservice teachers in the Madison PDS program and is dedicated to their growth and development. Her commitment to teacher education is greatly appreciated by the University of Wisconsin–Madison and the staff at Thoreau Elementary School. The author would also like to thank the PDS preservice teachers who agreed to be interviewed. Their feedback and insights on the portfolio have informed the process and continue to help us think about these issues more collectively.

APPENDIX A: UNIVERSITY OF WISCONSIN–MADISON TEACHER EDUCATION STANDARDS

Standard One: Incorporates Understanding of Human Learning and Development: Teachers design learning environments and pedagogical practices for students that are grounded in concepts and interpretative frameworks provided by disciplines that study human development and learning.

Standard Two: Understands the Social Context of Schooling: Teachers understand how local, state, national, and global social and political contexts differentially affect schooling and its outcomes for students.

Standard Three: Demonstrates Sophisticated Curricular Knowledge: Teachers understand the central concepts, assumptions, tools of inquiry, ways of reasoning, uncertainties, and controversies of the disciplines that they teach to students.

Standard Four: Demonstrates Pedagogical Knowledge in Specific Domains: Teachers are knowledgeable about the challenges and opportunities that commonly arise as students develop understanding of competence in particular domains.[1]

Standard Five: Explains and Justifies Education Choices: Teachers can articulate and defend their curricular choices and instructional choices with sound ethical and pedagogical justifications.

Standard Six: Connects School and Community: Teachers use the knowledge and abilities necessary for collaboration with individuals, groups, and agencies within the school and community. They base instruction of students on an understanding of curricular goals, subject matter and the community, and help the students make connections between community-based knowledge and school knowledge.

---

[1]The term *domain* was chosen because teachers are called on to teach "school subjects," not necessarily academic disciplines. Those school subjects include content and skills that fall within particular disciplines but often cut across those disciplines.

Standard Seven: Understands and Adapts to Multiple Forms of Communication: Teachers understand and adapt to students' multiple forms of expressing and receiving experiences, ideas, and feelings.

Standard Eight: Employs Varied Assessment Processes: Teachers understand and thoughtfully use formal and informal evaluation strategies to assess students' achievements, strengths, challenges, and learning styles for continuous development.

Standard Nine: Manages Learning Environment: Teachers establish and maintain an environment that engages students in learning while providing for their physical and socioemotional well-being.

Standard Ten: Employs Varied Instructional Strategies: Teachers understand and use a variety of instructional strategies to enhance students' learning.

Standard Eleven: Uses Technologies: Teachers appropriately incorporate new and proven technologies into instructional practice. They understand the major social, cultural, and economic ideas surrounding their implementation.

Standard Twelve: Accommodates for All Students: Teachers design educational environments and use instructional practices that accommodate students' achievements, strengths, challenges, interests, and learning styles.

Standard Thirteen: Reflective Practitioner: Teachers are reflective practitioners who evaluate the effect of their assumptions, choices, and actions on others (students, parents, and other professionals in the learning community) and who actively seek out opportunities to grow professionally. They examine assumptions enmeshed in ways of thinking and in familiar, institutional, and cultural lore and practices.

Standard Fourteen: Relates Well With Families and Communities: Teachers relate to students, families, and community members in a fair, respectful, and sensitive manner. They show an appreciation for the cultural[2] diversity of our society.

Standard Fifteen: Understands Legal Rights and Responsibilities: Teachers understand the legal rights and responsibilities of professional educators.

---

[2]*Culture* is broadly meant here to include the social patterns, arts, beliefs, institutions, and all other products of human work and thought characteristic of a community or population. Cultural patterns are related to language, sex/gender, race, national origin/ethnicity, social class, creed/religion, disability, and sexual orientation.

APPENDIX B: UNIVERSITY OF WISCONSIN–MADISON TEACHER EDUCATION STANDARDS AND INDICATORS—STANDARD SIX

Standard Six: Connects School and Community: Teachers use the knowledge and abilities necessary for collaboration with individuals, groups, and agencies within the school and community. They base instruction of students on an understanding of curricular goals, subject matter, and the community and help the students make connections between community-based knowledge and school knowledge.

Performance Indicator	Exemplary	Acceptable	Emerging	Unacceptable
	Consistently, over time, and in multiple contexts, you:	Regularly and in more than one content area, you:	One time and in one content area, you:	You do not understand and/or are unable to:
A. Identifies and uses knowledge of community cultures and resources to foster teaching that helps students make connections between community-based knowledge and school knowledge.	Use information within the current school/community context to design activities that connect learning to home and school experiences.	Use information within the current school/community context to design activities that connect learning to home and school experiences.		Use information within the current school/community context to design activities that connect learning to home and school experiences.
B. Participates in collaborative activities designed to make the school a productive learning environment.	Volunteer to work with others in planning and implementing community/school activities.	Volunteer to work with others in planning and implementing community/school activities.		Volunteer to work with others in planning and implementing community/school activities.
C. Establishes respectful and productive relationships with parents, guardians, and community members from diverse home and community environments in ways that support student learning.	Your professional conduct and communication style demonstrates an understanding and respect for diverse environments.	Your professional conduct and communication style demonstrates an understanding and respect for diverse environments.		Demonstrate that your professional conduct and communication style demonstrates an understanding and respect for diverse environments.

REFERENCES

AT (2000, Spring). Portfolio Interview.

BG (2000, Spring). Portfolio Interview.

BJ (2000, Spring). Portfolio Interview.

Booth, N. (2000). *Supporting the development of teacher education portfolios: Journeys in reflective thinking, assessment, and technology.* Unpublished master's thesis, University of Wisconsin–Madison.

Britzman, D. (1991). *Practice makes practice: A critical study of learning to teach.* Albany, NY: State University of New York Press.

Davidman, P. (1990). Multicultural teacher education and supervision: A new approach to professional development. *Teacher Education Quarterly, 17*(3), 37–52.

DB (2000, Spring). Portfolio Interview.

DJ (2000, Spring). Portfolio Interview.

Duckworth, E. (1997). *Teacher to teacher: Learning from each other.* New York: Teachers College Press.

Frykholm, J. (1997). A stacked deck: Addressing issues of equity with preservice teachers. *Equity & Excellence in Education, 30*(2), 50–58.

GM (2000, Spring). Portfolio Interview.

Gomez, M. L. (1994). Teacher education reform and prospective teachers' perspectives on teaching "other peoples" children. *Teaching and Teacher Education, 10*(3), 319–334.

Goodwin, A. (1994). Making the transition from self to other: What do preservice teachers really think about multicultural education. *Journal of Teacher Education, 45*(2), 119–131.

Gore, J. (1991). Practicing what we preach: Action research and the supervision of student teachers. In B. Tabachnick, & K. Zeichner (Eds.), *Issues and practices in inquiry-oriented teacher education* (pp. 253–272). London: Falmer Press.

Gore, J., & Zeichner, K. (1991). Action research and reflective teaching in preservice teacher education: A case study from the United States. *Teaching and Teacher Education, 7*(2), 119–136.

JB (2001, Spring). Portfolio Interview.

JD (2000, Spring). Portfolio Interview.

Ladson-Billings, G. (1994). *The Dreamkeepers: Successful teachers of African American children.* San Francisco, CA: Jossey-Bass.

LJ (2000, Spring). Portfolio Interview.

Meyer, R., Brown, L., DeNino, E., Larson, K., McKenzie, M., Ridder, K., et al. (1998). *Composing a teacher study group: Learning about inquiry in primary classrooms.* Mahwah, NJ: Lawrence Erlbaum Associates.

Nieto, S. (1992). *Affirming diversity: The sociopolitical context of multicultural education.* New York: Longman.

Saavedra, E. (1996). Teacher study groups: Contexts for transformative learning and action. *Theory Into Practice, 35*(4), 271–277.

SP (2000, Spring). Portfolio Interview.

SR (2000, Spring). Portfolio Interview.

University of Wisconsin–Madison, School of Education. (1998). *Teacher education standards*. Madison, WI: Author.

WP (2001, Spring). Portfolio Interview.

Wade, R. (1994). Teacher education students' views on class discussion: Implications for fostering critical reflection. *Teaching and Teacher Education, 10*(2), 231–243.

Wenger, E. (1998). *Communities of practice*. New York, NY: Cambridge University Press.

Wideen, M., Mayer-Smith, J., & Moon, B. (1998). A critical analysis of the research on learning to teach: Making the case for an ecological perspective on inquiry. *Review of Educational Research, 68*(2), 130–178.

Zeichner, K. (1994a). *Action research and issues of equity and social justice in preservice teacher education*. Paper presented at the annual meeting of the American Educational Research Association, New Orleans.

Zeichner, K. (1994b). Research on teacher thinking and different views of reflective practice in teaching and teacher education. In I. Carlgrin, G. Handal, & S. Vaage (Eds.), *Teachers' minds and actions* (pp. 9–27). London: Falmer Press.

Zeichner, K. (1996). Designing educative practicum experiences for prospective teachers. In K. Zeichner, S. Melnick, & M. L. Gomez (Eds.), *Currents of reform in teacher education* (pp. 215–234). New York: Teachers College Press.

Zeichner, K., & Hoeft, K. (1996). Teacher socialization for cultural diversity. In J. Sikula, T. J. Buttery, & E. Guyton (Eds.), *Handbook of research on teacher education* (2nd ed., pp. 525–547) New York: Macmillan.

Zeichner, K., & Miller, M. (1997). Learning to teach in professional development schools. In M. Levine & R. Trachtman (Eds.), *Making professional development schools work* (pp. 15–32). New York: Teachers College Press.

Chapter 6

Implementing Parallel Systems of Urban Teacher Performance: Assessment in Preparation and in Practice

Julie Kalnin
Donna Pearson
University of Minnesota

Ronna Locketz
Lynn Nordgren
Minneapolis Public Schools

Assessing teacher performance in ways that foster a teacher's development is, in any setting, a significant challenge. Creating whole systems of performance assessment within large urban institutions in ways that address the diversity of roles, purposes, and perspectives that participants hold is an even more complex endeavor. For well over a decade, the University of Minnesota (U of M) and the Minneapolis Public Schools (MPS) have been developing parallel systems of teacher assessment. Although each institution's experience has unique elements, these two cases of implementing teacher assessments in large urban institutions, seen side-by-side, draw a more complete picture of the issues involved in performance-based teacher assessment. A wide range of cultural, racial, and socioeconomic issues interacts within the urban educational setting. And if there is one lesson to be taken from these cases, it is that meaningful performance assessment within such a complex setting cannot be found in the direct application of standards or a swift adaptation of an assessment "tool" or teaching evaluation form. Rather, the development of a system of performance assessment is a process that takes much time to evolve—one that *should* ultimately become a shared expression of what is valued in the education of young people. The processes in which educators from MPS and U of M have engaged to imagine and implement their systems is, for this reason, as significant to an examination of urban assessment practices as the nature of the assessments themselves.

AN URBAN CONTEXT

Although Garrison Keillor's tales of German and Scandinavian immigrants in Lake Wobegon continue to amuse us, the Twin Cities of Minneapolis and St. Paul do not fit any stereotypical profile today. Religious and humanitarian organizations are carrying on their long history of actively sponsoring immigrants, resulting in a significant influx of refugees, most recently from Somalia. Hmong, Latinos, and Russians are the three other largest immigrant groups at this time (Wilder Research Center, 2000). According to census figures, Black, Hispanic, and Asian population groups have increased from 23% of the total population in 1990 to 34% in 2000 (U.S. Census Bureau, 2000).

The rapid diversification of the area has been reflected within the Minneapolis schools in sometimes dramatic terms. One high school enrolled 60 Somali students in one year; the next, the school enrolled 600. The student population is now about 44% African or African American, 29% White, 15% Asian American, 8% Hispanic American, and 5% Native American. Nearly one third of the district's schools have student populations in which more than 20% of the student population qualifies for English as a Second Language (ESL) instruction. The district is committed to high educational standards, yet struggles in changing times to meet the needs of all students. Significantly, fewer than half (44%) of the MPS students who enroll as freshmen graduate in 4 years; the failure to graduate clusters disproportionately among students of color (Minneapolis Public Schools, 1999).

Although its student population does not reflect the diversification of the wider metropolitan area, the University of Minnesota is situated literally at the heart of urban life in the Twin Cities. Urban issues are, therefore, fundamental to teacher preparation efforts in the College. Student teaching placements and hiring practices in the Minneapolis district figure prominently in the role of the University of Minnesota in the preparation of urban-bound teachers. In the 1999–2000 academic year, the College of Education and Human Development placed students in 185 practicum and student teaching experiences in the Minneapolis district alone (University of Minnesota, 2000). Adding data from neighboring St. Paul increases the number of urban placements to almost 300. Teacher preparation programs in the College of Education and Human Development at the University of Minnesota are offered primarily at the postbaccalaureate level. Students who seek an initial teaching license have earned a bachelor's degree in their content area prior to their entry into a "fifth year" master of education program of pedagogical studies and extended clinical experiences.

Whether in teacher preparation or in a K–12 classroom, preparing teachers to respond effectively to students within culturally and socioeconomically diverse settings poses a challenge for performance-based teacher assessment. In spite of their size and bureaucratic structure, urban institutions must create assessment systems that are fluid enough to accommodate the complexities of context, yet structured enough to ensure a standard of education deserved by all of the children in our nation's schools.

DIMENSIONS OF DEVELOPMENT

The development of systems of performance assessment at the U of M and MPS has been a slow and deliberate journey into new ways of thinking about teaching and learning and how it is assessed. In presenting these cases, we have chosen to emphasize the role of mandated standards, the nature of collegial interactions, and the development of structures to demonstrate how integral these elements are to an institution moving toward meaningful assessments of teaching.

As Zeichner (chap. 1, this volume) suggests, mandated teaching standards can lead to reductionistic assessments; long lists of indicators meant to "capture" teaching in actuality miss the holistic complexity of teaching and ironically recreate the behavioristic assessments so familiar in education's recent past. However, we suggest the reductionism is not necessarily located in the standards themselves, but in the ways individuals understand the relationship of those standards to the activities of teaching and learning. We contend that if the "performance" of teaching is understood on multiple levels as inherently social, spontaneous and planned, cognitive and affective, and ever imbedded in context, then the standards can inform and potentially enrich that fundamentally integrated understanding of professional activity. Teacher assessment is anchored by the people who participate in it. The artifacts generated or imported to serve that assessment purpose are—or in their use become—expressions of their assumptions, theories, and orientations toward teaching and learning.

Our discussion of the U of M and MPS cases in this way echoes the activity-theory perspective espoused by Conway and Artiles (chap. 2, this volume) and illustrates a number of the design principles identified by Peterman (chap. 3, this volume). We identify these dimensions:

- *Contextual sensitivity and responsiveness.* Performance assessment is an ever-evolving interaction that must be in balance with the pragmatic nature of the teaching enterprise. Community demographics, geographic location, political environment, and economics are examples of factors that have influenced its development and implementation. Individuals bring these factors into consideration as they observe and reflect on instruction. Peterman describes this as the "situated" nature of performance assessment in urban settings.
- *Agreed-on philosophical and theoretical foundations.* Through collaboration, core values are expressed, both in what is assessed by each institution, and perhaps more significantly, in how the assessment process is linked to professional development. Conway and Artiles discuss the importance of articulating a vision of teaching and learning that can serve as a touchstone for all participants in the process of assessment.
- *Performance assessment linked to professional development.* The overall goal in these institutions is to develop processes that support teacher learning and subsequently bring about the improvement of education for students. In both cases, evaluation is subordinated to professional development. Peterman's discussion of capacity building is evident in this dimension.
- *Time.* Performance assessment, as Peterman suggests, should be longitudinal. It takes time—it happens over time. The assessment processes implemented in both institutions afford a pathway for life-long teacher development from student to novice to experienced teacher; however, there is constant tension between the time needed to support teacher development and the constraint time has on what, in actuality, can be accomplished. The dimension of time also relates to the creation and evolution of the system itself; that may take years in development, in implementation, and in practice.

As we hope to demonstrate, these dimensions are essential aspects to consider in the development of a system of assessment. Making whole educational systems situated and responsive, oriented to shared visions of teaching and learning, and dedicated to capacity building is extremely difficult. We have challenged ourselves, in presenting these cases, to create an accurate portrayal of the development of our system— to give enough information to encourage others while acknowledging the difficulties. In discussing the process of teacher assessment at the U of M and in MPS schools, then, we acknowledge that the aims of these systems, to remain true to the complexity of teaching, have not been fully achieved. What has become evident to us is that the perceived benefits of moving in this direction have been compelling enough to keep us dedicated.

PERFORMANCE ASSESSMENT
AT THE UNIVERSITY OF MINNESOTA

It is essential to urban schools that preservice programs prepare student teachers to transition into their profession in ways that bring success and meaning into the first year of urban teaching. To begin, we identify the forces that have converged to provoke and influence the development of a system of performance assessment within the College of Education and Human Development at the University of Minnesota, as represented in Fig. 6.1. This figure supports the primary thrust of our case, which is to provide the reader with some insight into how whole systems of performance assessment develop and, thus, demonstrate that performance assessment involves much more than the development of a single instrument to measure teaching ability. It bears repeating that the College's

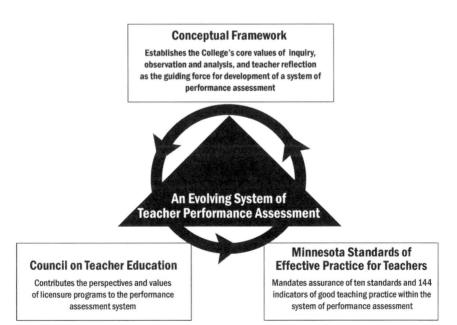

FIG. 6.1. Major forces in the development and implementation of performance assessment at University of Minnesota, College of Education and Human Development.

performance assessment system continues to evolve and, importantly, that influencing factors within each of these major forces continue to impact its implementation.

Responding to the Standards

Central to the message of our case is that external standards, although a significant force, were utilized as a beginning point for developing a system of performance assessment for teacher preparation programs at the university. Faculty felt it was essential that the development of a system be grounded in the college's conceptual framework to provide an essential foundation of theory and research. The conceptual framework, which focuses on inquiry, observation and analysis, and teacher reflection, has evolved from a growing understanding and consensus in the college of "who we are" and "what we value about teaching and learning." It has become the umbrella under which the mandated standards are addressed (University of Minnesota, 2000), and in this way, the college has retained its own special identity and mission. This aspect of development has been key in assuring that the system of performance assessment will remain open and fluid, unencumbered by potentially static standards and consistent in the ebb and flow of accountability demands.

The Minnesota standards, derived from the ten standards developed by the Interstate New Teacher Assessment and Support Consortium (INTASC), are accompanied by 144 indicators of good teaching practice. This state-mandated accountability measure, coupled with systematic review by the National Council for Accreditation of Teacher Education (NCATE), provided an impetus and a foundation on which the college began its development of performance assessment. Specifically, the call to demonstrate how programs and courses actually *assess* each of the mandated standards and indicators contributed significantly to the recognition of the need for development of a college-wide system of performance assessment—one on which each program could lean to assure quality preparation, and yet appropriately adapt to their specific content area. As one faculty member observed:

> I would like to think we were doing a quality job and I think ... we were by and large doing a good job of preparing teachers. But if we had to come up with the documented evidences of [teaching performance] in this area or that area, then we didn't. It was more of a global or general response ... now when we sit down with the student teachers and supervising teachers we need to hold ourselves accountable so we are sure we are addressing these standards.

Nevertheless, addressing mandated standards was neither swift nor problem-free. As we undertook the tedious alignment of each of the college's licensure programs, course by course, program by program, there was an ever-present tension evoked by the mandates, and an understandable resistance to developing what Zeichner (this volume) refers to as an "orgy of tabulation" (Saylor, 1976).

Collaborating to Develop a System:
The Council on Teacher Education

The most critical aspect in the development and implementation of performance assessment across the college has been and continues to be the work of NCATE. The Council is a unique body of representatives from 15 initial licensure programs from six different instructional units across the college. Within a large and diverse college, the Council has succeeded in promoting a collegial atmosphere and in building consensus around key issues in teacher preparation. As noted in a recent accreditation report, "Increasingly the Council is serving as a communications tool and an advisory body for making curricular as well as program changes" (NCATE, 2000, p. 23). The Council has been instrumental in building inclusiveness and responsiveness through implementation of task forces within the college, and through utilization of advisory meetings with a wide range of representation of school administrators, hiring officials, parents, cooperating teachers, current and former students, and more. The Council has assumed a key role in providing professional development for faculty and has offered a much-needed forum in which faculty may openly express their concerns and differences about performance assessment. As one Council member noted, "I value having a voice in the process … and I want to stay involved as much as I can because it is the heart of what I'm about."

A Task Force on Clinical Experiences was appointed by the Council to create the performance assessment processes and forms. It was through this task force that the "urban" voice was heard. Three of the task force members served concurrently as the College's UNITE team, bringing the perspectives and concerns of urban education into the development phase of the assessments. Notably, the task force drew from on-going work in the Institute of Child Development that provided the foundation of developmental theory and research and a supervisory instrument with which to start. This task force succeeded—it developed assessment processes and forms for use by all programs in the college. Importantly, all of these forms and processes point to the same categories and indicators of good teaching practice (see http://education. umn.edu/SPS/Clinical/Performance/formative_ assessment.pdf). In totality, they are developmental and longitudinal and, by establishing expectations for student teaching experiences to include the whole school setting, families, and communities, are sensitive to the urban context.

Practicing Preservice Teacher Performance Assessment

Beginning with their orientation sessions, students are introduced incrementally to the college's performance processes and the forms that will be used to guide and assess their progress. Throughout the program, students engage in multiple forms of assessment activities such as developing professional teaching portfolios, initiating action research projects at their school sites, and participating in structured inquiries within their student-teaching cohort groups. These types of activities are intentionally dovetailed into their concurrent University courses and on-site teaching responsibilities so as to join theory to practice in the year-long clinical teaching experiences. Faculty articulates alignment to the standards explicitly on syllabi and through a wide variety of assignments and readings within their core courses. This assists preservice teachers in understanding the mandated standards and allows them to begin internalizing a sense of how they are moving toward expressing these standards in the classroom. University supervisors, in collaboration with cooperating teachers in the schools, assess student teachers' performances throughout their year-long clinical teaching experiences. Student teachers also take an active role in self-assessment both at their teaching sites and in their university classes. To support communication and understanding about the clinical experiences and performance assessment, a handbook has also been created. It is widely distributed to all who are involved in the process of student teaching including district administrators, building principals, cooperating teachers, university faculty, university supervisors, and the students.

A formative assessment form is used to benchmark the student teachers' growth over the entire year of the teaching experiences. Although initially appearing to be cumbersome, this "long form" includes multiple indicators that are beneficial to students, cooperating teachers, and supervisors in finding a common language to identify areas of strengths and areas of needed improvement. The formative assessment is not designed to serve as an observational checklist; however, shorter versions of the long form have been adapted to support scripting of single visits by supervisors. Ideally, the formative assessment becomes a way to query the scripted observations; different indicators come to prominence across time, reflecting the supervisor or cooperating teacher's understanding of the student teacher's growth. A supervisor described how he thinks of this process:

> That's what the instrument does … it constantly calls me back that these are all of the dimensions of this thing called teaching, "Well, look, what have I left out?" "Oh! I better pay attention to that" … It's useful to have something that allows you to focus on what matters, versus what *I* think matters.

Other supervisors also pointed out that focusing on the indicators that appear on the assessment forms reminds them *and* their student teachers to refrain from using their personal experience as the sole basis for making judgments about teaching and learning. As a faculty member observed:

> [Prior to using the formative assessment] we were all assessing performance, but we were doing it in our own little worlds—every field was doing it, maybe 20 of us, were all doing it based on our own eyes … at least now we are all on the same page.

There is constant tension between the desire to score a student in a behavioristic way and the need to talk about teaching descriptively to support growth in teaching performance. We have been challenged to use the formative assessment "formatively," as a tool for dialogue and development. In order to have a meaningful assessment, it is essential to educate ourselves, the cooperating teachers, and our student teachers about what performance assessment is—that it is about development and not a score. To that end, professional development workshops are offered regularly to the supervisors and the cooperating teachers. University supervisors are also encouraged to provide opportunities for pre and postteaching conferences that engage the student teachers in reflecting on their teaching strengths and those areas where they have yet to develop.

As with any change, buy-in has not been automatic, and there have been both spirited disagreements and quiet dissensions. Buy-in by supervisors and cooperating teachers has been growing, but slowly. Some resist passively and simply approach performance assessment as another bureaucratic form to be filled out. Others give it a nod, but then dismiss it as something irrelevant; as one individual indicated, "Who cares what the scores are? It's *only* formative." The final letter of recommendation has more obvious importance.

The move to performance assessment has taken considerable time, and has demanded consistency and persistence of those who participated in its development. And, in the end, the assessments are only as good as the individuals who practice them. We anticipate that implementation will continue to raise questions about teaching and learning, and by engaging ourselves in these questions, we will emerge and evolve a system to continuously bring the best assessment practices to the fore.

Assessing Preservice Teachers in the Urban Context

Although the college maintains its commitment to support the improvement of urban education, urban schools admittedly are not the sole destination of its licensed graduates. This poses an ever-present challenge for publicly funded institutions with comprehensive programs, such as the university's, that are bound by land-grant missions and other state-mandated initiatives to serve *all* people. Admittedly, this tension will not subside; however, we attempt to show how this tension was acknowledged and addressed as the college moved to implementing a system of performance assessment.

As we indicated in our introductory comments, the system of performance assessment at the University of Minnesota has not been reduced to a single assessment form. Thus, implementation of preservice teacher assessment in the urban setting is found in maintaining a sensitivity and adjustment to the context, rather than in technical changes to the forms. One of the most important ways in which the assessment is contextualized is through establishing ongoing relationships among faculty, university supervisors, and cooperating teachers. The complexities of the urban setting make finding strong placements essential, one supervisor stated, "We try to align ourselves with the very best teachers who model well, teach well, and mentor well." Through the relationships that have been built over time, placements can be made that ensure that the student teacher can be assessed fairly, despite the complexities. Another supervisor described the process he uses as he considers potential placements:

> I went to some classrooms, and I said, "If I placed a student teacher in this classroom, they would have been killed," because of the classroom management that that teacher had, they wouldn't have been able to do anything ... I've been in rooms, in urban schools, where the teachers are just incredible, and they set up the classroom management for the student teachers and it runs perfectly. The student teacher rides on the coattails.

There is ongoing attention and relationship building to bring student teachers into urban classrooms that allow the student teacher to focus on the needs of the diverse student population.

However, because the condition of the urban setting, or any other, cannot be presumed, it is critical that assessment processes and instruments are inherently just and lend themselves to use in complex situations. The supervisor's and cooperating teacher's interpretation of evolving events are for this reason a critical factor, as they situate the teacher's performance within a particular classroom and school. Noting that the same day-to-day classroom issues experienced by teachers in suburban classrooms are more frequent and complex for those in the urban classroom, one supervisor emphatically observed: "The complexities of the urban setting *permeate* the duties of the teacher." This complexity calls for teaching responses that are suited to the demands. One supervisor described a depth of planning being required in some urban classrooms as being categorically different from that demanded in the suburban setting. He took this intensification of planning into account when assessing the instructional dimensions of the formative assessment. Another supervisor candidly remarked that the assessment form had caused him initially to focus on developing a more rigorous internal discipline, but emphasizing equality in judgment meant not attending reasonably to the multiple dimensions of the urban teaching situation:

> It's very easy to start to make "excuses" [for the urban teacher] or to have "higher expectations" [for the suburban student teacher] when things are "easier" on the [suburban] teacher ... It's a different ballgame. And does that then beg the question "Is the strike zone a strike?" and I'd say that [in the urban school] the strike zone's bigger.

A number of university supervisors have similarly suggested that the benefit of the formative assessment is that it helps them maintain high standards and expectations for teaching while it allows them to draw on their knowledge of the place and the people to situate their assessments.

The system of performance assessment developed in the college bears all the features that Peterman (this volume) earlier brought to our attention. It is longitudinal and reflective, capacity building, and situated and responsive. Although not explicitly advocacy based, it gives context—work with families and communities—a primary place of importance. Because cooperating teachers in the Minneapolis schools are approaching teaching and assessment in similar ways, these practices work together to ensure consistency and enable student teachers placed in the Minneapolis district to draw on the feedback of the university supervisor and their cooperating teachers with confidence. Having participated in this process of assessment in their student teaching experiences, preservice teachers from the University of Minnesota are well prepared to continue their professional development as they begin to teach in the Minneapolis Schools.

PERFORMANCE ASSESSMENT
IN MINNEAPOLIS PUBLIC SCHOOLS

The process of developing a system of performance assessment in the Minneapolis Public Schools (MPS) has been distinguished by nearly two decades of collaborative effort. Since the mid-1980s, when the teacher's association successfully negotiated to establish a joint labor/management committee, teachers and administrators have jointly led the district's professional development and assessment efforts. Among their collaborative efforts, the union and the district have articulated standards for teaching performance and student achievement and implemented a peer review system that replaced the administrative appraisal system based on Hunter's observational forms (1985). The current system is a unified, district-wide approach that is contextualized at the school level, situated in long-term relationships among colleagues and administrators, and dedicated to developing an individual's teaching abilities and to building the capacity of a faculty in that building. The assessment of teachers in the district is integrally tied to ongoing professional development.

Collaborating to Establish a System

Collaboration between teachers and administrators played an essential role in allowing the district to develop an assessment system that incorporated mandated standards in ways that were responsive to the realities of urban teaching. A joint union/district panel reviewed and synthesized standards from multiple national organizations (e.g., New Teacher Assessment and Support Consortium [NTASC], National Board for Professional Teaching Standards [NBPTS], NCATE) and then created the Minneapolis Standards of Effective Instruction (see http://par.mpls.k12.mn.us/). The collaborative decision-making processes in the district effectively created a forum where legislative mandates and standards could be interpreted and acted on in ways that are aligned with the district's core values and the needs of its teachers and students.

Through continued union/district collaboration, a new system of professional development and assessment was developed in concert with the MPS Standards of Effective Practice. The Professional Development Process (PDP) reflects the content of the MPS Standards of Effective Instruction by integrating three main emphases: developing a teacher's ability to self-assess, creating multiple forms of documentation of teaching performance, and establishing shared assessment decision-making processes. Guided by the fundamental belief that change cannot be mandated but must be linked to processes of structural change and individual learning, leaders in the professional development/assessment reform structured a 5-year implementation plan. The PDP system was phased in gradually and voluntarily, and was accompanied by extensive and ongoing professional development efforts. At the end of the 5 years, union members voted almost unanimously that the PDP process supplant the previous administrative review in the teaching contract.

The Professional Development Process (PDP) is notable for the way its creators realized that assessment standards take root only through an assessment process that enacts the values they espouse. Retaining a teacher evaluation system in which an administrator was the sole judge of whether a teacher had met standards such as MPS Standard Four ("Teachers reflect systematically about their practice and learn from experience") and Standard Five ("Teachers participate as members of learning communities") would strip these standards of meaning. The Professional Development Process incorporates assessment into professional development, rather than as a separate outcome. All teachers in the district are assessed through the Professional Development Process, as well as by periodic administrative evaluations.

Practicing Performance Assessment Across the Career Span

With the overarching purpose of supporting a teacher's ongoing improvement and facilitating student achievement, an individual's PDP is designed to be aligned with a district-wide process that engages all stakeholders in goal setting, reflection, and assessment. The district, drawing on performance data, identifies areas where attention is needed in a District Improvement Plan. At the school level, administrators and faculty interpret these areas in light of their own context to identify a School Improvement Plan. Individual teachers then identify a single aspect of the school plan that they see as an issue that needs attention in their own classrooms.

In summary, each teacher establishes a professional goal, seeks out related professional development, collects evidence, and analyzes progress with the support of a self-selected team of two to three teachers and one administrator. Over the course of the academic year, the teams follow a cycle of planning, sharing of evidence, summarizing, and assessing results that leads to changes in the classroom and focuses ongoing professional development.

As the PDP was being developed, the union and district were also collaborating to establish a rigorous tenure review. Teachers entering the district participate in a 3-year process of preparing for an evaluation that is conducted by a team of teachers and administrators at their school. Requirements for Achievement of Tenure (A of T) in the district are aligned with the Minneapolis Standards of Effective Instruction. The process is designed to ensure that teachers new to the district receive guided assistance in learning to reflect, to develop substantive relations with colleagues, and to document their developing competence in the classroom. The Achievement of Tenure process aims to induct novice teachers into the MPS/MFT vision of professionalism and to prepare them for full participation in the teaching profession.

The primary process for the Achievement of Tenure assessment process is the Achievement of Tenure plan, which is developed with the support of a team of colleagues. The professional portfolio provides a structure in which the teacher can document progress toward achieving the A of T plan. In the portfolio, nontenured teachers must document how their instruction meets professional standards. Student work samples, lesson plans and curriculum maps, feedback from students, parents, and colleagues are accompanied by written reflections and self-assessments. The portfolio also demonstrates the teacher's participation in the A of T PDP as well as ongoing professional development, such as an action research project. Near the end of the third year, the teacher presents the portfolio and responds to questions at a formal tenure review. For the purpose of this case, we focus on the intensive system of support and assessment developed in the Achievement of Tenure process for teachers in their first year.

Practicing Assessment in the Entry Year.   A new teacher in the MPS enters a system structured with multiple forms of formative assessment and support designed to assist entry into the profession and to foster productive collegial relationships (see Fig. 6.2). Two main processes are used to assess the novice teacher: the Pathwise assessment, and the Achievement of Tenure (A of T) Professional Development Process (PDP), which includes observations by an administrator and a teaching colleague.

Mentoring and the Pathwise © Assessment.   On entering the district, each teacher is assigned a mentor teacher who has experience in that subject area or grade level. The mentor's emphasis throughout the year is on providing nonevaluative feedback and focused assistance. In addition to conferencing with and observing the entry-year teacher multiple times during the year, the mentor may co-teach, demonstrate lessons, seek out relevant resources, and arrange visits to classrooms of skilled demonstration teachers. Once or twice during the course of the year, the mentor also conducts a formal assessment using the Pathwise © framework of structured observational cycles linked to the MPS Standards of Effective Instruction. The fact that the mentor, and not an administrator, conducts the Pathwise assessment is essential to the formative nature of that instrument. The mentor's ongoing relationship with the entry-year teacher and familiarity with the classroom context allows him or her to situate the standardized observation form within the broader landscape of the entry-year teacher's practice. Only a fraction of entry-year teachers interviewed indicated that the formal Pathwise observation was not effective. In those cases, interviewees indicated that professional relationships fundamental to the process had not been developed. If a mentor focused solely on meeting district requirements and was not able to provide consistent nonevaluative feedback, entry-year teachers often felt little investment in writing the reflections about their instruction to prepare for the Pathwise observations, and regarded the evaluation as "just a number." In contrast, those who participated in the assessment within the scope of an established and ongoing series of observations reported that the targeted feedback was rich in detail and effective in targeting areas for growth.

Achievement of Tenure Professional Development Plan.   With the support of his or her mentor, the entry-year teacher also participates in the Achievement of Tenure Professional Development Process (A of T PDP). A

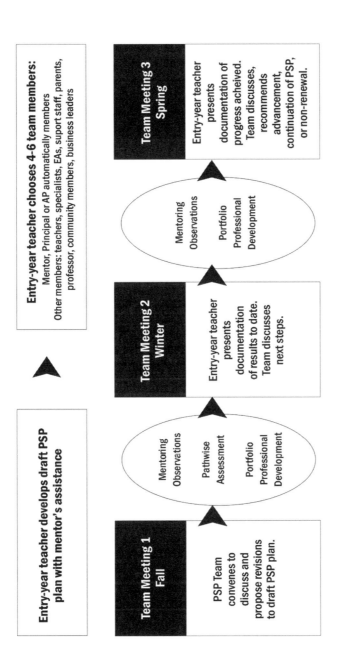

Entry-year teacher develops draft PSP plan with mentor's assistance

Entry-year teacher chooses 4-6 team members:
Mentor, Principal or AP automatically members
Other members: teachers, specialists, EAs, suport staff, parents, professor, community members, business leaders

Team Meeting 1
Fall

PSP Team convenes to discuss and propose revisions to draft PSP plan.

Mentoring
Observations

Pathwise Assessment

Portfolio
Professional Development

Team Meeting 2
Winter

Entry-year teacher presents documentation of results to date. Team discusses next steps.

Mentoring
Observations

Portfolio
Professional Development

Team Meeting 3
Spring

Entry-year teacher presents documentation of progress acheived. Team discusses, recommends advancement, continuation of PSP, or non-renewal.

FIG. 6.2.   MPS entry-year assessment.

141

district-wide workshop introduces the Professional Development Process, mentor assists in creating the A of T PDP plan, and the school's PDP coordinator provides guidance in constituting the team. Records of meetings and a colleague's observation augment the evidence the teacher presents to demonstrate progress toward his or her professional goal. In addition, at least one formal administrative observation is conducted. At year's end, after a final team discussion, summative reports indicating the level of achievement on the teacher's PDP plan are developed by the entry-year teacher and by all team members and forwarded to the district office.

Rooted in the teacher's individual attempts to improve on issues related to the school and district improvement plans, and supported by the Achievement of Tenure Team, this ongoing process allows the teacher the flexibility to respond to the demands of a particular group of students or a pressing concern in a specific year, but also offers the opportunity for a teacher to sustain and continually deepen a learning focus over many years, should that issue remain a vital concern. Personally documenting how one is influencing student achievement and reflecting on that influence with colleagues puts the focus of teacher development and collegiality on the core issues of education. The element of Peterman's (chap. 3, this volume) design framework that emphasizes the longitudinal nature of assessment and its relationship to learning "in action" are reflected in the year-long PDP and the three-year Achievement of Tenure processes.

The strength of the Professional Development Process clearly lies in the way in which it is situated within a school context, imbedded in professional relationships, and responsive to the needs of an individual teacher. The flexibility of the assessment system is also its Achilles heel. Although almost all teachers in the district write a PDP plan and provide minimal documentation of their involvement on a PDP team every year, the effectiveness of this process varies from school to school. With one district coordinator overseeing the entire process for more than a hundred schools, it is clear that the level and quality of implementation can vary. A school may devote tremendous time and energy to the PDP process; meetings to review goals and documentation are held more frequently than required and treated as significant opportunities for professional dialogue and support. About half of the entry-year teachers interviewed expressed how the PDP reinforces their sense of professionalism, as one novice teacher does here:

> With the PDP, it's very professional to start showing the public that we're definitely taking professional measures as teachers. So that's definitely wonderful. We want our students to be authentically assessed but we also want ourselves to be authentically assessed. I think that's a step in the right direction.

In the best case, A of T Professional Development Process allows the experience and expertise of all participants to be directed toward supporting the entering teacher in serving students' needs.

At the same time, the system only works if those involved believe that the activity of collaborating to support the entry-year teacher in defining an area of inquiry and examining student work is meaningful to the improvement of education. Even if the mentor developed a strong relationship with the entry-year teacher, if the school culture was not supportive of the A of T PDP meetings, an entry-year teacher's colleagues could, by their formulaic approach to the process, cause the entry-year teacher to lose faith in the integrity of the PDP. At one extreme, in a school where administrators or faculty do not support it, the PDP process can devolve into paperwork. A teacher may write a plan, provide some documentation, and gather necessary signatures without engaging in any reflection or collegial discussion. One first-year teacher commented, "I feel like it's another hoop to jump through. I know they were really excited about getting it in the contract. For the life of me, nobody has ever sat down with me and explained to me why that's important" (Carrie, MPS entry-year teacher). Despite the wide variation in implementation, it is worth noting that the PDP process offers a level of adaptability that can, when understood and embraced, significantly and simultaneously support accountability and professional development.

Pulling the Elements of the System Together. In late spring the mentor will draw from multiple sources of information to write up a summative assessment of the teacher's performance that is shared with the teacher. Some mentors interviewed identify a tension within their role between providing supportive assessment and participating in formal evaluation of a new teacher. They express concern that these two purposes are at odds. Other mentors believe that although their responsibility is to guide the entry-year teacher toward success, as professionals they also have a responsibility to uphold standards. Also, mentors point out that their evaluation is only one part of the final evaluation. A first-year teacher's final evaluation is based on at least three assessments gathered throughout the school year: the principal's summative statement, the mentor's summative assessment, and the summative report of the Achievement of Tenure team. These are shared with the teacher and with the A of T team members. The team then collectively makes a final recommendation to the district's Human Resources Department about the entry-year teacher's continued employment, as well as the level of support the teacher would need to teach successfully in the coming year.

In its design, if not wholly in its execution, we argue that the performance assessment system that has been collaboratively developed in the Minneapolis Public Schools effectively accomplishes a critical role in allowing novice teachers to personalize standards and focus their learning. From the A of T PDP system to the portfolio requirements, teachers are encouraged to make decisions about what they most need to know to serve their particular students well.

CREATING SYSTEMS SIDE BY SIDE

The creation of these systems through deliberate collaboration between the faculty and staff from the two institutions has contributed to each becoming a more significant force in the improvement of urban education. Collegial relationships, formal and informal, have been built on a shared commitment to the improvement of urban education and have provided a basis of understanding and agreement as both systems of assessment have developed. A long-term partnership between the college and Patrick Henry High School as a professional practice school and the subsequent development of a residency program at that site have provided a basis of understanding and agreement as both systems have emerged.

University faculty who teach on-site courses in the residency program for the Minneapolis Schools also serve on the college's Council on Teacher Education and the Clinical Experience Task Force. Their dual roles have been invaluable in increasing the college's understanding and sensitivity to the needs of the urban context. University faculty have participated in Pathwise training with the MPS mentors. In turn, cooperating teachers have been invited on a regular basis to participate in professional development activities and performance assessment seminars hosted by the college. In some programs, such as the elementary education program, cadres of teachers from the Minneapolis district work closely with on-site supervisory college faculty. They are regularly invited to attend seminars and workshops. In other programs, cooperating teachers are acting in advisory capacities, and some serve as adjunct faculty.

These collaborative experiences in the development, acceptance, and implementation of side-by-side systems of performance assessments in the Minneapolis Public Schools and at the University of Minnesota have yielded these essential features in and across both systems:

- *Structured collaboration.* Within and across the two institutions, collaboration was the essential starting point for responding to mandated standards in ways that were grounded in their central institutional missions. Both the Minneapolis Public Schools and the University of Minnesota created formal structures to facilitate collaboration within their large and diverse institutions.
- *Inclusiveness.* Development and implementation of performance assessment has been an inclusive process—one in which both institutions

have been intentional in identifying stakeholders and utilizing multiple levels of advisory committees and task forces for this purpose.

• *Collegiality*. Fostering of collegial relationships is based on a shared interest in improving urban education and education for all students. Relationships, both formal and informal, continue to serve as bridging mechanisms between the two institutions and contribute to the intellectual vitality of both.

In looking across the two institution's evolving systems of professional development and assessment, we see that both are grounded in core values and aligned to standards and that the role of standards shifts as the teacher grows in understanding and competence. Within the university's assessment system, as preservice teachers are introduced to professional and curriculum standards for the first time, external assessment of explicitly stated standards is essential for the teacher to initially develop a sense of what the standards mean in a particular teaching setting. Simultaneously, through methods courses and portfolio development, the preservice teacher is learning to self-assess and to document progress toward achieving standards. As a teacher moves through the initial years of teaching in a system like the Minneapolis Public Schools, the explicit statement of standards becomes incorporated into the process of the assessment itself as the teacher draws on an internalized sense of the standards in goal setting and engages in reflection, self-assessment, and peer review.

SUMMARY

These two cases indicate that mandated standards are not necessarily roadblocks in the development of performance assessments that are meaningful in the urban setting. The system of performance assessment for preservice teachers at the University of Minnesota continues to evolve from a growing understanding and consensus about best teaching practices. The experience of first developing and now implementing this system has pointed to the opportunity found in using mandated standards as a foundation, as a common ground, for moving toward beneficial, symbiotic relationships with urban schools in the preparation of new teachers.

Built on an extended and significant collaboration between the union and the district, the MPS/MFT assessment system exemplifies how performance assessment within an urban context succeeds with student achievement and teacher development at its heart. In a setting where diversity is the norm, assessments of teachers must be open-ended enough that individual teachers and administrators can specify broad standards for their students and their schools. When teachers are allowed the flexibility to determine how they need to grow and to be assessed based on goals that make sense to them, external standards can become meaningful.

As we described the U of M and MPS cases, we came to understand that developing systems of assessment in the urban context is not as much about finding ways to address a specific set of standards as it is about sustaining substantive conversations that examine the complex and multifaceted nature of teaching and learning. Each institution faces the challenge of engaging hundreds of individuals in the process to avoid reducing teacher assessment to discrete characteristics. The fluidity required by such a system is, then, both its greatest strength and it greatest weakness, for shared understandings about teaching and learning ultimately cannot be mandated, but must be continuously cultivated. The professional relationships that support teacher assessment in urban schools are the key to transforming assessment from a bureaucratic requirement to a shared process of professionalization and a foundation of educational reform.

REFERENCES

Hunter, M. (1985). What's wrong with Madeline Hunter? *Educational Leadership, 42,* 57–60.

Minneapolis Public Schools. (1999). *About Minneapolis Public Schools*. Available: http://www.mpls.k12.mn.us/about/report_2000/schools.shtml

National Council for Accreditation of Teacher Education. (2000, November). *Board of examiners report: Continuing accreditation visit to the University of Minnesota, Twin Cites*. Washington, DC: Author.

Saylor, J. (1976). *Antecedent Developments in the Movement to Performance-Based Programs of Teacher Education: An Historical Survey of Concepts, Movements, and Practices Significant in the Development of Teacher Education*. Washington, DC: American Association of Colleges for Teacher Education.

University of Minnesota, College of Education & Human Development (2000). *Distribution of student teaching placements by district*. Unpublished raw data.

U.S. Census Bureau. (2000). *Census 2000* [Online]. Available: http://factfinder.census.gov/

Wilder Research Center. (2000). *Speaking for themselves: A survey of Hispanic, Hmong, Somali, and Russian immigrants in Minneapolis–St. Paul*. St. Paul, MN: Amherst H. Wilder Foundation.

Chapter 7

"Whose Standards Count?": Practice-Oriented Urban Teacher Preparation

Micky Cokely
Peter C. Murrell, Jr.
Northeastern University

We use case studies to explain, analyze, understand, and hopefully solve complex problems. We use *situated* case studies particularly when there is a complex dynamic of human interaction complicated by the influence of situational variables. Most socially structured settings, whether they are classrooms or boardrooms, have their own set of symbols, relationships, and interactional patterns, making each situation dependent on the contextual interplay of these situational variables (Brown, Collins, & Duguid, 1989). The term *situated case study* denotes the use of case studies to find a *way out of a complex problem* embedded in such settings with its myriad of contextual variables, and find a *way into a consistently effective practice* that is generalizable beyond particular instances of the problem setting. This chapter uses that particular kind of case study as a tool for systematic inquiry into practice-oriented teacher preparation and performance assessment.

The following set of vignettes form a case study based on an actual school–university joint enterprise created to produce a cadre of accomplished urban teachers. The vignettes, and the situated case study they comprise, articulate the all-too-real problems and issues of trying to assess teaching performance in ways that really produce effective urban teachers. The specific problem concerns teacher performance assessment—and the

147

question of whose standards of professional practice we use if our aim is to prepare excellent teachers for diverse urban environments.

THE SETTING

Most schools of education have partnerships with public schools that attempt to coalesce the activities of professional development with preservice teacher training. Our situation is slightly different in that we attempt to make our teacher preparation for initial licensure and professional development of the school faculty extensions of the same basic enterprise—that of improving teaching practice school-wide. Our setting is a particular version of the professional development schools (PDS) model (see Murrell, 1998) in that it attempts to create a new *community of practice* (Lave & Wenger, 1991; Wenger, 1998). The notion of the community of practice, or CoP, connotes a collective of people whose prolonged engagement in common practices, professional interaction, and commitment to common aims creates a *collective identity* based on what they do together—their teaching practice. A CoP connotes a *collective identity* circumscribed by the *practices* that people share as a result of their engagement in a common enterprise. So in our case, we explicitly declare our partnership to be a CoP that includes higher education faculty, parents, school administrators, and teachers. As a CoP, the members involved share a dedication to the common enterprise of educating young people.

The more specific enterprise of university–school partnership is field-based teacher preparation taking the form of a teaching internship. Included in this sphere of activity are not just the clinical faculty of the university and the cooperating teachers of the school, but the entire school faculty of the partnership school. The term we use to characterize the CoP for practice-oriented, urban-situated teacher preparation in our partnership is *Institute*. The Institute features a yearlong, intensive, and practice-immersed teacher preparation program that runs concurrently with a whole-school professional development system. Both the professional development system and teacher preparation in the Institute are guided by the use of professional teaching standards, not unlike those used in many states nationwide. However, the development of professional standards that truly elevate practice in urban environments required considerable clarification of meaning, cooperation, collaborative inquiry, and negotiation, detailed in the discussion to follow.

Prior to our partnership, the faculty in the high school had enjoyed relative freedom from any consideration of performance assessment. They had not experienced any sort of standards-based evaluation and, therefore, any consideration of professional teaching standards. Charter schools in this state had not required that its teachers possess initial licensure, and about

85% of the school faculty did not. However, the recent No Child Left Behind legislation has changed all of that, and the state now requires an initial license for *all* classroom teachers. Consequently, our Institute activity was also aimed at assisting the school's faculty in completing a development plan that specifies when and how they will complete the state requirements for initial licensure. Thus, one major difference between our Institute and the typical professional development school is the responsibility it assumes for the teaching faculty. The Institute assumes as much responsibility for the professional development toward *licensure of the faculty* as it does for the teacher *preparation of the interns* in the program. In short, teacher preparation and teacher professionalization-to-licensure are conjoint enterprises in the Institute.

The professional teacher preparation program offered in the Institute features a developmentally designed sequence of scholarly study—in both content and pedagogical knowledge—that is systematically embedded in the field experience. The Institute is called the Community Teachers Institute or CTI, and weaves strands of human development, learning theory, curriculum and assessment, special needs, and motivational theory as through-lines of the yearlong curriculum. The teacher preparation program in the Institute is designed to prepare educational leaders who understand, and are committed to, improving the contemporary conditions of schooling in high need, low performance urban schools.

The *Institute* model is based on the Community Teachers' (CT) framework (Murrell, 2001), which in turn is predicated on the idea that preparing effective urban teachers requires a focus on *practice*. The CT framework is about the systematic, thoughtful, and regular use of both theory and systematic reflection on the results of putting theory to use. Becoming an accomplished teacher requires actual teaching practice in the company of more experienced teachers who are committed to assisting performance in the actual professional contexts that simulate all of the demands and conditions of urban teaching and learning. According to the CT framework, the quality of teaching practice is always appraised in terms of how well it benefits student achievement and development.

Candidates are immersed in practice and are called *teaching fellows*. The rest of the faculty are regarded mentor teachers and mentors-in-training, but given a special name—*primary consulting teachers (PCTs)*—to avoid the state Department of Education's definition of a mentor as someone who has been licensed for 3 or more years. The Institute, therefore, consists of an integrated program of co-teaching, guided practice, and systematic inquiry into teaching and learning. It is through their reflection on practice, *co-practice* with a PCT, and the guided assistance they receive from a team of more capable practitioners, that candidates become community teachers—exemplary and effective educational leaders in urban settings. The CTI combines practical and theoretical preparation and helps *all* faculty become more flexible in their teaching and learning styles, more knowledgeable in their subject areas and more capable in their inquiry into the lives, cultures, and heritages of students in diverse urban communities.

The Institute's program of study is based on a *co-teaching model* where teaching fellows and PCTs work together and take the lead in the day-to-day delivery of instruction as appropriate. This collaborative model is a deliberate repudiation of the apprenticeship model with its exclusive mentor–novice pairing, which erroneously assumes that the PCT has all the knowledge to be imparted to the novice teacher in an exclusive one-to-one relationship. Educational research has recently demonstrated the importance of broadening the contexts of professional learning so as to include multiple relationships and multiple settings for professional interaction. Although teaching fellows interact with a number of teachers in the school, the PCT (mentor teacher) in the Institute is the primary contact for the teaching fellow and is the primary person in guiding instructional and professional practice.

There are two settings for which teaching fellows receive guided assistance to their practice: *instructional activity settings* (i.e., teaching, planning, assessment, etc.) and *professional activity settings* (i.e., clinical practice appraisal, doing rounds, team meeting, faculty meetings, committee work, program development, etc.). The instructional activity settings consist of actual classroom teaching. The professional activity settings are scheduled in collaboration with connected faculty (i.e., PCTs, at-large faculty, and personnel), and school events (e.g., town meeting, advisories, etc.).

THE PROBLEM OF PERFORMANCE ASSESSMENT FOR EFFECTIVE URBAN TEACHING

According to the CT framework, there is a subtle but important difference between the *assessment* of teaching practice and the *appraisal* of teaching practice. We return to this distinction after it is developed in the vignettes to follow. Suffice it to say at this juncture that there are two warring visions of teacher assessment. One model is *evaluation*, for which the questions organizing performance assessment are: Does the teacher adhere to the policies, procedures, and expectations articulated by the school administration? and Does the teacher have control of the class? This is assessment of teaching practice. The other model is *assisted performance*, for which the questions organizing performance assessment are: Does the teacher improve his or her teaching? and Does the teacher draw on and receive productive feedback on his or her teaching practice in a way that shows demonstrable progress toward meeting standards of performance that will earn him or her licensure? and Are they learning from their professional experience in ways that show improvements in their practice? This is appraisal of teaching practice.

We at the university *thought* we were clear about what we wanted to achieve in the new partnership arrangement with the high school. We constantly had to reinforce our strong preference for the assisted performance or *appraisal* model, as opposed to the evaluative model. For a number of reasons—particularly time resources and structuring of professional meeting time—there was ample opportunity to observe practice and collaboratively examine teaching practice. This meant that there were many people doing observation in the school, but not much consistency on the aims, the uses, and the value of observational feedback given to both fellows and faculty. The school's flexible schedule, the need for a large proportion of the staff to work toward earning initial licensure (more than 85%), and the value placed on collaboration in multiple venues were all factors.

At the university we had ample access to means of communicating what we wanted to accomplish and to fully understand what the school community wanted to accomplish. The problem was that the message was *heard*, but not acted on. The accomplished urban teacher, the community teacher, the STAR teacher, never became a shared concept. We invoked the concept of the STAR teacher articulated by Haberman (1993, 1995, 1999) so that we could emphasize the type of practitioner we were aiming to produce in the CTI. Haberman (1993) defines a STAR teacher as someone who, "by all common criteria, are outstandingly successful: their students score higher on standardized tests; parents and children think they are great; principals rate them highly; other teachers regard them as outstanding; central office supervisors consider them successful; cooperating universities regard them as superior; and they evaluate themselves as outstanding teachers" (p. 1). A distinction from the STAR teacher framework that we wanted to make explicit at the beginning of the partnership was that ours was an enterprise of *development*, and not *selection and recruitment*. Rather than select those who seem to have certain qualities, our enterprise was about a process of teacher preparation that produced effective urban teachers. Using our own framework of the community teacher, we began the process of teacher preparation with the aim of developing the qualities and proficiencies toward becoming a community teacher. *Community teacher* is the term we used to refer to the teacher who meets not just national board standards or the professional teaching standards of their state-approved program, but urban practice standards where there is evidence that they systematically reach all students.

The key to the whole CTI enterprise is the *appraisal of teaching practice* and *urban teaching standards* that are derived from an appraisal of practice. The urban teaching standards we use were the result of a long, systematic appraisal of urban practice in a variety of different schools and contexts. Prior to starting the Institute, we had created a practice-oriented set of standards for the community teacher (these are referred to as the *Urban Practice Standards*, or *UPS*, in the following case study). Originated as a polemic to get people thinking differently about how to use standards in improving practice, we increasingly eyed the UPS as a means for shaping culturally responsive practice. Our initial thought was that it might be best to consider that the trajectory to becoming a community teacher or STAR teacher has two tiers. Tier one is the basic proficiencies people need to get an initial license. We call this *competent practice*, the corpus of real proficiencies one needs to be able to enter a school classroom and "do no harm." Tier two concerns the stuff of which STAR teachers or community teachers are made. This we call *accomplished practice* (as does the National Board of Teaching and Professional Standards, although we think there are some differences in the usages that we describe later). To get to accomplished practice of the STAR teacher or the community teacher, one must hold performance up to urban practice standards.

What are urban practice standards? They are standards that attempt to more concretely describe the proficiencies of effective practice in terms of the requirements of exemplary practice in urban contexts (see Appendix A). Just as Haberman (1993, 1995, 1999) organized a set of necessary and critical qualities of urban teaching from years of experience in urban classrooms, we organized a set of performance outcomes. This is backward mapping—working back from the particulars of what is required for successful practice in a particular setting to *identify qualities* (Haberman, 1995) or *performance outcomes* (Murrell, 2001). The next step in our work is to map the performance outcomes to *demonstrated proficiencies*. In terms of the program of teacher preparation, the backward mapping that produced our urban practice standards "maps back" to a point earlier than screening potential candidates for urban teaching jobs. It maps back to the point of specifying the performance criteria for those just entering a yearlong immersion program with an assumed trajectory of becoming successful urban teachers.

VIGNETTE ONE—SMALL LEARNING COMMUNITY MEETING

The practice standards (see Appendix A) and the notion of the community teacher looked good on paper. But a number of questions arose as we attempted to realize this vision in the Institute. How does teacher development and preparation happen in practice? Isn't instituting a new set of standards at the same time you are using them to assess teaching practice a bit like piloting and building an airplane at the same time? How are people going to receive this? That is, if these are standards that are the result of backward mapping, doesn't it imply a set of qualities generated on the basis of what teachers *cannot* do? How do teachers feel about the implication that they are not yet community teachers? Isn't it possible for them to construe urban practice standards as a *deficit model* for White, culturally mainstream, and suburban-socialized prospective teachers?

These are questions our partners are beginning to pose in more concrete forms. In the beginning-of-the-year orientation, this aspect of urban teaching standards and practice-oriented development sounded reasonable to the teachers—as most reasonable sounding ideas do when few have the expectation of ever having to implement them. It sounded good to the clinical faculty, especially when they learned that the idea received verbal support from Ken Zeichner and others as a viable approach to the project of generating standards to shape preparation of accomplished urban teachers. But how will this work? Over what period of time? Is it reasonable to simply proclaim, as we have done, that the practice standards are *the* tool of choice? The following is a professional activity setting where these concerns emerge.

Teacher A: Okay, here we are at this Small Learning Community meeting trying to determine what our mode of operation will be for observing, assisting, and assessing the performance of our faculty in working successfully with the students who come to our school. [*Turns to Co-director A*]. I think I understand your distinction between "assessing" teacher practice and "appraising" teacher practice. But let me check my understanding before we get going.

Co-dir. A: Sure.

Teacher A: Is the basic difference that when you are *assessing*, you are making a *judgment about the teacher's performance* according to criteria, but in *appraising practice*, you are not looking to see how the teacher is meeting some preset behavioral indicators. Instead, you are sort of taking *stock of the productive activity* of the teacher and the *sustained effective effort of the students* that seem to constitute effective teaching and learning. Is that right?

Co-dir. A: That's right. And I would add that, when you are *appraising practice*, you not only avoid making an evaluative judgment of the person, but you are *taking stock of the whole instructional setting*. It's the difference between asking whether the teachers' "moves" look right, or whether the teachers' activity is producing results or likely to produce real measurable learning achievement.

Teacher B: So, you are judging the entire instructional context, not just the discrete behaviors of the teacher.

Co-dir. A: Right.

Teacher D: And you're not judging the teacher, but really getting data to offer productive feedback on the effectiveness of the teaching.

Co-dir. A: Right. And so it might be just as important to be collecting data relating to *what should be* in the teaching and learning as it is noting what *is* there. Identifying new criteria as you observe what's going on in an instructional setting is also a part of *appraising practice*.

Teacher A: It's sort of what we do in designing performance assessments. It is the same thing when you design a rubric for a performance assessment on a proficiency. Rubrics are always modified to better capture what we want to see evidenced in a student's demonstration of proficiency.

Suppose, for example, we take one of the subgoals for the proficiency on writing—namely, writing an informative, well-researched term paper. The first time that you use your performance assessment, and each time thereafter, you find things you wish you had made as criteria and you plan to include the next time. That's the nature of developing good performance assessments that guide instruction.

Teacher B: Is it fair to say that the quality of teaching performance is determined by what the person does in the context *and* how the context "responds," so to speak? I mean, in appraisal, you are looking at both what the teacher does and "how things go."

Co-dir. A: That's the central idea here. But the "how things go" judgments you make ought to be guided by quality criteria related to student achievement. The quality of professional activity—whether in the classroom or in settings like this—should only be judged by its results. And the results we are after are demonstrable indications of student understanding.

So it's really the difference in the questions you ask or are thinking about when you observe someone's teaching. What questions you ask has everything to do with the kind of *data* you get, and whether you are getting the data you need most for *productive feedback*. In the case of *assessing practice*, the question is, "Is this teacher doing what he or she is supposed to be doing?" And if your criteria for what teachers are supposed to do aren't complete or appropriate, you're not going to ever really help that teacher improve. In the case of *appraising practice*, the question should be something like, "Is what's going on here engaging students, eliciting their participation and effective effort in a worthwhile learning activity, and resulting in a demonstrable learning achievement?"

Teacher A: So when we are *appraising practice*, part of what we are doing is noting any new or additional criteria for shaping more effective teaching.

Co-dir. A: Exactly.

Teacher C: Now I see why this ... the *appraisal of practice*, I mean ... isn't done in most public schools. In order to appraise practice, you have to do and know some things about a person's teaching that many, maybe most, administrators don't bother to find out.

Teacher B: Like what?

Teacher C: Well, like really ascertaining what's going on in the classroom, or what's supposed to be going on, in the classroom you're observing. You'd have to know the context of a classroom. To do that you have to spend more time than most AP's do when they evaluate teachers—which is like a couple of class periods.

You know, I was at Central City High before I came here. I served as the acting assistant principal for a year and my job was to handle a backlog of unfinished teacher evaluations. I can tell you that the way we did those evaluations, and looked at practice, wasn't *appraisal of practice*. What we did was the furthest thing from it. You wouldn't even call what we did *assessment of practice* because of the one or two days during the school year we'd see a teacher, we weren't always operating from a set of criteria—or at least none which related to the question of "Is the teacher ensuring worthwhile learning achievement here?"

Teacher B: But surely you could tell whether a teacher had control of his or her classroom.

Teacher C: Well, of course! But what kind of standard is *that* for teaching or learning? Would you want the sole standard for the teacher teaching *your* kids to simply be "Can he or she control the class"?

All I'm saying is, whatever constitutes the best teaching, we ought to have standards for it so that we can expect that level of performance of ourselves and of each other.

I'm saying that if we want high levels of learning going on, then that ought to be part of the feedback we are giving each other as teachers. Back at Central, the thing that really bothered me was that there was practically no feedback we gave teachers that even touched the fabric of kids learning. We didn't even really find out what the teacher had as achievement goals—either short term or long term. The only thing we expected was that the teacher put the lesson goals on the board before the beginning of class. And the quandary did cross my mind more than once—especially when the people I knew to be good teachers received lower ratings than less capable teachers because of something like not putting their objectives on the board.

Teacher B: Sounds like you are talking about just getting a good baseline of teacher performance and student behavior.

Teacher C: That *is* part of what I mean, but I mean more than that. As a person in the role of evaluating a teacher, I feel like I ought to know more about the whole setting of the classroom and the instructional aims of the day. How can you tell whether the excited talk of kids in a new group project is a matter of being too noisy and boisterous if you don't know where the teacher is in developing classroom community? Suppose the one day that the AP makes his "too boisterous" inference is a day that the students have *actually improved* on how well they comport themselves when excited?

Don't get me wrong. I think that it's worlds better here than at Central because, as the lead teacher, I actually can be a part of your practice—I have a working sense of what you're doing in world history and U.S. history and where students are in their learning achievement.

[Co-teacher A hands out a sheet with the Urban Professional Standards as Teacher C is finishing her comments]

Teacher B: Oh, that's cute! We get to good practice via UPS.

Co-dir. A: Yeah, but they deliver reliably and on time!

Teacher A: All right. Now the next thing we need to talk about is what *co-teaching* is. I know that it is something to be worked out, negotiated, whatever, but we need *some* guidelines. The students are already here and I for one would like to get the arrangement a little more settled than it is.

Co-dir. A: I hear that. As we have said before, there are a number of co-teaching models. We are at the point of having to feel our way through a bit in order to get this going. Ideally, we would have had things set up based on the needs of each teacher— both fellows and consulting teachers. Ideally, we would have set up the *system of mutual assisting of performance* based on each person's development plan.

Teacher B: Development plan? What's that?

Co-dir. A: Well, technically speaking, every faculty member should have a plan for development toward some set of professional goals. For most folks, one major goal should be to get initial licensure. Actually, the state DOE requires it. I think what we want to develop together is a system of how we do the same procedure we do with developing proficiencies for our students. The main difference is that we already have the proficiencies in the form of the Urban Teaching Standards and the Licensure Standards. But getting a data stream is essential. So is the feedback and strategies. How are we going to do it?

Teacher A: Well, shouldn't we first decide which set of teaching standards we're going to use?

Co-dir. A: That would make things simpler, but I don't know that it makes things better. Actually, the teaching fellows have to use both. I should point out that they represent two different levels of preparedness. The endpoint for the fellows is not simply licensure, but readiness as accomplished urban teachers —ready to move into city public schools. We use the urban practice standards to assess that. Fellows have to meet licensure standards by the middle of the year, and UPS by the end of the Institute.

Teacher M: Wait a minute. I just don't get how all of this is supposed to work. I get that the biggest parts of this *appraisal of practice* stuff are the two things. The co-teaching to assist each other's performance thing and the getting good or rich evidence or samples of teaching performance. But these two things already seem like too much. I mean, just the *co-teaching* thing has already been an issue. In the class my fellow is assisting, I want to be the recognized authority in the classroom. I didn't want to start off with a split authority because I don't want that relationship with my students—not if I'm going to be the instructor of record. If I have the full responsibility for the class, than I want the full authority.

Teacher A: You're right. That last part really captures it. It is risky for us. When I am the instructor of record, that means I have the responsibility for student learning, but when the intern takes the lead I worry that I am splitting or diminishing my authority. That's the opposite of being empowered—having the responsibility without the authority.

Teacher B: *[Directing her comments to Co-director A]* Say what you will about the tiredness of the old model—that … what did you call it again?

Co-dir. A: *Triadic model* or the clinical triad.

Teacher B: *[continuing]* Yeah, say what you want about the triadic model. But for me it worked. More than that, it made sense to me. It was clearer what the roles were. I am the senior person in terms of the authority in *both* classrooms—both the one I assist in and the one I'm the lead in. It's my call about what's taught and you come to confer with me about the progress of the intern or fellow. But now, it's not so clear.

Teacher A: *[Chiming in]* How are we supposed to appraise practice? I mean, what really is the mechanism that we're supposed to use to look at teaching? It seems to lack an organizational structure and a focus.

Co-dir. A: Well, what is it that you do that is most immediate to improving your practice?

Teacher B: What do you mean?

Co-dir. A: What I'm asking is: What is it that every teacher is committed to working on to improve teaching and learning?

Teacher B: I still don't know what you mean. Like improve MCAS scores?

Co-dir. A: *[with some irritation in her voice]* Is that an activity of teachers or is that an outcome, or potential outcome, of some concerted professional activity?

Teacher B: This is getting ridiculous. This seems so pie-in-the-sky to me. With every question I ask, this seems to get more complicated and abstract.

Co-dir. A: I feel and appreciate your frustration. I'm frustrated too. What's ridiculous to me is that you are three weeks into the beginning of the year and nobody is teaching anything worthwhile yet. How are you explaining to kids why they are being tested *prior* to being taught? There are a lot of frustrated youngsters in here, and for some of them this process looks like child abuse to me. How do you know what good teaching is when nobody is doing any?

Teacher A: Hold on, now. Let's cool this down some. We have already explained why we had to approach the school year this way, your analysis of the problems our approach poses for teaching and learning notwithstanding.

Co-dir. A: You're right. What's done is done, and we should move from here. But I want people to take this into account. If you are going to evaluate either the Primary Consulting Teachers or the Fellows on the basis of classroom comportment, I hope you'll remember that some of the animosity you see from students is of your own creation.

Teacher A: Let's try to take this in a more positive direction. Can we start with just a clear definition of what co-teaching is?

VIGNETTE TWO—MEETING OF UNIVERSITY SUPERVISORS

Ms. Clark: Are we going to have to go another year with this same old grid? I don't think I can face another semester having to explain what each of these indicators means to the cooperating teacher.

Ms. Iry: Yeah, and then have to listen to their stuff about how arcane they are and how they do fit the feedback that the student teachers really need or get from them.

Ms. Clark: Right, then they start in on telling you how they do it at this college and that college. Do you think that their evaluation forms really make more sense than ours? I presume they are based on the same state professional teaching standards.

Mr. Earnest: I taught in a lot of those other places, and it was the same thing—only the cooperating teachers were comparing us unfavorably to a different set of teacher preparation programs.

Ms. Clark: Well really, isn't there something we can do to improve these forms as tools? I'll tell you the truth—I feel like I have to do this conversion or translation from what I have in my field notes to something that will fit according to the state standards myself. And I'm tired of it.

Ms. Clark: But you know, a committee of this supervisors group redid these forms four years ago. So it should be related to the state standards.

Ms. Iry: Well, why do they seem so out of whack now? How could it be that something that seemed satisfactory for them to use in their clinical supervision feels so clumsy to us now?

Ms. Clark: It could be that the state professional teaching standards changed as well.

Ms. Iry: Yeah, except they always seemed out of whack.

Ms. James: I think that most of the placements back then were in suburban schools, and now most of our placements are in urban schools.

Ms. Iry: So? Why should that make a difference?

[Both a Black supervisor and a White supervisor have the same question and the same irritation but for different reasons.]

Ms. James: *[Defensively]* Well, I don't know. Maybe they just fit the situation of those placements better. I'm not implying that the standards for teachers are or should be different for our urban placements than for our suburban placements.

Mr. Earnest: *[Black supervisor]* Well, that would be all right, because I think that the standards *are* different—we have to expect more of our teacher candidates to be successful in urban schools.

Ms. James: Well, that may be. But I just think that there is something to the idea of "fit." I think that when people try to take the state frameworks and translate them into basic expectations of teaching performance, they are *not* likely to end up with something they can work with. When a different set of people, or maybe the same set of people in different teaching contexts, try to use those indicators, it feels less useful.

Ms. Clark: In the state I taught in, the INTASC standards were basically the same as the state professional teaching standards. And even though they were long and had a lot of indicators, we used them in three-way conferences for student teachers and interns.

Ms. Iry: What do you mean, they were long? Aren't there only 10 INTASC standards?

Ms. Clark: There are, but each one has a whole bunch of indicators for the knowledge, dispositions, and performance for each standard—and all of them were on the evaluation form. It took forever to do the three-way conference using that form when I was a cooperating teacher. After I came here, I heard that the university working with our school went to a system by which the cooperating teachers kind of fill out the ratings form in advance on their own, along with the student teacher, and then in the three-way the only items that got talked about was when there was some significant disagreement between the three people in the conference.

Mr. Earnest: We do that here. But you know what bothers me about that? It's that the patterns of disagreement are so predictable. The candidate always rated lower than both the cooperating teacher and me, and my ratings were almost always higher than the cooperating teacher. How is that, when he or she is only here less than a half-dozen days in a marking period? Anyway, you were saying about the instrument that had all of these indicators?

Ms. James: Well, did you feel that it was a good instrument to evaluate teachers?

Mr. Earnest: Well, not really. I mean, I always felt that all the bases were covered so to speak. But I don't really know if there was any differentiation of growth or development. Using the form, if the candidate met a sufficient number of the indicators on the form, I felt that they were competent enough to begin teaching. But whether it really was useful in guiding practice—I don't think so. One thing bothered me. I had two student teachers last year, one in each semester. I kept my records from the first semester and compared the performance of the two student teachers using those forms. The young woman in the fall semester was a much better teacher—a natural, so to speak. She was ready to teach from day one and she actually got better and better. But her ratings on all but one of the five evaluation sheets were lower than the guy in spring semester. That's when I realized that there was a way that I really wasn't truly representing my student teachers' actual proficiencies as teachers by the ratings on the form.

Ms. Clark: Well, the thing about the INTASC standards, you know they were developed by a whole lot of people with a whole lot of discussion to cover the whole gamut of teaching practice that we should expect of teachers. I mean, you look at them and go, "Oh yeah, a teacher needs to do that to be good!" But then, other times you don't know exactly what, in concrete terms, you got to do or show in order to meet this standard or that standard. That's why people—departments, I guess—need to make up their own indicators.

Mr. Earnest: Can't they, like, be narrowed down? I feel like we need to do something that makes it speak to actual practice.

Ms. Clark: I mean, I think you put your finger on it. How to use what the powers that be say is good practice in a way that keeps it real? You know what I mean? You have to be able to say what each indicator is about in a way that is real to you, your students, and the cooperating teachers in the school … everybody.

Ms. James: Well, now how is this supposed to work with the new PDS school that is working on this new teacher evaluation system?

Ms. Clark: It is system in which everything is based upon student data. That's all I really know.

Mr. Earnest: Oh, I know what you mean! It is that guy from Oregon. I can't think of his name, but I have seen him present a number of times at these AACTE or ATE meetings. You know, that thing where samples of student work are somehow incorporated into how the teacher gets evaluated. So you measure how good the teacher is by how much learning the children demonstrate.

Ms. Clark: Well, I don't think it's that, but the idea seems similar. But anyway, as we look at what we are actually going to use, [Co-director A] wanted us to consider these five urban practice standards …

[Ms. Clark passes out the single sheet of paper and they are all looking at them for a few moments in silence.]

Ms. James: So now, explain to me again how this works? I mean, if these new practice standards are to specify behaviors, how do we know what we are looking for in the candidate's teaching?

Ms. Clark: Well, try to think of these practice standards as specifying the outcomes and ongoing conditions of teaching and learning in the classroom.

Ms. James: But still, how do I know what counts as "Participation and Engagement" in the candidate's classroom? We are stuck with the same basic problem—the actual performances and behaviors that count as evidence for the standard.

Ms. Clark: Here is where the contextual nature of these standards comes in. I think all of us can recognize some common moves of inexperienced teachers that reflect a shortfall on this practice standard. For instance, if you walk into a classroom where someone is doing a cooperative learning activity in groups, and one or more members of each group is not involved in the groups' activity, it is a safe inference that there is work to be done on this practice standard. Like it says here, the outcome —the joint product or conditions generated by learner and teacher interaction is …

Ms. James: Look here. I teach mathematics. "Engagement" to me is when my students are paying attention when I explain a new concept. "Participation" is when they work the practice problems when I direct them to. Is there anything more to it than that?

Ms. Clark: Well, I should hope so! You can determine the degree of "participation" as a practice criterion if not everyone is paying attention and not everyone does the practice problems. But I can tell you from experience, I have been in mathematics classes as a student and done both of these things—paid attention and did my work—and still felt unengaged and did not understand much.

Ms. James: You mean, there is a sort of higher order type of engagement, right? Like whether a student is really into imaginary numbers or differential equations.

Ms. Clark: That's right. But you won't see standards that really relate to that kind of engagement. How do you know your students are engaged at the level you're describing? I'll bet you couldn't see it looking at a videotape. You can tell some things, but

	what behavior, action, gesture, or sign would reliably reveal to you that type of "into-it-ness" you're talking about?
Ms. Iry:	That speaks to some limitations to video records of teaching.
Ms. Clark:	It sure does.
Mr. Earnest:	Then why do you want us to do *so much* of it? It seems that's all my intern does. The video camera is always in the classroom and seems to be running nearly all the time. But you know, I was just looking at this last standard. This one that has social justice, and has it in the inquiry and reflection of teachers, is pretty interesting. Now if we could do that we could do a lot!

CONCLUSION

Practice standards do have a greater contextualization—a greater situativity to the real work and challenges of teachers—than do the state performance standards that we have appropriated (see Appendix B). We have found the urban practice standards useful to point out the unseen practices that are particularly detrimental to the African American students in the school. For example, the practice standard of engagement and participation is the means by which we directly contest the too often uttered phrase, "Well, you can't reach everybody." The value added of the urban practice standards is that of holding both practicing teachers and new interns accountable for a broader and deeper understanding of institutional racism and how it plays out in the everyday instructional activities and professional practices of the school.

There is also a value added for envisioning the community teacher as a particular kind of accomplished practitioner and using the practice standards to reinscribe the vision of the accomplished practitioner who is effective by virtue of his or her impact in, and on, the cultural environment of the school. In this way, the urban practice standards offer a different perspective on the idea of *accomplished practice* as it is used by the National Board for Professional Teaching Standards (NBPTS). A person could ostensibly meet all of the requirements of National Board Certification and still not have the individual's practice manifest in well being of the school he or she taught. In the CT framework, by contrast, you cannot be an exemplary teacher by being successful with some or even most of the students in your classroom as long as there remain some who are not being reached (especially those historically and systematically underserved).

The value added for the community teacher goes beyond an ethic of caring to agency toward social justice combined with a sense of advocacy on behalf of historically underserved populations in America. In a sense, the candidate adhering to the urban practice standards meets a higher level of accountability. The currently operating notion of teacher preparation seems to regard teacher quality as a matter of merely having the right stuff, as determined by performance assessments for a range of skills and demonstrations of teaching performance. What is left out of consideration is whether these demonstrations actually mean that the teacher will be successful with the population of students most underserved by public schooling in America.

The disadvantage in using the urban practice standards is that they always seemed to be in flux. It was clumsy to work with our school faculty as the UPS always seemed to require an explanation whenever they were invoked to talk about teaching. Trying to use them as the shared system for appraising the practice of the teaching fellows feels like a continuous negotiation of meaning. Part of the difficulty might be that they try to do too much. That is, criteria of performance at a micro level that tap into meso and macro levels as well may be too much to expect in a system of teacher performance assessment. At this point, it still seems worth pursuing.

When we talk about the quality of teachers and teaching practice, our measures ought to include all of the dimensions of agency that teachers must exhibit on behalf of students in order to promote their development as learners and as people. To do this, we created the UPS in order to be mindful of more than just the micro level of activity—instructional activity and interaction in classroom instructional settings. We would need to be just as thorough about teachers' capacity in mesolevel settings of professional activity where they interact with the many other social systems in the school—curriculum committees with colleagues, parent groups, administrators, and mixes of these groups engaged in the work of schooling.

The accomplished teacher who meets urban practice standards is ethically responsible and morally accountable for what happens to his or her students, and to their families and communities. In other words, it is not enough for a teacher to be competent in his or her classroom practice, but he or she must act in ways that contest the destructive and often contradictory teacher education agendas. Accomplished teachers have the moral responsibility for systems of practice that are effective, just, and focus initiative in precisely those areas where it is needed most.

APPENDIX A: PRACTICE STANDARDS
FOR THE COMMUNITY TEACHER INSTITUTE

Performance Standards	Practice Standards
Pedagogical knowledge— Ensuring that every student "finds a way into" the inquiry and the subject matter. The means to ensure full engagement and participation of learners and teachers in a learning enterprise.	**Engagement and Participation** **Teacher Role:** On the part of the teacher, these are actions and arrangements that encourage and promote the interest, engagement, and participation of every student—with one another and with the learning enterprise. **Outcome:** These practices aim to provide *sustained effort and commitment* with respect to the learning activity, and *sustained interpersonal engagement* with the community of learners. **Learner Role:** On the part of the learner, the practice results in strategies and other means by which the learner mobilizes himself or herself to engage productively with others, put forth effort, and participate in the activities of learning.
Knowledge of the learner in social context—Ensures that each student finds meaning in his or her experience of curriculum, through action, through ideas, or through relationships. The knowledge about children and contexts to promote their identity in activity, as people (learners) construct themselves as worthy in the activity, enterprise, or social setting. Know what is significant and important to learners as individuals so as to allow everyone a "way in" to the learning community, into the domain of knowledge and skills, and into a productive role in both.	**Identity Development** **Teacher Role:** On the part of the teacher, these are actions and arrangements that result in healthy identity development and self-construction as an able learner. **Outcome:** The beneficial outcomes for students are productive *self-exploration* and *self-definition* in the context of meaningful rich inquiry about the world. Literature selections and topic selections related to social justice and the students' backgrounds are particularly important for the teacher. **Student Role:** On the part of the learner, these are actions that involve trying out different roles, representations, and expressions of self by discourse, stance, dress, and particularly, language. In general, learner practices of identity development include all means of self-definition and redefinition.

Performance Standards	Practice Standards
Knowledge of community	**Community Integrity Practices**
Social coherence in community in conducting productive, worthwhile conjoint activity that benefits individuals and the group.	**Teacher Role:** On the part of the teacher, these are activities and arrangements *for organizing the intellectual and social life of a community of learners.* The teacher creates a setting of social cohesion and cultural richness. **Outcome:** The teacher incorporates cultural features (e.g., fictive kinship, communicative styles) and knowledge (e.g., the intellectual traditions of the African American heritage). These practices also identify and support students' initiative in building community integrity. **Learner Role:** On the part of the learner, these practices involve forming relationships and maintaining membership in a learning community. The learner participates in community integrity practices by joining, belonging, supporting other members in whatever the core activities of the group are.
Knowledge of subject matter	**Meaning Making**
Deep interpretation, deep interrogation of meaning, and sign systems (especially of one's subject matter) to create meaning. Metaunderstanding of one's discipline or subject matter to assist conceptual newcomers in finding meaningful points of entry and connection.	**Teacher Role:** On the part of the teacher, these are activities and arrangements for making explicit cultural models (especially sign and symbol structures) and cultural patterns to amplify the interpretative frameworks of learners. **Outcome:** These practices are particularly important for discourse practices and for engaging students in what Freire calls "reading the world." They result in demonstrations of understanding through complex and rich activities, not just on paper and pencil achievement tests. **Learner Role:** On the part of the learner, these are practices of inquiry that involve appropriation (taking for their own use), interpretation, and consumption of cultural forms, signs, symbols, and other forms of symbolic representation. The aim for learners is to develop deep skills in analysis and interpretation of information and ideas, as well developing a critical regard of how and for what purposes they were produced.

Performance Standards	Practice Standards
A Social Justice Perspective as Part of Inquiry and Reflection	**Critical Inquiry Standard**
Deep inquiry of complex problems, symbols systems, and forms of communication; critical reflection on one's own practice in light of student outcomes.	**Teacher Role:** On the part of the teacher, these are activities and arrangements for critical inquiry. This involves making students aware of their appropriation of symbols, signs, and other representations of meaning in the act of expressing and creating new meaning. **Outcome:** The outcomes are students adept at interrogating the use and consumption of signs, symbols, and other symbolic representations. They develop the critical capacities to analyze, reflect, critique, and act to transform the conditions under which they live. **Learner Role:** Learner practices of inquiry are conceived as various forms of recursive reappropriation—they take on and use (or sample) the phrases, signs, and images of others for their use in their own expressive and reflective repertoire.

APPENDIX B: CLINICAL PERFORMANCE STANDARDS*

State Competency from Regulations	Indicators
Competency I: Plans for Curriculum and Instruction	1. Incorporated content from the appropriate curriculum frameworks in the planning of instructional activities and the assessment of students' achievement. 2. Instructional plans clearly delineated the development of skills, together with the content to be understood in the form of proficiencies required for high-level work in the discipline. 3. Assessed reading and writing fluency of students in anticipation of the work required for successful achievement of learning performances required for the course of study. 4. Instructional designs were coherent and organized in ways that make explicit how student knowledge and proficiency is systematically advanced. 5. Documented advancements in students' learning achievement by the use of both formal and informal assessments that are linked to instructional goals in the course of study. 6. Developed a system for engaging every learner in sustained effective effort.
Competency II: Delivers Effective Instruction	1. Planned learning activities appropriate for the full range of students within a classroom. 2. Communicated high standards and expectations when beginning the lesson or instructional setting. 3. Made learning objectives clear to students. 4. Communicated clearly in writing and speaking. 5. Found engaging ways to begin a new unit of study or lesson. 6. Built on students' prior knowledge and experience. 7. Wrote and spoke with appropriate clarity and meaning. 8. Specified and assessed worthwhile learning achievements.
Competency III: Manages Classroom Climate and Operation	1. Created an instructional environment that is conducive to learning and included a range of learning activities. 2. Maintained appropriate standards of behavior, mutual respect, and safety. 3. Managed classroom routines and procedures without loss of significant instructional time and without loss of student esprit de corps, enthusiasm, and participation. 4. Planned and organized instruction appropriate to the specific discipline and to the age and cognitive level of the students in the classroom. 5. Sought resources from colleagues, families, and the community to enhance learning.

State Competency from Regulations	Indicators
Competency III: *(continued)*	6. Incorporated appropriate technology and media in lesson planning. 7. Used information in Individualized Education Programs (IEPs), as appropriate, to plan strategies for integrating students with disabilities into general education classrooms.
Competency IV: Promotes Equity	1. Encouraged all students to believe that effort is a key to achievement. 2. Works to promote achievement by all students without exception. 3. Assesses the significance of student differences in home experiences, background knowledge, learning skills, learning pace, and proficiency in the English language for learning the curriculum at hand and uses professional judgment to determine if instructional adjustments are necessary. 4. Helps all students to understand American civic culture, its underlying ideals, founding political principles, and political institutions, and to see themselves as members of a local, state, national, and international civic community. 5. Assigns homework or practice that furthers student learning and checks it. 6. Provides regular and frequent feedback to students on their progress. 7. Provides many and varied opportunities for students to achieve competence.
Competency V: Meets Professional Responsibilities	1. Conveyed knowledge of and enthusiasm for his or her academic discipline to students. 2. Took responsibility for legal and moral responsibilities of teaching. 3. Evidenced an interest in current theory, research, and developments in the academic discipline and exercises judgment in accepting implications or findings as valid for application in classroom practice 4. Worked actively to involve parents in their child's academic activities and performance, and communicates clearly with them. 5. Reflected critically upon his or her teaching experience, without defensiveness, and identified areas for further professional development as part of a professional development plan that is linked to grade level, school, and district goals, and is receptive to suggestions for growth. 6. Recognized legal and ethical issues as they apply to responsible and acceptable use of the Internet and other resources.

*Adapted from Massachusetts Department of Education Professional Standards.

REFERENCES

Brown, J. S., Collins, A., & Duguid, P. (1989). Situated cognition and the culture of learning. *Educational Researcher, 18*(1), 32–42.

Haberman, M. (1993). Predicting the success of urban teachers: The Milwaukee trials. *Action in Teacher Education, 15*(3), 1–5.

Haberman, M. (1995). *Star teachers of children in poverty*. West Lafayette, IN: Kappa Delta Pi.

Haberman, M. (1999). Increasing the number of high quality African-American teachers in urban schools. *Journal of Instructional Psychology, 26*(4), 208–212.

Lave, J., & Wenger, E. (1991). *Situated learning: Legitimate peripheral participation*. Cambridge, UK: Cambridge University Press.

Murrell, P. C., Jr. (1998). *Like stone soup: The problem of the professional development school in the renewal of urban schools*. Washington, DC: American Association of Colleges for Teacher Education.

Murrell, P. C., Jr. (2001). *Community teachers: A new framework for effective urban teaching*. New York: Teachers College Press.

Wenger, E. (1998). *Communities of practice: Learning, meaning and identity*. Cambridge, UK: Cambridge University Press.

Part III

THEORY INTO
SITUATED PRACTICE

Chapter 8

Context Matters:
Situated Assessment Practices
in Urban Teaching

Virginia Navarro
University of Missouri, St. Louis

> *Half of the instructors supported by special programs designed to help*
> *poor children were teachers' aides, among whom only 19% had a*
> *bachelor's degree; this figure was 10% in the schools with the highest*
> *poverty rate.*
>
> —*Lott* (2002, p. 102)

The process and practice of assessment in American institutions reflect conceptual schemes deeply rooted in the competition of material capitalism, efficiency models of production, and a conservative ideology with lingering theoretical ties to positivism and behaviorism. As a result of this state of affairs, efforts to improve educational outcomes for children are mired in a discourse of accountability under a banner of intellectual meritocracy that glosses complex and situated realities (Apple, 2001). This text has offered both a theoretical tool to reframe assessment issues and a practical guide of basic design principles focused on urban settings. Case studies of university–school partnership efforts and activities in preparing and evaluating developing urban teachers provide illustrations of assessment-in-action. This chapter attempts to highlight a few conceptual strands in these reflected accounts of practice.

Despite divergent perspectives in the literature about the uniqueness of urban teaching, the authors here identify a set of skills, dispositions, and knowledge that support successful urban teaching. Demographic studies confirm that an increasingly White, middle-class teaching force must be prepared to educate an increasingly diverse, multilingual student population. Teacher education curriculum, intentionally designed to prepare urban teachers, should include opportunity for self-reflection, cultural consciousness raising through integrated readings and fieldwork, strategies for negotiating bureaucracies, immersion into community and technology resources, and broad conceptual content knowledge. Few would argue that all teachers need such preparation to successfully teach diverse learners; what is often absent in evaluating teacher and student performance is a recognition of the sociocultural environment and system within which the teaching/learning activity occurs.

Sadovnik and Semal (2001) highlight this point in their review of Anyon and Wilson's (1997) *Ghetto Schooling:*

> It [school reform] continues to be oversimplified by experts in fields like curriculum and pedagogy, who often are ahistorical, sociologically and politically naïve, and fail to understand the complex relationship among schools, families, and the larger society to which they are inexorably linked. (p. 30)

For example, the visual image of teachers planning creative lessons around district curriculum guides represents a portrait that is rarely painted in urban districts (Davis, Pool, & Mits-Cash, 2000). The central office often reassigns teachers to new buildings and grade levels as late as 8 weeks into the year because of shifting student populations. Some new teachers begin the year without ever getting the curriculum guide or class books because they are misplaced in some warehouse. Few mentors are available in buildings where substantial numbers of teachers are permanent substitutes, aides, or new to the school. By 2 months into the year, as much as half the class represents new faces, new learning challenges, and new beginnings for shaping the community. In early spring, many students migrate yet again as weather becomes warmer and housing needs change. Learning outcomes might be improved more by committing resources to inexpensive housing, job opportunities, and stability in teacher–student contact than by spending big bucks for standardized assessments. In order to fill in the brush strokes for a picture of successful teaching in urban contexts, special techniques and color blends are needed, but the final picture can be brilliant and beautiful because of its complexity and significance. The microethnography, *The Complexities of an Urban Classroom: An Analysis Toward a General Theory of Teaching*, offered by Smith and Geoffrey (1968) some 35 years ago, provides us with the still valid metaphor of teacher as "ringmaster," overseeing multiple, simultaneous, and situated events.

SHAPING ASSESSMENT TOOLS FOR REFORM

The process of evaluation relies on identifying the relationship of complex variables to stated goals and outcomes. One needs to understand design principles that acknowledge that context can transform not only the meaningfulness of collected data from situated practice, *but also the actual data itself*. Urban teachers and administrators are cautious about collecting and sharing data because they have experienced the ways it can be misrepresented and used against the children they seek to help. This presents challenges to authentic assessment for change. Developing urban teachers with sophisticated observational and assessment skills who can document student learning in multiple ways is a necessary balance to overemphasis on decontextualized, high-stakes tests.

An additional challenge to successful evaluation practice is the multidimensional nature of collaborative work within Professional Development School (PDS) partnerships (Teitel, 2000, 2001; Fountain, 1997; The Holmes Group, 1990). Meaningful assessment leading to effective practice must embrace all system components. Teitel (2000) invokes Newmann and Wehlage's (1995) notion of concentric circles with student learning at the core, circled by authentic pedagogy, the schools' organizational capacity, and its external support (p. 3). Over reliance on self-report measures and/or test scores from preservice teachers undercuts collecting data on simultaneous changes in the practice of university faculty, practicing teachers, and school administrators, as well as board and community members. The Holmes Group Principles (1990) for institutionalizing partnerships include reciprocity between partners, experimentation with new forms of practice, systematic inquiry to validate practice, and teaching strategies for student diversity; this early set of goals still resonates with those seeking school reform through partnership work. Teacher quality is intertwined with system goals.

Although the bottom line of P–12 student achievement, a reasonable fixation of policymakers, remains an underdocumented outcome of school reform, reductionist models of assessment practice that are based only on comparative high-stakes testing ignore the way children and their teachers actually grow and develop in their zones of proximal development (ZPD). Measuring student or teacher learning at the level of independent mastery ignores the need for instruction that scaffolds help by a more competent other within an individual ZPD. How can these teachers and students begin to imagine themselves in the role of learners, engaged in authentic inquiry, with a learning rather than performance orientation, if the only feedback available reifies labels of failure, personal deficit, and incompetence? Amrein and Berliner (2002) document unintended deleterious effects when assessment data is used punitively in real persons' lives, including increased dropouts, more special education referrals, and erosion of quality teachers in poor districts.

Informal talk with practicing urban teachers and administrators at Holmes Partnership and the Urban Network to Improve Teacher Education (UNITE) conferences highlights why student performance averages are inadequate in understanding actual learning outcomes in complex systems. For example, a high school social studies teacher at an exemplary PDS describes her current reality in one class:

- six English as a Second Language (ESL) students (almost *no* English),
- drop-in students who make it to class on average once a week,
- 40% of students with special need diagnoses with pull-out schedules,
- many students working 30+ hours a week, and
- a student with an electronic cuff for probation purposes.

She admits to being distrustful of outsiders coming in to "assess" her students; she feels fairly overwhelmed in just getting through the day despite years of experience and high expectations for student outcomes. Reducing the nature and quality of her situated teaching to student test scores, or evaluating a student teacher's performance through GPA and PRAXIS scores, amounts to naive folly in her eyes. Her beliefs are supported by recent research on urban teacher attributes as predictors of success (Sachs, 2002).

Some state departments of education are moving toward certification based on passing PRAXIS-type tests as a marker for achieving proficiency, even for school counselors—no reflective clinical supervision required. Cognitive knowledge does not equate to skilled counseling practice with vulnerable young people; urban teacher retention and success cannot be predicted by looking at one test score; content knowledge is a necessary but not sufficient base for quality teaching. Except in the case of high school mathematics, Wayne and Youngs's (2003) meta-analysis found that the links between degrees, coursework, and certification to increased student learning was inconclusive. Defining criteria for quality professional teachers is anything but obvious.

A recent analysis of ACT entrance scores and PRAXIS exit scores in teacher education programs in a Midwestern state showed a moderate correlation (.67) between the two. A strategy to raise PRAXIS exit scores by raising the ACT entrance requirements would ironically result in screening out huge numbers of current teacher candidates: 45% with one point ACT increases (62% students of color) and 58% with two point increases (76% students of color). With an anticipated shortage of qualified teachers to meet the *No Child Left Behind* mandate and evidence that many students admitted at the current score levels have become successful professionals, it seems reasonable to conclude that preparing and inducting enough quality teachers for the nation's children will require strategic gate-keeping and multiple measures of competence. Yet competing voices reflect deep ideological divisions on what constitutes quality teacher preparation and evaluation.

DISCOURSE GAMESMANSHIP: PROFESSIONALIZATION AND DEREGULATION AGENDAS

The tensions around competing discourses on reform and assessment issues discussed by Zeichner (chap. 1, this volume) are thoughtfully articulated by Cochran-Smith and Fries (2001), who remind us of the essentially political context of schooling rhetoric, often designed "to attack and dismiss social theories that conflict with one's own will to power and to suggest that one's opponent is an ideologue, operating within a closed system and unwilling to consider other points of view" (p. 6).

Assessment practices are very much about voice, power, and access to higher education; about who is taught higher order thinking skills and who gets to fill out skill and drill worksheets (Anyon, 1995). Two distinctive discourse strands are currently competing to map the road toward quality teaching for policymakers, yet both groups appeal to a political warrant, an accountability warrant, and an evidentiary warrant; citing empirical findings rooted in scientific data to argue their cases (Cochran-Smith & Fries, 2001; Darling-Hammond & Youngs, 2002). The *professionalization agenda* promoters support work by Darling-Hammond (2001) and Berliner (2002), whereas those advocating the *deregulation agenda* affiliate with Michael Podgursky and/or the Abell Foundation. The *professionalization* discourse argues for rigorous teacher preparation and expanded professional development opportunities such as "working with diverse learners, meeting the special learning needs of students, providing positive learning environments, collaborating with parents and colleagues, thinking systematically and critically about practice, and functioning as members of learning communities" (Cochran-Smith & Fries, p. 9).

In contrast, the *deregulation agenda* followers believe colleges of education are a barrier to reform, reflect a liberal bias, lack academic rigor, and focus too much on pedagogy; they believe public education will improve if schools are privatized and made accountable to market competition. Good students who want to teach can learn what they need to know in the classroom without extensive course work. Unfortunately, many well-intentioned, content-competent, alternatively certified teachers leave urban teaching after brief tenures in the classroom. Recent data on student learning outcomes with Teach for America recruits also provides evidence that being a successful student oneself does not necessarily translate into success in motivating others to learn (Laczko-Kerr & Berliner, 2002).

Publicity on comparative district and school test scores creates political environments that are punitive toward teachers and students who may be engaged in heroic efforts to build communities of practice, so learning can occur in classrooms despite instability, high-need children, and poverty. School reform involves complex systems; change initiatives, to be effective, cannot isolate the work of teachers from wider community issues. A recent analysis of standards-based reforms and accountability initiatives highlights this point:

> Researchers identified a need for coherence between policies and action at all levels, a need to build organizational and teacher capacity for better instruction with standards, a need to build resilience and consistency against political instability, and a need to devote energies toward learner development. (Chatterji, 2002, p. 373)

Without addressing these multiple issues, standards-based reform will not succeed. Schools must engage in activity beyond narrow assessment goals covered in yearly standardized tests if true reform is the goal.

Bush's *No Child Left Behind* (2001) legislation, however, mandates yearly testing with an operational definition of "proficiency" for all student populations in order to evaluate adequate yearly progress (AYP). There is evidence, however, that actual individual progress in learning, even in homogeneous, stable schools using a standards-based curriculum, does not mirror AYP expectations of incremental score increases (Ding & Navarro, in press). Problems also are created when individual states define "proficient" to mean different things compared to the National Assessment of Educational Progress (NAEP) data (see Berliner, 2002; Linn, Baker, & Betebenner, 2002; Shepard, 2001). Further equity concerns include the structural aspects of school districts, beliefs about diverse students, and classroom processes (Allexsaht-Snider & Hart, 2001). Such contradictions set up a Catch-22 for successful compliance, especially with insufficient resources to achieve the universal proficiency mandated by this bill. Once again, American schooling will be subjected to the rhetoric of failure based on unrealistic goals during an era of state budget crises. The real disappointment is the missed opportunity to engage in the hard work locally of forming partnerships to actually address systemic urban issues such as housing, jobs, mobility, retention, and mentor support. Lashway (2002) succinctly summarizes the present climate: "Today, standards-based accountability is the 800-pound gorilla of school reform—highly visible, hard to control, and impossible to ignore" (p. 15).

STANDARDS: GOOD NEWS OR BAD NEWS FOR ASSESSMENT

Every major accrediting body, both state and national, has now adopted a standards-based approach to performance outcomes. Although the case studies and design principles for assessing teachers in urban environments shared here resonate with the professionalization camp, Zeichner (this volume) worries both the deregulation and professionalization arguments. He documents previous bids historically to enact each of these perspectives. Will standards-driven preparation lead to hegemonic replication of an unjust schooling system? Can advocacy-based teaching achieve demonstrable academic gains for poor children? What is the appropriate relationship between public schooling and issues in the larger society? What political and measurement issues arise because individual state and federal definitions of "proficiency" are often contradictory?

Rothstein (*The New York Times*, May 1, 2002) writes about what is obvious to most educators: "… most tests are poorly matched to state standards," and later, "teachers preparing for tests mostly of basic skills will not do much to train students in higher-order thinking" (p. A21). Rothstein makes the point that many standards cannot be assessed with inexpensive, mostly multiple-choice tests, even if the tests ask for a few short-essay answers (p. A21). Quality assessment of complex skills cannot be done "on the cheap."

CHALLENGES TO REFRAMING ASSESSMENT TALK

For those who believe that standardized test scores are a responsible measure of learning outcomes and that they can be raised through market competition for schools that produce high scores, a sociocultural assessment system that honors the situated nature of the teaching/learning process will not have much allure. Those with "teacher as technician" beliefs will continue to locate the problem of children not learning in a failure to institute scripted predictable routines to deliver test-based content knowledge and in a deficit model of children's intelligence.

In a similar vein, Peterman's *Design Principles for Urban Teacher Assessment Systems* (chap. 3, this volume) will probably not interrupt the worldview of those interested exclusively in competitive models of achievement. Struggling with ways to creatively name and assess messy, layered process variables in urban contexts is challenging; no simplistic pen-and-pencil outcome measure will sufficiently document the learning that does go on above, beyond, in between, below, and on top of the academic curriculum. Yet the long-term solution to low test scores and "achievement gaps" flow out of these sociocultural realities in which schooling takes place. The effect of huge migrations of students and teachers to different schools when the weather turns cold and housing needs dictate relocations is not on the radar of those who live in less mobile environments. Judging teaching success by a test score when many of the students just arrived in that classroom seems naïve folly to those in the trenches.

Many criticisms of urban schools are legitimate and refocus on student learning, which is appropriate. Unfortunately, the argument to "focus relentlessly on results" does not illuminate pathways to success in the day-to-day activity of the urban teacher's classroom. Perhaps efforts to engage in alternative assessments will increase our understanding of the complexities of a given context despite demands of time to collaborate on portfolio artifacts, consult with parents and colleagues, and dialogue with individual students. Taking a postmodern perspective that questions the "knowability" of human beings, Hargreaves and Earl (2002) write:

> The cultural perspective examines how alternative assessments are interpreted and integrated into the social and cultural contexts of schools. The political perspective views assessment issues as being embedded in and resulting from the dynamics of power and control in human interaction .... The postmodern perspective is based on the view that in today's complex and uncertain world, human beings are not completely knowable and that "authentic" experiences and assessments are fundamentally questionable. (pp. 69–70)

Might the educative process be about "composing a life" and becoming a responsible citizen in a pluralistic democracy, as well as preparing to compete in the marketplace? Individualistic competition and free market practices are not solutions to urban education, according to the controversial report, *What Matters Most: Teaching for America's Future* (National Commission on Teaching and America's Future, 1996):

> The challenge extends far beyond preparing students for the world of work. It includes building an American future that is just and humane as well as productive, that is socially vibrant and civil in its pluralism as it is competitive. (cited in Cochran-Smith & Fries, 2001, p. 11)

Here, the discourse of the political warrant is linked with the accountability warrant using highly evocative language. Assessment practice often is more than establishing whose knowledge is of most worth; it is about naming the worthy and unworthy, the stars and slackers, the morally superior and the socially bankrupt. The third work cycle of UNITE addresses the accountability warrant by gathering educational data from urban partnerships to inform policymakers in usable data-rich ways. This book provides some valuable collective wisdom about how to participate responsibly in the accountability and evidentiary values discourse of teacher reform. Framing discourse around linguistic hooks such as *democracy, school choice, and ac-*

countability does not always translate into rational advocacy for students and teachers in urban settings. Too often, the situated, contextual successes and failures are obfuscated by assessment principles that do not acknowledge the limited perspective and middle class bias inherent in many "objective" measures within a test environment that is individualistic, deficit-focused, and culturally biased. This assertion in no way glosses the very real problems and issues in large bureaucratic systems that need reform; it is the tools chosen to do reform work that are being critiqued.

SOCIOCULTURAL DESIGN PRINCIPLES FOR URBAN ASSESSMENT

The Vygotskian notion of a zone of proximal development (ZPD) calls our attention to distinctions between things we know, things we are learning with some guidance by a more competent other, and things presently beyond our imagination. Learning to teach in urban contexts, particularly for an increasingly white, middle class, monolingual, and disproportionately female group of preparing teachers, means stretching beyond a familiar comfort zone into the challenge of being wholehearted, open-minded, and responsible. Dewey (1910/1991) provides early insights into the qualities of mind necessary to foster resilient, efficacious advocates of children:

> Reflective thinking is always more or less troublesome because it involves overcoming the inertia that inclines one to accept suggestions at their face value; it involves willingness to endure a condition of mental unrest and disturbance ... the most important factor in the training of good mental habits consists of acquiring the attitude of suspended conclusion, and in mastering the various methods of searching for new materials to corroborate or refute the first suggestions that occur. (p. 13)

Teachers learn to resist invisible assumptions inherent in a discourse of deficiency through guided mentoring in their zone of proximal development. Identifying "right answers" on a standardized paper-and-pencil test may actually subvert their growth in naming and reframing the nature and scope of teacher-advocate work.

If, from a set of learning principles, it were possible to formulate an activity script for the teacher (as is advocated by literacy programs such as Slavin's *Success for All*; Slavin & Madden, 2001, 2002), then assessment could be reduced to demonstration of knowing the script. Tharp's research on standards for professional development (CREDE http://www.crede.ucsc.edu) offers a broader notion of teacher competency based on evaluation of "joint productive activity, collaborative reflection, and instructional conversations" (see chap. 2 by Conway & Artiles).

The evaluation of teacher performance connects integrally to a philosophy of teaching/learning (Gallimore & Goldenberg, 2001; Shepel, 1995). By acknowledging the sociocultural roots of this process, one quickly recognizes the limitations of exclusive reliance on solo performance as sufficient evidence of competence. Using a sociocultural perspective demands that we situate the curriculum, activity, and assessment pieces in teacher education programs to prepare teachers to recognize, name, and adapt to the historical, cultural, linguistic, and institutional forms of life that empower and constrain student learning (Wong & Rowley, 2001). Assessment practice within a dynamic ZPD gathers a variety of process data points to gauge the teacher's ability to pose problems, seek resources in dialogue, and implement responsive reflected practice in a situated system. Collaborative planning enhances teacher and student outcomes (Pasch, 1990).

The tools of assessment, both for teachers and P–12 students, are not morally neutral instruments of objectivity about knowledge (see Wertsch, 1998, *Mind as Action* on this point); rather, they represent powerful "message systems" about authority, possibilities, and the nature of truth. Two critical ideas to internalize from the sociocultural chapter (Conway & Artiles, this volume) include the following: (a) culture mediates the activity of a community of practice by assigning meaning and possible identity roles within a system of teaching/learning statuses; and (b) higher order thinking is acquired first through human relationships interpsychologically and then becomes internalized intrapsychologically within the individual person. Assessment activity needs to support learning within an individual's ZPD.

While acknowledging that the urban context presents distinct affordances and constraints, it is important to emphasize that urban children are not seen as different from other children in their developmental trajectories, in their capacity to learn, or in their need to be affirmed and taught academic content by qualified teachers. Successful teaching within the urban setting, however, does depend on strategic and dispositional skills and knowledge that must be assessed with appropriate urban design principles in mind.

RESPONSIBLE PROBLEM SOLVERS AND ADVOCATES

Peterman (chap. 3, this volume) offers a close-up look at the capacities that must be nurtured developmentally in teachers through urban assessment practices. If educating children of poverty successfully were a matter of better curriculum or scripted teaching, the many resources spent to date to improve test scores would have had more of an impact. As it is, urban teachers are the most likely to be uncertified, to leave the teaching profession after a few years, to spend more of their own money on basic classroom supplies, and to have minimal induction and professional development opportunities (Lott, 2002). For urban teachers, on-going mentor support and incentives to stay in urban public education are especially critical to quality teaching. Networks of partnerships with universities, local social services, other urban teachers, and businesses become critical for survival and sustaining teaching effort (Zeichner & Hoeft, 1996). Naïve judgment of performance and negativity about the children of poverty cannot sustain growth and development within an emerging ZPD.

In a recent presentation on assessment of Professional Development School partnerships, Teitel (2002) raised issues about the audience for data collected on teachers and learners. Too often, efforts to assess take on sinister meanings far different from the stated goal of improving performance. He develops a four-tiered conceptual framework that echoes the themes in this text. In order to look at improved learning measures, one has to also take a look at organizational innovation and partnership development, adaptations in roles, structure, and culture, and establish best practice in teaching, learning, and leadership (Teitel, 2002). In other words, only by acknowledging the impact of the whole can we make reasonable sense of the individual parts. When data is used as a tool of communication, it can validate one's vision and shape outcomes positively.

Naming the realities of urban schooling, in chapter 3 by Peterman (this volume), provides a blueprint for teacher preparation needs because urban schools *are* bureaucratic and contradictory, poverty-bound, diverse, and underresourced. Like Peterman, Teitel's (2000) work on PDS assessment practices provides maps for thinking creatively about designs for assessment that honor context yet focus on documentation of outcome attributes in collaborative ways among community, school, and university participants.

At a recent Urban Partnership day at my institution involving university, school, and community people focusing on urban issues, I shared Peterman's assessment system for urban teaching success (situated and responsive, reflective in action, capacity building, and advocacy based) and facilitated a 2-hour brainstorming dialogue session to design a course, Urban Teaching 101. The list generated by this group of educators and social service workers mirrors many of the insights offered in the case studies included in this volume. Those with accumulated day-to-day tacit knowledge of urban schooling can name the components necessary for good urban teaching, as well as identify ways to foster these characteristics. This text represents an effort to share ideas and insights with those not working in urban contexts.

Looking across the diversity of settings, problems, and creative structures that exist in the case studies, one quickly concludes that solutions to urban issues must be negotiated within historical, political, and organizational realities that are situated and unique. Meaningful assessment should be goal-directed, data driven, and ultimately improve the teaching/learning opportunities in situ. With the current high-stakes standardized testing mind-set, policymakers can confuse competitive bottom line mean averages of test scores with authentic, systemic reform progress.

CONTEXTUAL SENSITIVITY AND RESPONSIVENESS

The Minnesota case study, *Developing Systems of Performance Assessment in the Urban Context* (chap. 6, this volume), identifies the necessary components of successful urban partnerships to improve student learning: "structured collaboration, inclusiveness, contextual sensitivity, and responsiveness." It is not possible for assessment to be linked with professional development in reflective, collaborative ways if we turn over control of assessment to professional statisticians and large corporate structures far removed from day-to-day realities and priorities. Using standards in dynamic and changeable ways through shared activity and reflection in partnership can produce systemic change to improve teaching/learning opportunities. Yet such assessments are not only more responsive but may also be more valid in that they represent the shared vision and values of the community that practices them. In the Minnesota case, the formative assessment documentation was intentionally left out of the permanent file in order to highlight the developmental role assessment must play in mentoring new teachers.

ASSESSMENT-IN-ACTION: ELECTRONIC FRONTIERS

Web-based electronic portfolios, like other evaluation tools, mediate a set of affordances and constraints as professional development experiences. The portfolio as a product evolves in close relationship with a set of peers, supervisors, and teachers. The electronic portfolio folder titles (*teaching philosophy, teaching and learning, school and community, technology, my story,* and *standards*) used at University of Wisconsin–Madison (chap. 5, this volume) reflect a set of shared priorities: Although for many the technology learning curve is steep, it is imperative that teachers for tomorrow are technology literate in order to transform work preparedness of urban students. At the University of Wisconsin–Madison, with deep roots historically in the social reconstructionist tradition, efforts to meld technology into the assessment mix brings new insights into documentation as assessment-in-action.

The urban experience is a chosen option at the University of Wisconsin–Madison. Focus on diversity, social justice, and urban needs is explicit and scaffolded throughout three field semesters. Commitment to a community of psychological safety creates a climate of trust that fosters "critical dialogue." Another important feature of this program is the ownership of the standards used in assessment, a document negotiated in partnership with the Madison

Metropolitan School District—an admirable achievement. Citing journals from preparing teachers, this case captures the irreducible tension around the intent of standards to improve teacher quality and the actual meanings assigned to such standards to organize portfolio assessments. Honest confrontation with "difference" is foundational to growth.

A powerful example in the Wisconsin case of Peterman's notion of teacher-as-advocate tells the story of a student teacher who includes a unit on voting rights in her portfolio. She herself becomes a voter registrar and takes a class into a school neighborhood to help register people to vote. There is no objective test that can capture the unique ways that teachers, especially in an urban context, impact their community norms of practice. One of my own students reported on her efforts, despite many obstacles, to create a community garden across from her urban middle school to teach science and involve students. Persistence led to success and eventually the naysaying building administrator basked in his school's recognition from the community. Such initiatives are hard to capture on standard assessment forms that note whether the day's lesson is posted on the board or not.

HIGHER EDUCATION AND URBAN SCHOOLS: TRUST AND ACCESS ISSUES

At Cleveland State University, efforts to provide quality teachers for urban areas has led to an innovative MAT program that hopes to apprentice mature learners into successful career teachers. Marquez-Zenkov's (chap. 4, this volume) analysis draws parallels between urban public schools and urban public universities that often have uncomfortable similarities in their climates of underfunding, understaffing, and fragmented personnel agendas. This honest story about the challenges of developing a viable portfolio assessment process for the MAT resonates with my experience around teacher education reform at a large urban institution. Both the preservice teachers and the professors that work with them in the trenches through the Cleveland State partnership model Peterman's concept of resiliency. We really do know a great deal about how to help teachers grow and develop, but too often the efforts toward quality assessment practices emerge from a few committed true believers who develop programs through overload rather than institutional and state policy. By modeling how one stays engaged and hopeful in one's own reflected learning despite major challenges, urban teachers may be teaching urban students the most important lessons of all.

CONSENSUS THROUGH DIALOGUE: SHARING VISION

Power of collaboration across universities and PDS sites has resulted in a unified set of standards and practices to prepare professional educators who function effectively and reflectively in multicultural urban schools, an amazing feat as some programs are graduate only, some are undergraduate focused, and some have alternative certification paths. Many tensions and problems exist when developing productive discourse patterns around the label *urban*. Multiple dialogue opportunities and drafts insured a high level of buy-in as standards for urban teaching evolved.

In the final analysis, better systems of assessment practice are only possible through collaboration among stakeholders with a vested interest in improving schools for learning. Paradoxically, the most successful stories of "best practice" emerge from reframing discourse practices to recognize and build on learners' many strengths and from resisting individualistic, behavioral language embedded in deficit labeling. By naming good work, by understanding more deeply the concept of developmental growth within a learner's ZPD, by designing learning activities supported in myriad scaffolded ways, teachers and students engage in intricate dance steps and blend cacophonic sounds into a more coherent song. The process of assuming the identity of a successful teacher is linked to the nature and quality of this dialogic process:

> The social knowledge or experience that is created between speakers and listeners is always collaborative, a mutual effort. And since language is never neutral but inflected with people's beliefs and values, then the dialogic process affects the individuals' internal states and external social conditions as well. Dialogue, for Bakhtin, is necessary for ethical and socially responsible communities to thrive. Through dialogue, meaning is negotiated jointly, every voice is "animated" by other voices, and individual experience is collectively interpreted through a shared body of cultural assumptions. (Danielewicz, 2001, p. 145)

It is incredibly important to question the purpose of any assessment system that purports to name others' performances from an imagined outside place removed from the community and discourse within which the teaching/learning activity takes place.

Urban children will learn if their teachers can imagine a way to create a space in which assuming the role of "learner" makes sense. Discourses of failure, deficit, and bad behavior produce failures and internalized deficit behaviors. Accountability as a current concept seems to me to be saturated with critical judgment and assumptions of wrongdoing, and is often indirectly punitive in its structure. The authors of these chapters hope to provide developing teachers, university professors, and questioning policymakers with complex tools of assessment to counter linguistic games of accountability by documenting the reflexivity and common sense of their day-to-day experiences in guiding learning in urban contexts. Cokely and

Murrell (chap. 7, this volume) discuss the "value added" from their community teacher idea that emphasizes advocacy, agency, and care. They believe accountability to a social justice agenda means urban teachers meet a higher level of accountability. By using shared standards for urban teaching success as a yardstick, administrators, board members, and parents can then responsibly calibrate the success of the teacher-made case for activity that leads to learning (Airasian & Horn, 2000). Participation in school communities and neighborhoods as sites of learning insures that the mission of public schooling—to model good citizenship in a democratic society—is met. (Ladson-Billings & Darling-Hammond, 2000; Mason, 1999).

EFFECTS OF POVERTY ON SCHOOL CONTEXTS

Another way that comparing teachers and schools across contexts becomes a problem is suggested in the quote that began this chapter (Lott, 2002). In the poorest schools, Lott tells us, half the instructional personnel are aides and only 10% of those people have college degrees. She further states that 41% of the aides report that they teach students on their own with no supervision. The rhetoric around accountability fails to address such irreducible tensions around situated realities in assessment contexts. For example, suburban schools define "aide" to mean personnel *in addition to* a certified classroom teacher, not *instead of one*.

Continuing to compare apples and oranges in superficial ways results in the degradation of the status and autonomy of trained professional teachers struggling with overwhelming demands and priorities, mostly constructed by others. The messy, challenging, and sometimes discouraging search for responsible and meaningful ways to teach successfully in urban settings is documented in many ethnographic texts such as Weiner's (1999) thoughtful book *Urban Teaching*, Ladson-Billings's (1994) *The Dreamkeepers*, and Delpit's (1995) *Other People's Children*. Vicarious stories and reflective analysis can help us bridge gaps between different cultural contexts.

SOME CLOSING RUMINATIONS

Quality urban teaching can be achieved through an intentional curriculum with well-designed opportunities for mentored practice and time for reflective processing. Partnerships with Black churches, ethnic advocacy groups, after-school and athletic organizations, and local businesses represent creative outreach for preparing competent urban teachers.

Adopting sociocultural theory to rethink assessment-in-action systems means adapting the following tenets to prepare teachers collaboratively:

- commit to the labor intensive work of negotiated dialogue to identify standards to support a shared vision,
- recognize and nurture community connections beyond the walls of a classroom,
- insure that teachers value and are equipped to document student learning,
- provide some choice to teachers and students around professional development needs,
- interpenetrate university, school, and community cultures by institutionalizing reflexive tools and processes of assessment, and
- cultivate strategic connections to advocate for student success.

Our goal is to build bridges between evaluative standards and to improve teaching and learning in urban settings; however, the meanings surrounding situated activity are always local. Because of the complexity of urban settings, collaboration across partner stakeholders becomes both more necessary and more fragile. The discourse around assessment in school settings must shift away from dominant discourses of deficiency, based on competitive social comparisons, to a more generative language of situated informational feedback and hope.

REFERENCES

Airasian, P. W., & Horn, S. (2000). Consortium for Research on Educational Accountability and Teacher Evaluation (CREATE). *Journal of Personnel Evaluation in Education, 14*(4), 319–327.

Allexsaht-Snider, M., & Hart, L. E. (2001). "Mathematics for all": How do we get there? *Theory and Practice, 40*(2), 93–101.

Amrein, A. L., & Berliner, D. C. (2002, March 28). High-stakes testing, uncertainty, and student learning. *Educational Policy Analysis Archives, 10*(18). Retrieved May 25, 2002 from http://epaa.asu.edu/epaa/v10n18/

Anyon, J. (1995). Race, social class, and educational reform in an inner-city school. *Teachers College Record, 97*(1), 69–94.

Anyon, J., & Wilson, W. J. (1997). *Ghetto schooling: A political economy of urban school reform*. New York: Teachers College Press.

Apple, M. (2001). Markets, standards, teaching, and teacher education. *Journal of Teacher Education, 52*(3), 182–195.

Berliner, D. C. (2002). Educational research: The hardest science of all. *Educational Researcher, 31*(8), 18–20.

Chatterji, M. (2002). Models and method for examining standards-based reforms and accountability initiatives: Have the tools of inquiry answered pressing questions on improving schools? *Review of Educational Research, 72*(3), 345–386.

Cochran-Smith, M., & Fries, M. K. (2001). Sticks, stones, and ideology: The discourse of reform in teacher education. *Educational Researcher, 30*(8), 3–15.

CREDE http://www.crede.ucsc.edu

Danielewicz, J. (2001). *Teaching selves: Identity, pedagogy, and teacher education.* Albany, NY: State University of New York Press.

Darling-Hammond, L. (2001). *National Commission on Teaching and America's Future Refutes Abell Foundation Report.* Retrieved October 15, 2001, from http://www.nctaf.org/whatsnew/abell_response.pdf

Darling-Hammond, L., & Youngs, P. (2002). Defining "highly qualified teachers": What does "scientifically-based research" actually tell us? *Educational Researcher, 31*(9), 13–25.

Davis, D. R., Pool, J., & Mits-Cash, M. (2000). Issues in implementing a new teacher assessment system in a large urban school district: Results of a qualitative field study. *Journal of Personnel Evaluation in Education, 144*(4), 285–306.

Delpit, L. (1995) *Other people's children: Cultural conflict in the classroom.* New York: New Press.

Dewey, J. (1991). *How we think.* New York: Dover. (Original work published 1910)

Ding, C., & Navarro, V. (in press). What standards-based tests can tell us about student mathematics learning: A longitudinal look. *Studies in Educational Evaluation.*

Fountain, C. A. (1997). *Collaborative agenda for change: Examining the impact of urban professional development schools.* Paper presented at the Annual Meeting of the American Association of Colleges for Teacher Education, Phoenix, Arizona.

Gallimore, R., & Goldenberg, C. (2001). Analyzing cultural models and settings to connect minority achievement and school improvement research. *Educational Psychologist, 36*(1), 45–56.

Hargreaves, A., & Earl, L. (2002, Spring). Perspectives on alternative assessment reform. *American Educational Research Journal, 39*(1), 69–95.

The Holmes Group. (1990). *Tomorrow's schools: Principles for the design of professional development schools.* East Lansing, MI: Author.

Ladson-Billings, G. (1994). *The dreamkeepers: Successful teachers of African American children.* San Francisco: Jossey-Bass.

Ladson-Billings, G., & Darling-Hammond, L. (2000, May). *The validity of National Board for Professional Teaching Standards (NBPTS)/Interstate New Teacher Assessment and Support Consortium (INTASC) assessments for effective urban teachers: Findings and implications for assessments.* National Partnership for Excellence and Accountability in Teaching, Washington, DC. Retrieved from http://www.ericsp.org/digests/NBPTSvalidity.htm

Laczko-Kerr, I., & Berliner, D. (2002). *The effectiveness of Teach for America. Educational Policy Analysis Archives, 10*(37), 56 pages. Retrieved November 23, 2002 from http://epaa.asu.edu/epaa/v10n37/

Lashway, L. (2002). The accountability challenge. *Principal, 81*(3), 14–16.

Linn, R. L., Baker, E. L., & Betebenner, D. W. (2002). Accountability systems: Implications of requirements of the No Child Left Behind Act of 2001. *Educational Researcher, 31*(6), 3–16.

Lott, B. (2002). Cognitive and behavioral distancing from the poor. *American Psychologist, 57*(2), 100–110.

Mason, T. C. (1999, Spring). Predictors of success in urban teaching: Analyzing two paradoxical cases. *Multicultural Education, 6*(3), 26–32.

National Commission on Teaching & America's Future. (1996, September). *What matters most: Teaching for America's future.* New York: Columbia University.

Newmann, F., & Wehlage, G. (1995). *Successful school restructuring: A report to the public and educators.* Washington, DC: Office of Educational Research and Improvement.

Pasch, S. H. (1990). Collaborative planning for urban professional development schools. *Contemporary Education, 61*(3), 135–143.

Rothstein, R. (2002, May 1). States teeter when balancing standards with tests. *New York Times*, p. A21.

Sachs, S. (2002). *Evaluation of teacher attributes as predictors of success in urban schools.* Unpublished dissertation, University of Missouri, St. Louis.

Sadovnik, A. R., & Semal, S. (2001). Book review of J. Anyon & W. J. Wilson, *Ghetto schooling: A political economy of urban educational reform. Educational Researcher, 30*(9), 27–32.

Shepel, E. N. L. (1995). Teacher self-identification in culture from Vygotsky's developmental perspective. *Anthropology & Education Quarterly, 26*(4), 425–442.

Shepard, L. (2001, April). *Protecting learning from the harmful effects of high-stakes testing.* Paper presented at the 2001 annual meeting of the American Educational Research Association, Seattle, WA.

Slavin, R. E., & Madden, N. A. (Eds.). (2001). *Success for all: Research and reform in elementary education.* Mahwah, NJ: Lawrence Erlbaum Associates.

Slavin, R. E., & Madden, N. A. (2002). *Success for all and comprehensive school reform: Evidence-based policies for urban education.* U.S. Department of Education, Office of Educational Research and Improvement, Educational Resources Information Center. ED 1.310/2:459301.

Smith, L. M., & Geoffrey, W. (1968). *The complexities of an urban classroom: An analysis toward a general theory of teaching.* New York: Holt, Rinehart & Winston.

Teitel, L. (2000). *Assessment: Assessing the impacts of Professional Development Schools.* AACTE Professional Development School Practice Series. New York: American Association of Colleges for Teacher Education.

Teitel, L. (2001, February). How professional development schools make a difference: A review of research. *National Council for Accreditation of Teacher Education.*

Teitel, L. (2002, May). *Suggestions for designing PDS research.* Paper presented at the Professional Development School Collaborative Meeting. St. Louis, Missouri.

Wayne, A. J., & Youngs, P. (2003). Teacher characteristics and student achievement gains: A review. *Review of Educational Research, 73*(1), 89–122.

Weiner, L. (1999). *Urban teaching: The essentials.* New York: Teachers College.

Wertsch, J. (1998). *Mind as action.* New York: Oxford University Press.

Wong, C. A., & Rowley, S. J. (2001). The schooling of ethnic minority children: Commentary. *Educational Psychologist, 36*(1), 57–66.

Zeichner, K., & Hoeft, K. (1996). Teacher socialization for cultural diversity. In J. Sikula (Ed.), *Handbook of research on teacher education* (2nd ed.). New York: MacMillan.

Author Index

Subject Index